2,000 MILES TOGETHER

2,000

miles together

the story of the
largest family to
hike the appalachian trail

Ben Crawford

with Meghan McCracken

FFT
PRESS

2,000 MILES TOGETHER
The Story of the Largest Family to Hike the Appalachian Trail

ISBN   978-1-5445-0242-7   *Hardcover*
       978-1-5445-0240-3   *Paperback*
       978-1-5445-0241-0   *Ebook*
       978-1-5445-1632-5   *Audiobook*

*This book is dedicated to all the thru-hikers
who have walked away from comfort and chose
homelessness with intention. You are my heroes.*

CONTENTS

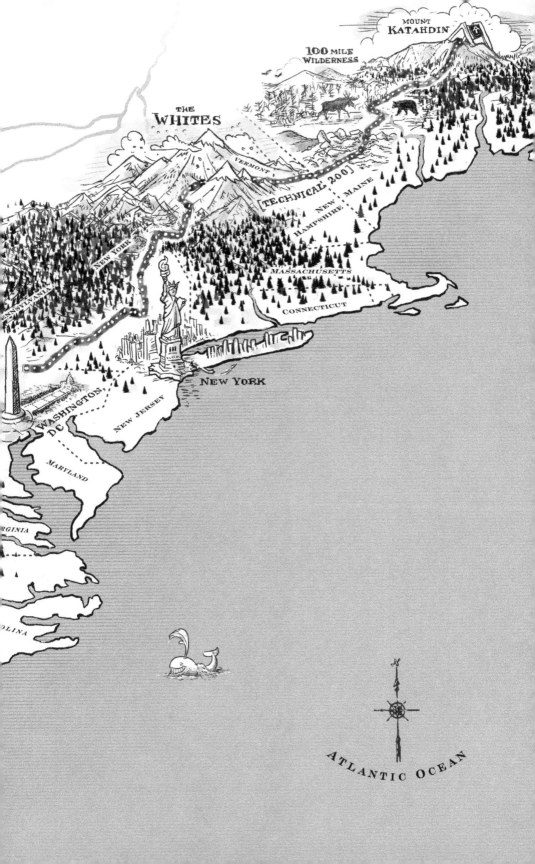

2018 witnessed an extraordinary group expedition up the Appalachian Trail, an undulating patch of green extending close to 2,190 miles connecting the summit of Springer Mountain in northern Georgia to the majestic summit of Mount Katahdin in central Maine. This footpath should represent freedom of movement through public spaces; freedom to take risks in the true spirit of outdoor adventure; freedom from the institutional pollution of liability and fear-mongering; and the potential to find oneself in relation to ourselves, our loved ones, our fellow travelers on the way to becoming, and within our "civilized" cultural conditioning.

What made this group expedition extraordinary is that it consisted of the largest family to ever attempt a thru-hike. The Crawford family hike was undertaken by middle-aged parents and their six children aged two to seventeen years old (four daughters and two sons). Not only was theirs the largest family to hike the trail, but each family member completed what they set out to do, and learned many valuable lifelong lessons along the way. These lessons can only be learned through the hardships, suffering, pain, frustration, joy, and elation endured and experienced by walking for 161 days in bone-chilling rain, snowstorms, heat, and humidity.

I have personally organized, as a labor of love to fulfill my calling as a social change educator, ten groups to hike the entire trail with phenomenal, historic completion rates. But in doing so, we were day-hiking with van support. Our youngest was fifteen years old; our oldest, sixty-eight years old. We didn't have any youngins, nor the challenges inherent in backpacking with family members. I believe that hiking the entire trail with a group has a different set of challenges then hiking it alone or with a friend. That is why you probably can count on two hands the number of groups of over four people that have accomplished this enormous undertaking.

This book is the Crawfords' story—raw and unvarnished, and truthful in a sensitive, caring way. It is radical and rambunctious; thought-provoking and intelligent; and full of questioning, of oneself and the world. It is a tale of a different type of "family values" that isn't based on religion or Republicans. It is about the joys and challenges of striving together.

This narrative is neither sugar-coated nor sanitized. (Thank goodness it will be self-published!) Prepare yourself for a read that includes freezing, self-doubting, frustrated people; a family campout in a public bathroom in the middle of a blizzard; the social media haters/guilters (which has also especially been a problem in the 2020 A.T. COVID season); visits by Child Protective Services and National Park Service rangers; institutional injustices; and collective familial barfing.

But also look forward to reading a celebration of the wonderful acts of kindness and encouragement that the Crawfords received from fellow hikers, trail angels, and hostel owners along the way. Bask in how this family grew and learned along this sacred pilgrimage, and how they overcame setbacks that would have stopped others' forward progress.

They won the hard fight for "togetherness"; they are certainly worthy of my respect and admiration for this, and hopefully you, the reader, will feel the same way.

—Dr. Warren Doyle
Member of the Appalachian Trail Hall of Fame;
Founder of ALDHA, the Appalachian
Long Distance Hikers Association;
38,000-miler, a record 18 traverses of the
entire A.T.—more than anyone in history;
Director of the Appalachian Trail Institute

PREFACE

When I sat down to write this book, the story of our family hiking all 2,189 miles of the Appalachian Trail, I had no idea what kind of book I was writing. I just knew that my family had a story to tell, and that enough people had told us we should share it.

But how?

I didn't want to write a how-to book or a guide to thru-hiking—mostly because we're not typical thru-hikers. As a family, we enjoy hiking...sometimes. It's always been more of a means to an end for us, a way for me and my wife, Kami, to build closer relationships with our kids. We don't believe in a one-size-fits-all model for parenting, and even if there were one, we wouldn't say it's thru-hiking.

I also didn't want to write a memoir, a book that was all *my* story. The first thing we heard from people when they asked if we were writing a book about our hike was, "We want to hear from the kids!" Well, it turns out that writing a book is hard (surprise!) and something our teenagers didn't really want to do. After working through ten versions of this manuscript, I can understand why. For a time in the creation of this book, my wife, Kami, and I were co-authors, writing our family's story together. Her experience on the trail was just as important, and just as compelling, as mine, and at times it was difficult to tell where her opinions ended and mine began. The same goes for our four daughters and two sons: Dove, Eden, Seven, Memory, Filia, and Rainier, who was only two years old when we hiked. Their unique thoughts and feelings about our trip are just as interesting—probably more interesting, honestly—than mine. What Kami and I found when we started writing, though, is that this is a complicated story with a huge, sprawling setting and a giant cast of characters—kind of like *Game of Thrones* but with gummy bears. We saw right away that we needed one unifying voice to tell such a complex story, and since I was doing the bulk of the writing, the voice that came through the clearest was mine. So, while this book primarily represents my viewpoint, I've done my best to incorporate as much insight and perspective from Kami and our children throughout the story as possible. To do this, I've included entries from their journals and quotes taken from over 120 of our trail videos.

Originally, I started off writing an adventure book. People seemed most interested when we told stories of bears, snakes, snowstorms, and Child Protective Services busting in on our family's camp. All of those things happened to us, and then some. It would be pretty easy to write about any number of hardships we faced, and the courage we had to find to overcome them and come out on top like heroes.

I was equally passionate about writing an outside-the-box, counter-cultural approach to parenting because it's a huge part of our lives—and was a huge part of our hike. Over the years, Kami and I have faced a lot of criticism for the way we parent our children. The criticism has come at us from all sides, from our own family and friends as well as strangers on the internet. I originally intended to defend our way of life by providing background information for some of our decisions, to counter being written off as "crazy" and use our success as the ultimate defense of being right in our philosophy. The book started out that way. But somewhere around draft number eight, I couldn't stand to hear myself preach about parenting anymore. The book read like a tone-deaf sermon, and felt like one of those Halloween festivals that churches invite you to by offering you a bunch of free candy (but really they just want to lecture you about hell). Besides, Kami and I have changed our minds so many times about what's best for our family that there was a good chance our sermon would be obsolete by the time this book made it to print. I decided to limit the parenting talk unless I absolutely couldn't help myself.

In the end, I decided to stick with what I was good at: telling the truth in all its gory detail, and then letting you, the reader, decide what conclusions you want to draw. This story includes the ways we were tested and challenged. I wrote about the times we fell apart and came back together. I wrote about our haters and the vitriol that made us doubt ourselves. I wrote about my identity as a father, and how the trail transformed me. I wrote about my fears, my disappointments, the times we howled with laughter, and the times we cried, overwhelmed with emotion. I also wrote about my mistakes. I'm not going to defend my actions—Kami and I have never lived defensively—but I will offer explanations so that you can better understand what was going on for us in the moment.

Including vivid details of our mistakes means that, most likely, you'll read things in these pages that you disagree with. That's wonderful. What I hope comes through is that there is more than one way to live life and experience relationships to the fullest. My aim is that this book can be a new lens through which to consider your own relationships. Even the things that you disagree with can prompt conversations that lead you to change, and I would expect your change to look completely different from my own.

In order to weave together the opinions and experiences of eight different people, content that spanned six months, fourteen states, and over two thousand miles, I needed help. I hired Meghan and her team to help translate 161 days of journal entries, videos, and emotions into the story you're about to read. Meghan watched our videos, interviewed me for hours, and went back and forth with me on more than ten drafts before we arrived at a manuscript that we thought did my family's experience on the Appalachian Trail some justice.

We're the Crawfords, and this is a story about our family. We're also thru-hikers; this is the story of how we got accepted into that community. And it's a story about every person we met who helped us along the way.

This is a true story. As a result of living it, our lives were changed. Our relationships with family, friends, and neighbors were changed. Even our identities, and how we saw our personal stories, were changed.

My hope is that, by reading this story, maybe some of those same things will happen to you.

"I think that people who do the Appalachian Trail for reasons that aren't intensely personal are going to get weeded out in the first few days, if not weeks."

—Joe "Stringbean" McCounagey

It had been more than five months since we'd left home.

We'd all lost more weight than was healthy. My cousin would later tell us, "You look like meth addicts, except for your teeth!" Kami's ribs were showing, and her thin shoulder bones jutted out awkwardly. The kids had started calling her Gandhi, even though each of them had lost weight too. When we had the energy to hug each other, we felt each other's spines poking through our shirts. We hoped the weight would return after our trip, but we had no way of knowing what the lasting effects would be.

Our legs were steel trunks. We could each see eight distinct muscles in our calves and thighs. We were used to waking up before sunrise and hiking for more than sixteen hours, often in the dark. We had walked through blizzards and rattlesnake pits; we'd dealt with vomiting, Lyme disease, bee stings, and falls. We didn't feel pain in the same way anymore—it was more a constant companion than something to notice or remark on. We'd been reported to two national park services and interviewed by Child Protective Services after sleeping on the floor of a women's public restroom.

After 161 days of hiking, we were machines. Our family had walked an average of 13.6 miles a day up and down some of the steepest, most rugged trails in the United States. We accomplished that distance— more than a half-marathon per day—while carrying thirty-pound packs, camera gear, a laptop, and a two-year-old human. We had crossed state lines thirteen times and traveled a total of 2,189 miles, not including the nineteen miles that were impassable due to a forest fire.

That distance is the equivalent of driving from Tijuana, Mexico, up the I-5 to Vancouver, Canada, and then turning around and driving more than halfway back. We'd covered it entirely on foot.

We were told that if we finished, we would be the largest family ever to have completed the Appalachian Trail. There were eight of us: two parents—me, Ben, age thirty-eight, and my wife, Kami, thirty-seven—and our six children. Dove, our eldest, was sixteen when we started; Eden was fifteen; Seven, our eldest son, was thirteen; Memory was eleven; Filia was seven, and, if we completed the trail, she would be the youngest female ever to do so; Rainier, our youngest son, was two. He would need to be carried the entire way.

The A.T., as the hiking community calls the famous route, is the longest hiking-*only* trail in the world. It runs from Georgia all the way up to Maine, with the official "finish line" at the summit of Mount Katahdin. "Thru-hike" is the term used to describe hiking the full A.T. within the course of one year.

As a family, we had hiked through three seasons. Now our journey was coming to an end.

It wasn't the end we'd hoped for.

We hadn't completed the trail; there were two miles left. Just two, after more than two thousand. But we had decided to not go any farther. Mere steps from the destination we'd been focused on for months, we stopped. For the first time in six months, we went south instead of north. We turned around and walked away from the famous A-frame sign at the top of Mount Katahdin, with no plans to return.

THE VOICES AGAINST US

A year later, as I started writing the story of our hike, the first things that popped into my mind to recount were all the scary things we encountered on the Appalachian Trail. And there were *many*. If I'd been hiking alone, it would have been scary enough; but I was hiking with my wife and our six children, which meant that every decision called into question not only our personal safety but also my qualifications as a parent.

After I wrote out all the scary stuff, though, I realized something. The scariest thing was never the mountains or the weather, the bears and snakes, the falls, sickness, and trying to get to the finish.

The scariest thing about hiking the Appalachian Trail was starting.

Because I knew myself. I knew that if I started the hike, nothing would keep me from finishing. Not snow, not animals, not sickness, not cold or heat or miles. I'm a driven, competitive person. I had spent my whole life learning how to ignore feelings of pain and push projects through to completion. On the trail, I could ignore my own pain, discomfort, and misgivings—but would that lead me to ignore my kids? Would I push them past their breaking points, in pursuit of a goal that probably only mattered to me?

The scariest thing for me was that we *would* finish the trail, all two thousand-plus miles of it. And that someday my kids were going to hate me for it.

In order to begin a journey like this, you have to ignore voices—the voices of the general population, the voices of the media, the lesser voices screaming for comfort in my head. Loudest were the voices of my children. No kid wakes up and wants to go do something hard. Kami and I have never parented traditionally, and over the years we've bribed, cajoled, and outright sprung on our kids many different tasks of varying levels of difficulty. Up until we started the hike, we had mostly gotten away with it. Our kids seemed to enjoy the "Crawford family adventures"—or at least, they got pretty good at tolerating them, which is as much as any adventuring parent can hope for.

But hiking the Appalachian Trail would be a trip too long for the kids to fake tolerance, let alone enthusiasm. The stakes were too high. The kids wouldn't be able to hide what they felt when it got hard. They might end up feeling defeated, pushed for hundreds of miles for months past their desire just because they couldn't speak up loud enough to say no.

And my capacity for listening to them would have to be at an all-time low, just to keep the family moving forward.

I recalled something I'd read in *Into Thin Air* by Jon Krakauer: the last five hundred feet of Mount Everest are the most dangerous because of a phenomenon called "summit fever." People ignore every agreed-upon term and condition that's designed to protect their safety in order to get to the top. The call of the summit is just too loud. With how much they've invested, they can't help themselves.

The concept of being so driven toward a goal that you ignore your own safety, and the safety of others, haunted me. Being driven toward goals and ignoring outside voices was how I had accomplished most of the things in my life.

I had the loudest voice of anyone I knew; would my kids be loud enough to shout over me if needed?

If they didn't, they would follow a pattern Kami and I had seen with many other families. Kids comply with the parents until they don't have to anymore. Then they leave, both physically and emotionally.

I knew that with my loud voice, I could get my family to finish the A.T. all together as one—but when it was over, would my kids ever talk to me again?

These were my biggest fears before we started out on our months-long, 2,200-mile hike as a family of eight people. Looking back on it now, the story I sat down to write was never one of nature, snakes, snow, and external threats. It's the story of how, as a family, we had to fight. The worst threats came not from the outdoors, but from inside us: staying together, holding on to our love for each other, and not getting summit fever.

OUR JOURNEY, TOGETHER

At the very end of our hike, after five months of walking, we were in Baxter State Park on Mount Katahdin only two miles from the official northern terminus of the A.T. We could see the top of the mountain, where the A-frame sign sat—the sign that every hiker touched, and then took their picture with to signify their success and the end of their adventure.

But as it turned out, that would not be our story. We would not complete the Appalachian Trail. We would have to find satisfaction beyond touching the sign.

As we walked down the mountain, and in the days that followed, we wondered: Were we failures? Did we really *finish* the Appalachian Trail? Should we be outraged that we were judged so harshly for trying? Why did so many people think we endangered our kids? Were we crazy?

Kami and I knew that in the grand scheme of our children's lives, they would draw their own opinions on what they had gained and lost. We couldn't decide that for them. All we could do was give them something to fight for, and allow them to forge their own paths from Georgia to Maine. In the end, our journey wasn't about whether we physically took every step—although the physical component was crucially important to us. It wasn't about the choices we made on the hike, and the many ways in which we carved our own path through the woods of the Eastern Seaboard, creating a hike that was as much about our family as it was about the actual dirt footpath that stretch ahead of us for 2,200 miles. What mattered most was our fight, the fight for together against nature, weather, other people's judgments, and our own doubts. And at the end, what mattered most as we walked down Katahdin was that we walked down together.

This book is the story of our fight.

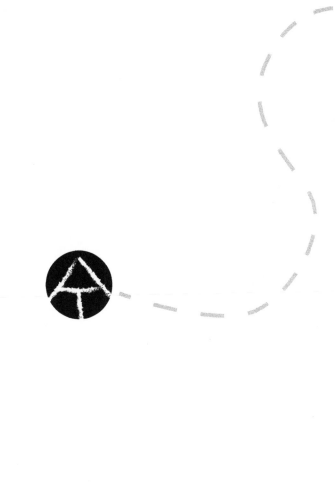

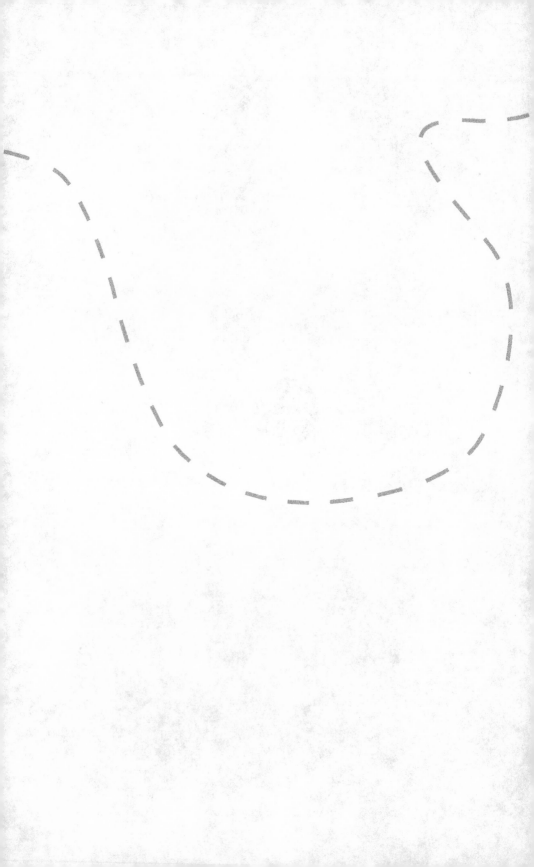

CHAPTER ONE

No Turning Back Now

"I want to repeat one word for you:

Leave.

Roll the word around on your tongue for a bit. It is a beautiful word, isn't it? So strong and forceful, the way you have always wanted to be. And you will not be alone. You have never been alone. Don't worry. Everything will still be here when you get back. It is you who will have changed."

—Donald Miller, *Through Painted Deserts: Light, God, and Beauty on the Open Road*

Every parent believes on some level that they know what's best for their kids.

We make our kids go to school, we don't allow them to eat candy nonstop, we teach them not to play with matches, and we don't let them run into traffic. Parents enforcing their will upon their children is an accepted practice.

But what happens when your beliefs aren't something you see practiced in the mainstream? What happens when your will as a parent is something that most people disagree with?

Before we set out to thru-hike the A.T., our kids were no strangers to backpacking. Kami and I had taken our kids on extended backpacking adventures enough times that we knew it was good for them—that it had a profound impact on their health and moods. Back when we first started having kids, we were not "outdoorsy" people; we were more the restaurant-loving, Disneyland-vacation-going type. But as we took our growing family into the outdoors more and more, Kami and I noticed the huge positive impact it made on how we all related to each other. We fell in love with the results of being challenged together. Hiking was one of the easiest ways to all spend time together outside, and the thrill of banding together to confront the wild unknown made us feel a type of togetherness we couldn't seem to replicate back at home. We'd also seen firsthand the amount of self-confidence our kids developed when they faced, and conquered, difficult things that the entire world said was impossible.

Every time we returned from a short hiking trip, we felt good, but we dreamed of doing something longer and bigger—a journey that would bring our family closer than ever, a story we would tell the rest of our lives.

But hiking the entire Appalachian Trail with six young kids was, we knew, way further outside the norm than taking them on backpacking trips. And we knew from past experience that when you step outside the norm, and push your kids to do things that make them uncomfortable, the stakes are *much* higher if you turn out to be wrong.

Kami and I knew the critics would be out in force. One broken bone, and people would call us reckless, selfish, tyrannical. Even our friends were just waiting to say, "I told you so."

In the months of prep leading up to our thru-hike, we'd told our kids as much as we could about what the Appalachian Trail would be like. We made clear what a huge commitment and true lifestyle shift it would be. They weren't total strangers to the concept of a backpacking trip, but the longest hike we'd previously completed as a family was twelve days, which is a *completely* different beast from hiking the A.T. for five months. Twelve days is a "trip." Five months is akin to moving, living somewhere new. We'd given our oldest kids—Dove and Eden—the choice to stay behind if they wanted. The decision to join us on the hike was ultimately theirs. The range of emotions our kids displayed as the hike drew nearer was everything from incredibly excited and positive, to anxious at the idea of being cut off from their friends and world of comfort for the six months we anticipated the journey would take us. But when it came down to it, they all wanted to go.

Secretly, Kami and I were dealing with our own questions. We had no idea how the kids would react once they were actually *on* the trail. What if they revolted once they got an idea of how hard it was? Would they want to quit before we could get used to it? Or, worst-case scenario: would they get used to it, then be gradually worn down and want to quit after we had hiked a substantial amount and had much more to lose? I dreaded a situation where I knew a kid had hit a mental or physical wall—I knew classic parenting tricks to push them through, everything from bribery to downright threats, but would I push a kid too far? Was it worth pushing one kid beyond health for the sake of the greater goal? Even if they were being shortsighted, did that mean that our vantage point and perspective as parents automatically won out?

You can't plan an adventure while obsessing about "what ifs," so instead of dwelling on future scenarios outside of our control, Kami and I focused on buying gear and packing up our house to rent it out.

Even the act of supplying ourselves for a six-month trek was different from the norm. Gear can be incredibly expensive (as it should be if you're literally going to depend on it to save your life), and most hikers invest tons of cash to buy gear just for themselves. We had to buy gear for *eight* people. This required getting creative, and often buying what was easiest and not necessarily optimal. We bought gloves at Costco. Instead of buying the perfect shoes for each person, we bought whatever was on clearance, which meant a hodgepodge of brands, colors, and styles.

We set aside living expenses to buy what we would need to survive on trail for six months with no income whatsoever. We did our taxes early. We told our family and friends we were doing it: we were finally going to attempt "The Hike."

By the time the big day arrived, Kami and I still had our secret doubts. If there were answers to our questions, we'd have to find them out there on the trail.

ON YOUR MARKS...

On February 28, 2018, our whole family loaded into our twelve-passenger van, and my parents drove us from our home in Bellevue, Kentucky—just outside of Cincinnati—to Atlanta, Georgia.

The drive took seven hours. Kami and I both grew up on the West Coast, so most of the scenery in the South and along the Eastern Seaboard was unknown to us. We were going to a place where we had no friends, no contacts, and if we wanted help, it would mean buying or hiring it. We were leaving home and going out on our own in the most literal sense of the phrase.

We arrived at a comfortable hotel outside Atlanta late at night and planned to wake up the next morning at 5:00 a.m. to go to Cracker

Barrel for breakfast. The kids love Cracker Barrel, and we hoped the promise of going would help inspire an early start. As the kids loaded up their new backpacks at bedtime that night, the general mood was excited, nervous, and ready for an adventure.

The next morning, miraculously, everyone woke up on time—even our thirteen-year-old son, Seven, who's a chronic oversleeper. Kami and I checked and double-checked everyone's clothing, packs, and supplies, and we managed to get everyone out the door on schedule.

We would soon find out that the smooth start was the calm before the storm. The rest of the morning was *far* from miraculous.

At Cracker Barrel, we were all too tired to eat. Dove and Eden, our teenage girls who could usually be found whispering and giggling together, were completely quiet. The younger kids were unusually still and sluggish. Seven was practically asleep at the table. And as the cherry on top, our two-year-old son, Rainier, was fussing non-stop and seemed sick. We feared he might be in the beginning stages of a virus, which only intensified our worries about maintaining the health of eight people at the beginning of the most physically difficult adventure of our lives.

As everyone picked at their food, I could feel the stares from my mom and dad—Halmonee and Papa to our kids—seated across the table from me. They knew better than to speak up anymore, but throughout the past few months of planning, they had made it very clear to Kami and me that they thought we were crazy, that this would be taking our counter-cultural parenting style too far.

I didn't want to meet their eyes. If I did, maybe the voice in my head that had been second-guessing myself would speak for them.

To make matters their absolute worst, it was also pouring rain outside. This was *not* how we had imagined our first day on our adventure.

Halfway through the lackluster meal, Kami and I gave each other a knowing look. *Maybe we should go back to the hotel?*

And just as quickly, we dismissed the thought. It wasn't the first time doubt had reared its head. There had always been a new excuse not to go in the years leading up to our grand departure; taking six months off work and schooling is disruptive no matter how carefully you plan it. Plus, we wanted to wait for the kids be "the perfect age" where they could all be self-sufficient and able to walk the whole trail—and at the very least, potty-trained. But after fifteen years of hoping and dreaming and putting it off, Dove's seventeenth birthday approached, and we realized this was the last year we were guaranteed a shot at taking this leap together, potty-trained or not.

Now, this morning, a new set of excuses had cropped up. The rain. Rainier's fussing. Everyone's yawning listlessness.

There would never be a perfect moment. I was suddenly struck by that old adage you always hear about when to have kids—"There's no perfect time, you'll never be ready!" Kami and I knew that all too well.

We had to put aside our feelings about the rain and Rainier's fussiness. Waiting out the weather was not an option. We couldn't waver. We had decided months ago, the moment we started spending money on gear, that it would all be worth it; it was too late to turn around now. Besides, if we quit now, we'd have to tell everyone we failed before we even started.

We steeled ourselves, paid the bill, and walked out of Cracker Barrel into the rain with half our pancakes laying uneaten on the table. After piling everyone into the van, we found ourselves driving east into black clouds, straight into the storm.

NOT EXACTLY A PICTURE-PERFECT START

The Appalachian Trail officially begins at the summit of Springer Mountain, in Georgia, and ends fourteen states later at the summit of Mount Katahdin, in Maine.

In other words, to begin the A.T., you have to climb a mountain. And to finish, you have to climb another mountain. (There's a lot of mountain-climbing in between, too, which you'll read about in later chapters.)

At the top of Mount Katahdin stands a weathered A-frame wooden sign that reads simply:

Katahdin
Northern Terminus
Appalachian Trail

It's not fancy. But if you make it all the way to Katahdin on foot and lay your hands on that famous sign, you don't care much about what's written on it. The moment is so significant that it speaks for itself.

Each year, around three thousand people set out to thru-hike the Appalachian Trail. Like us, most of them start in Georgia and work their way to Maine—they call themselves Northbounders, or NOBOs, as opposed to Southbounders, or SOBOs, who set out from Maine and head down to Georgia. The northbound route puts hikers in the south in early spring, when the weather is cooler and the heat of the southern summer hasn't taken hold of the area, and lets them move north as the summer unfolds, hopefully making it to Maine before the cold of fall and winter sets in. Weather-wise, it's the least miserable way to hike the trail.

But in the end, the weather is completely unpredictable. You just have to hope for the best.

Needless to say, pouring rain on our very first day couldn't have been *further* from "best."

That morning, our crowded van traveled down a series of ever-narrowing gravel roads, windshield wipers swishing loudly, before ambling into a small parking lot off Forest Service Road 42, about fifteen miles from the nearest major highway. We'd planned to begin our thru-hike by leaving the van in the parking lot and having my parents join us for the brief mile-long hike to the A.T. terminus on Springer Mountain. Then we'd officially "begin" our hike, backtrack to the van, say goodbye to my parents, and start walking to Katahdin.

We'd envisioned this as a fun sendoff, bringing my parents into the experience with a celebratory taste of the feat we were about to take on. It didn't work out that way.

As soon as we all started hiking up Springer Mountain, the ever-present rain turned to *freezing* rain. We each had a huge pack containing hundreds of items and a dozen zippered compartments. Months into our hike, our gear would be organized, there would be a place for everything, and we would all be well-trained in finding what we need quickly; today, though, we couldn't even remember where we'd packed the rain jackets. Instead of stopping to look for them, we increased our pace and hoped we didn't get hypothermia.

I felt terrible for my parents. They had signed up for a relaxing walk in fair weather to take some photos, not the miserable slog we found ourselves in. They didn't have rain jackets. My dad hadn't even tied his shoes.

That year, the trail would total 2,189 miles. The distance changes from year to year due to natural disasters, topography changes, park projects, and other variables. It was hard to even comprehend the distance we were about to cover on foot. We'd done no shortage of math to figure out a schedule, we'd read dozens of maps, and of course we knew that two thousand is a hell of a lot of miles. But it was such a big number that it was impossible to truly plan for all of those miles. All we knew was that, to have the best chance of completing a thru-hike with a group of our size, we needed to start our hike as early in the spring as possible.

When you think March 1 in Georgia, what comes to mind? I'd pictured mild springtime weather and peach trees in the breeze. Our research had indicated it would be around forty to fifty degrees during the day and maybe drop into the thirties at night.

Trudging the relatively short distance to the Springer Mountain terminus, getting wetter and colder by the minute, Kami and I just hoped that the stunning view on the top of the mountain would raise everyone's spirits. But when we got there, the scene was bleak. The sprawling vistas we had been looking forward to were completely blotted out by ominous rain clouds—to the extent that it was hard to tell we were even *on* a mountain.

Less than an hour into what would be a months-long hike, and we had already put our kids' tolerance to the test. It was written all over their faces how they felt. They'd never heard of Springer Mountain, they were restless, they were starting to wonder what we'd gotten them into, they were shivering, and maybe worst of all, they looked bored.

Here we were at the beginning of the longest, most difficult journey of our lives, Kami and I finally living our scary but beautiful dream, and no one cared.

We were supposed to be focused on a small metal plaque on a rock that marked the official starting point of the Appalachian Trail. The plaque was directly next to the first white blaze of the trail—a streak of white paint that marks the trail along its entire length.

None of us could focus on this important milestone, though. Kami was distracted by the search for Rainier's rain pants.

"I put them right here!" she griped as she spilled all of our clothes and supplies out onto the soaking ground.

"Are you sure you packed them?"

"I don't remember. If they're not here, then they're back at the hotel."

"Well, it's not going to help if we get everything else soaking wet too."

She shot me a desperate glare, then went back to rummaging around.

I pulled open the bag nearest to me and helped with the search. Almost immediately, I found Rainier's rain pants tucked into the far corner of the bag.

"Here they are," I said, holding them up. Kami snatched them out of my hand and silently started dressing Rainier. Everyone else was standing still, staring at the ground, clearly contemplating their soaking-wet shoes and wondering if we would ever see them dry for the next six months.

It's the trip of a lifetime, I reminded myself sarcastically.

While Kami got Rainier ready for the rain, I took the opportunity to shoot a quick video capturing the start of our hike.

"Okay, we made it to the top," I said to the camera, after trying and failing to un-fog the lens in the rain. "It's been a bit of a disaster. It's been absolutely pouring..."

I aimed the camera at Kami, now standing hunched over in her soaked jacket. She shook her head miserably into the camera, but I could see a flicker of humor in her eyes. Our situation sucked, but it was also pretty funny—the first day of our hike literally couldn't be *further* from our dreams.

We quickly lined everyone up around the plaque for a picture. We all put on our best fake smiles. Except my dad. He couldn't even fake it. To this day, the blatant frown on his face in that picture makes us howl with laughter.

And with that, we had officially begun our hike north on the Appalachian Trail.

By the time we got back to Mile 1 and the parking lot, everyone was soaked and hungry for lunch. We'd intended to walk past the van and keep going, but the decision was unanimous: more than anything, we wanted to be *dry*.

Inside the van, we blasted the heat and peeled off our wet clothes. The warmth was soothing, and we found ourselves saying "ten more minutes" more than a couple of times.

Eventually, we looked at the clock and realized we'd been in the van for almost an hour. Our clothes were about 50 percent dry, and the thought of walking right back into the wet and cold seemed more than we could handle. I knew my parents were going to have a tough time saying goodbye, and now they had to watch us walk into freezing rain, which would only deepen the concerns they had for us.

At this point, though, it was clear there was no "good time" or any point in waiting. We had to keep moving.

Kami and I looked at each other and nodded. "Okay," I said. "Let's do this."

THE HARSH REALITY

When people ask us what the hardest part of the trail was, we always say, "The cold." That was true from Day 1.

We knew we weren't exactly headed into a hot Georgia summer, but we weren't prepared for the level of cold we encountered. No amount of information could prepare us for how harsh that cold would be or how tiring it was to survive in such bitter temperatures.

My parents had offered to meet us at various points along the hike. Even though we knew we'd see them again soon, saying goodbye in that parking lot at Mile 1 felt serious and somber. By the time we all finished hugging, everyone was crying.

It was the first time, but not nearly the last, that the thought entered my mind: *This might be a mistake.* But like many other questions that would come up, I didn't have the energy to ponder an answer. At this point, all energy needed to be put toward keeping the family moving forward.

I knew I had to be the leader. I turned my back on the van and my parents with tears in my eyes, and I started walking. I knew the kids would follow.

"Call us if you need anything," my dad said to our retreating forms, his voice cracking. I didn't let myself turn around.

As we headed into the forest that first day, we wrapped Rainier's hands in a jacket because they were so cold. This created a problem, though, because his favorite way to self-soothe was to suck on his fingers, and with the jacket on, he couldn't. He was already cranky that morning, fussing and acting like he was getting sick. From that moment on, the whole day with him became a battle. He cried nonstop as we walked into the rain.

We all wore gloves and insulating layers, and hiking generated some heat, so moving felt better than standing still. This meant that we had to put extra layers on Rainier since he was being carried. By the end of the day, we knew what the first huge obstacle of our adventure would be: dealing with the freezing temperatures.

We had no way to calculate how long this hike would take us, but we knew that to make it to Katahdin when it was still warm, we needed to average thirteen to fifteen miles a day.

On Day 1, we hiked all of 8.4 miles.

We had pushed it as hard as we could, but we weren't even close to reaching the distance we needed to cover, even with a nice breakfast and the support of my parents. What made it worse was the sinking realization that the fewer miles we did now, the more we would have to make up later to keep our average on-target.

That night, we set up camp for the first time. It was still raining as we struggled with freezing fingers to set up the tents and cook dinner. On the trail we were introduced to a completely new way of eating: it was all about high calories and low weight. This meant dehydrated and simple. Foods like macaroni and cheese, ramen, dried potatoes, and powdered soup would be our dinner staples for the next five months. Instead of following the recipe and adding things like oil and butter, our only condiment was water. We couldn't even afford the extra weight of bringing along salt and pepper. Backpacker life is as simple and streamlined as possible—you're going to feel every ounce you're carrying every step of the way, so you don't want to carry anything you don't absolutely *have* to.

For lunches we looked for things that didn't need to be cooked because we couldn't afford the time. Big hits among thru-hikers are tortillas, foil-wrapped tuna, Nutella and peanut butter, and occasionally, if you want to splurge, a block of cheese. Totally nonexistent are meats and any fresh fruits or vegetables that are heavy in water weight or require refrigeration.

Cooking on-trail was a challenge. Without utensils, measuring cups, or a colander, cooking pasta for too long or with not enough water meant we were eating glue. Too much water meant we were eating soup. That first evening at camp, I was quickly discovering these unique difficulties. While I tried to figure out the cooking, the kids tried to collect all the camping gear scattered around in their packs. It seemed to take forever to set up the tents. Eden and Seven got in an argument about who was doing more work while Kami held Rainier to keep him warm. Once everything was set up, the kids' shared tent was a chaotic nightmare, with sleeping pads and sleeping bags everywhere.

We shoveled food in our mouths, barely tasting it, and went to bed at 7:00 p.m. Even though we had only hiked eight miles, everyone was so tired that we slept straight through for thirteen hours.

The next morning, we started again at 9:00 a.m.—a relatively late start, but dragging everyone out of their warm sleeping bags into the freezing cold had been our most difficult challenge yet.

On the trail, there would be no coffee. Many hikers take the time in the morning to boil water for coffee, and are happy to bear the packed weight of ground beans. At home, Kami and I were used to relaxing and sipping coffee while reading each morning. But on the trail, Kami and I had decided that since we adults were the only ones drinking coffee, it wouldn't be fair to make the kids sit around waiting in the cold while we made and drank it in the mornings.

As we trudged out of camp that morning, I was beginning to regret that decision.

Maybe today will be better, I thought optimistically.

In those first two days, we got into the groove of hiking the A.T., forming new routines for everyday life. Back home, our routines had been full of things that seemed completely superfluous on the trail—things like wiping down counters while waiting for coffee to brew, and reading or writing for an hour or more every morning while the family all sat and talked. Out on the trail, there was no time for any of that. Survival and forward movement were the foundation of every action we took.

We fell into a rhythm. There were three things we did over and over again:

We walked. Our bodies were still getting used to our shoes and backpacks, so from Day 1, everything was sore, especially our shoulders, hips, knees, and feet.

We ate. This was a chore, particularly at the beginning, when all our food was frozen and we were still figuring out where all our equipment was stored. Boiling freezing water took a long time. Sitting and shivering while we waited was painful.

We stayed warm. We were walking in twenty-degree windchill. Even when the temperature climbed to the forties and fifties, it was well below body temperature and dangerous if we didn't actively stay warm. Unlike back home, there was no "inside" to retreat to.

Every minute of every day was spent doing one of these three things. There were no breaks, and we had no mental energy for anything else. The first couple days, we didn't even brush our teeth. It was too cold and just took too much energy. We felt like we were becoming wild animals. Once we reached camp each night, all our energy went to putting up tents and trying to get warm. In the morning, it was hard to even think about pouring cold water into our hands to do something like brushing teeth. It was shocking to see the speed at which previously "necessary" creature comforts went right out the window in just two days of living on the trail.

"I DON'T THINK I CAN DO THIS."

Day 2 wasn't much better than Day 1. Setting up camp at night and packing in the morning each took a long time and were incredibly complicated. It was a good thing that the cold had created a sense of perilous motivation, because these tasks would have been frustratingly tedious otherwise.

I did most of the work breaking down camp while the kids stood around and Kami tried to keep Rainier warm. We left camp without eating breakfast; the cold had also frozen all of our appetites.

On Day 2, Eden, our fifteen-year-old daughter, made a declaration.

"This is too hard. I don't like it. I don't think I can do this for six months."

As parents, we wanted to be strong, but Kami and I had the same thought going through our minds, and we knew everyone else was feeling that way too. Eden was just the first one to say it out loud.

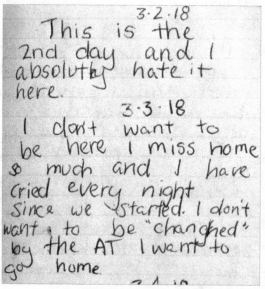

Eden's (15) journal from the first week.

At home, Kami and I are a step ahead of the kids, emotionally speaking; as the adults in their lives, they rely on us for advice and comfort. On the trail, though, our emotions were coming unhinged just as fast as theirs. The questions running through their heads were the same going through ours. *What did we get ourselves into? Will this ever get any better? Is it going to be this hard the whole way?*

I knew I had to be the family's cheerleader. "Things will get better," I told Eden. "Let's just take it one day at a time."

I said it just as much for my own benefit as everyone else's.

Kami and I both quickly fell into the role of coach. In sports, coaches yell all sorts of encouragement at the team, like, "You can do it" and "We got this!" They continue to encourage even if, in the backs of their minds, they don't believe what they're saying. But usually, the coach isn't playing the game. They have a different perspective and all sorts of energy to motivate their players, energy Kami and I didn't have. We were coaching and playing. Every hour, we'd stop and complain about our various aches and pains. Occasionally, we'd all just look at each other, and with one glance, we all knew what the others were thinking: *This is stupid. Why are we doing this?*

The main thing that kept us going that day was the path ahead of us. It was a single track through the forest with no easy way out. We had to walk to keep warm, so we just kept walking where the path took us. Having only hiked 8.4 miles on Day 1, we still had 2,180.6 miles left to go. It seemed like an impossible task.

We put our heads down, swallowed our fear and doubt, and just kept walking.

CHAPTER TWO

The Plan

"High sentiments always win in the end. The leaders who offer blood, toil, tears, and sweat always get more out of their followers than those who offer safety and a good time."

—George Orwell

Even though it was dry on Day 2, the temperature stayed in the freezing range. Kami had been carrying Rainier the entire time, and was really struggling; our baby boy was *way* heavier to carry on a hike than we'd expected. I carried the bulk of the gear for the three of us, which we thought would be heavier, so I couldn't help much with Rainier.

The kids were ahead of us and made it to camp around 5:30 p.m. while Kami and I still had half a mile to go. I could tell Kami was barely hanging on, totally exhausted and demoralized.

Then a glimmer of hope came walking back up the trail toward us.

"Hey, guys," Eden said, having doubled back from the campsite where her siblings were waiting. "I'll take Rainier for this last bit."

I saw Kami's face almost melt with relief. She gratefully lifted Rainier's backpack off her back and got him settled on his sister's back, and we all took off together to the campsite. Kami walked like a new person—she was faster, stood up straighter, and was smiling for the first time all day.

Most importantly, she didn't feel alone in her burden anymore. It couldn't have been easy for Eden to come back out to meet us; when you arrive at camp after walking all day and take your pack off, the last thing you think of doing is heading back out to the trail to optionally hike the same section two more times. But Eden was focusing on something besides comfort: she was focused on care. The trail had brought out the first glimpses of what we'd gone out there to see: our family caring for each other, while conquering a huge task together.

After walking in the cold for two days, we were emotionally raw. Things had been feeling bleak, and the inhibitions, logic, and patience we could put between our emotions and actions most of the time had been beat out of us by the conditions out on the trail. Little things that wouldn't have seemed like a big deal at home really stood out in the woods. Both of us, Kami and I, started crying with relief as we walked the last half-mile into camp.

We knew our family was capable of so much more than we ever imagined back home, and now we were seeing it. That snapshot of kindness Eden gave us offered us hope—something we didn't have much of.

If we were going to walk to Maine, we wouldn't be
able to avoid the cold or the rain or the difficult

miles. But one thing became apparent: we wouldn't be facing any of those things alone. Eden's gesture taught us the worst situations could be redeemed when you shared the moment with someone else.

While we hated being cold and wet and going without our beds or electricity, we thought back to our life one week earlier, when we had all those things but felt so isolated from each other. A week ago, it seemed impossible that one of our children could do something that would bring us to literal tears of joy. In that moment, we wondered why we had put off doing the trail for so long.

REASSESSING THE PLAN

The next morning, Kami and I tried to start the day off filming a vlog in our tent. But the camera lens was totally frozen from condensation caused by the cold.

We filmed anyway, cracking ourselves up with how bad the video was. "See that fog? That's *authentic*," Kami joked.

One highlight of the mornings on trail was that Rainier always seemed to be in a good mood when he woke up. The tent was an adventure to him. Every morning he woke up in a fort filled with sleeping bags, pads, and his brother and sisters. The nights were so cold that with down jackets and down quilts covering us, we were all huddled and shivering, and nobody got very good sleep. But we'd all slowly come awake in the morning to our toddler giggling and babbling away with his high-pitched, happy noisemaking, off in his own world.

It was our second day without coffee, and as Kami and I were packing up our campsite that morning, a couple of hikers walked past with more energy than any of us felt.

"Morning!" they called out cheerfully.

I tried to match their mood, but I'd had a long, exhausted night using a pack of diapers as a pillow, which is not as comfortable as it sounds, and my body was starting to scream from the physical output of the past two days. "Morning," I said, bleary-eyed, with all the false enthusiasm I could muster.

"Ready for breakfast? They're cooking for hikers about a mile down the trail."

Now I was awake! I looked at Kami, who mirrored my excitement.

Dove stuck her head out of her tent, her blonde hair messy from sleep and her blue eyes wide. "Did someone say breakfast? *Real food?*"

As fast as we all could, our family cleaned up the site, packed everything, and scrambled to get on the trail. The promise of hot cooked food was the boost of energy we all needed. I had a horrible vision of us all arriving at this supposed breakfast oasis just as they handed out the last meal, and hurried everyone along as fast as our legs could carry us.

We needn't have worried. Sure enough, a mile down the trail, the first thing to hit us was a delicious smell—sausage and eggs cooking on a grill. As we walked out of the woods toward the road, we saw a folding table set up with fruit snacks, breakfast sandwiches, and coolers of pop.

Behind the propane grill was a man in his early thirties wearing a blue baseball hat. "Morning!" he said as our whole family walked up. "Look at all of you! You hungry?"

We all gratefully filled paper plates with heaps of hot food, sandwiches, and anything else edible in sight. The kids sat down on the ground and tore into the food. I walked over to the man at the grill and introduced myself and Kami.

"I'm MacGyver," he said. "You all look like you could use some trail magic."

We'd heard the term before years ago in reference to leaving beer on the trail for other hikers to find on a hot day, but it had never occurred to us that we'd one day be the recipients of trail magic on this cold morning. And now, with the kids smiling and laughing, trail magic was the biggest highlight of the trip so far.

"I was a 2015 thru-hiker. My first two weeks were really disheartening, and Day 3, three years ago, I was thinking about quitting. Then I met a man standing right where I am cooking food. He went by Fresh Ground. That was the best breakfast I ever had, and I went on to finish the whole rest of the trail because of that moment. I wouldn't have made it without him. So I like to give a little trail magic back, and every year on this day, I come back to this spot and cook for hikers like you."

Kami and I were enthralled. We realized, maybe for the first time, that by hiking the trail, we were truly in a different world—a culture all its own.

MacGyver and Fresh Ground weren't their real names, obviously. They were trail names. We'd seen trail names in the logbooks placed along the route so far—people signing all sorts of weird aliases. Trail names are part of A.T. culture. You don't pick your trail name, you're *given* your trail name, and it's usually tied to a story, something notable that happened on the trail.

That morning's trail magic was enough to get us all back out in the freezing cold, walking determinedly with a spring in our step. Even with all that help, though, we were still only able to complete 8.5 miles that day.

Our first three days, we'd only done around twenty-five miles total. We'd been aiming for forty-five. Kami and I did the math in our tent that night—at this pace, it would take us more than eight and a half months to get to Mount Katahdin, arriving in mid-November.

Eight and a half months. We were horrified and felt totally deflated.

Lying back in our sleeping bags, Kami spoke aloud for the first time the big question that had haunted us internally.

"What if we can't do this?"

We would only ever ask these questions where the kids couldn't hear us. Our family's resolve and determination were like a fragile soap bubble in those first few weeks on the trail. If the kids saw us or heard us waver, the bubble would pop all too easily, and doubt and dejection would spread.

The next morning, Kami and I got back in our coach roles. We got the kids up, got them fed, packed up the camp, and got back on the trail. We tried not to think about the math anymore. We had to just put one foot in front of the other and keep our kids focused and determined.

On Day 4, we arrived at our first bit of civilization since leaving Halmonee and Papa at Mile 1. It was a road crossing that passed in front of a gear and souvenir shop called Mountain Crossings, a hostel, and a row of accommodations called the Blood Mountain Cabins. We walked eagerly up to Mountain Crossings, anxious to take our packs off and be in a building for the first time in three days.

As we drew closer, we saw an eerie sight: a giant oak tree outside the shop with hundreds of pairs of hiking boots hanging from its branches.

We knew right away what it was. We'd heard about it from other hikers. The shoes were the shoes of hikers who had decided to quit.

There are infinite reasons why someone might spend months, if not years, prepping for a hike like this, and then quit in the first week. People will come up with seemingly concrete reasons—*I packed the wrong gear. I got injured. I didn't train right.* The net result is the same, though: they give up because it's too hard. It's as simple as that.

I want to say that as we approached the shoe tree, we felt compassion for those who had faced the challenge and lost. But honestly, at that moment of extreme fatigue, our lizard brains took over. *Look at all these people who quit. That's not us.* All we felt was relief and superiority. In the midst of an almighty struggle, cold, exhausted, and still so far from Katahdin, superiority was all we had to cling to. *We have what it takes, and all these people didn't.*

MacGuyver had said something during our Day 3 breakfast that had stuck with us. "Everybody thinks that the Appalachian Trail is about sacrifice, about taking things away. But it's not about taking things away. It's about revealing what's really underneath."

For us, our mindset had always been that quitting was *not* an option. I wasn't willing to announce to our friends and family that we couldn't handle four days of pain. We could handle four days of *anything*. Our family had also learned a trick about endurance that had helped us previously: *Don't even think about quitting.* You can't afford to even allow yourself to ask the question. Once you go down that path, the pressure of your pain will speak louder than the long-term reward, so it's best not to entertain that voice at all.

But now, after hiking through four days of bone-chilling cold, I started to become aware that there could be a much higher cost to keep going under these conditions. Katahdin was still so far away, and we weren't making our miles, not by a long shot. Such a far-away goal offered us no immediate satisfaction or motivation. And our days were about constant suffering. Suffering from the walking, suffering from the adaptation to no electricity, suffering from the cold. There was no pleasure, no enjoying anything.

We'd dreamt of the trail in a totally different way—walking in the heat, finding streams to explore, taking three-hour lunches while swimming and lying in the grass. We'd imagined work, but we'd also imagined joy. So far, our hike had only been pain.

If we allowed the pain to linger too long in our minds, it would be over. We'd toss our shoes into the tree. We'd give up. We'd go home.

So instead, we pushed the pain out of our minds, rallied around the tree and laughed at the crazy sight of so many hiking boots hanging there.

Our family was too big for the hostel attached to the store—a problem we'd find ourselves facing many times on the trail—so we decided to splurge on one of the cabins. Spending some time indoors with the heat blasting watching the rain from inside of a window would be a huge boost for our morale.

But no sooner did we get indoors than disaster struck. One by one, all the kids started barfing.

Rainier's fussing three days earlier appeared to be as we'd feared—we thought he'd picked up a bug. And now all the kids had it.

From Day 1, even when we didn't feel like we were making enough progress, at least we were still moving forward. Now, with the kids so sick, we weren't going anywhere. We had almost nothing to show for our months of sacrifice, saving, and planning to do the A.T.

The shoes in the tree suddenly struck us differently. The reasons to quit didn't just feel like excuses anymore—instead of seeing weakness, we saw wisdom. After all, pushing the pain out of our minds meant that we weren't actually *dealing* with it; in a way, we were lying to ourselves. Now we were asking ourselves if it was wise or healthy, physically or emotionally, for six kids under our care to go farther. This was dangerous territory to be in, mentally and physically.

With everyone sick and more freezing rain falling, we decided to take an unexpected "zero day," which is a day when you hike zero miles. Most hikers on the A.T. do everything in their power to avoid unnecessary zero days. Zero days are usually reserved for resupplies or intentionally planned days of relaxing in nicer weather with friends in a town. When your only job is to keep moving forward, it's seriously demoralizing to hike zero miles in a day for reasons completely out of your control. Doing it in our first week was *not* part of our plan—yet here we were.

With morale at an all-time low, it was time to stop and think.

MUCH-NEEDED MOTIVATION

Many people had told us how brave we were for starting the A.T., but sitting there in the Blood Mountain cabins watching our kids throw up into every available sink, toilet, and trash can, we didn't feel brave at all.

Knowing I had to record something for the vlog, I pulled out the camera and said the only honest and positive thing I could think of. I was mostly talking to myself.

"We didn't start the A.T. *because* we were brave, but we did believe it would make us brave."

It was my way of asking for help.

You can't enter into a journey like this without being changed. If there was any superpower we had developed, it had nothing to do with hiking. It had to do with wanting positive change, even when we didn't know what that change was going to look like. We hoped the trail would make us the type of people who could finish, to teach our kids that they could accomplish huge things. We didn't need to know we could finish the trail when we started it. We started only knowing we could take the next step. The ability to finish would have to come from the journey.

> We didn't start because we knew we had what
> it takes. We were just confident we'd pick
> up what it would take along the way.

But in that rustic cabin far from home, I started to fear that the change wouldn't come quick enough. One more day under these conditions seemed daunting.

At the Blood Mountain cabins, we felt trapped. It was incredibly remote—no internet, no cell coverage, and no cable—and because it was the off-season for day hikers (who wait until spring to hike, when the weather is good), all we found to eat were frozen pizzas and Pop-Tarts. The office had a bunch of VHS tapes, but we couldn't get our TV/VCR combo to work. The lady behind the reception desk felt so bad about the lack of supplies, she offered to do laundry and give us clean blankets. As we had been wearing the same clothes for three days and the kids had thrown up on all the blankets, we gratefully accepted her offer. From this point forward, we took eager advantage of any chance to machine-wash our clothes, since it would prove to be the exception, not the rule.

So, with at least one small problem—clean laundry—taken care of, Kami and I decided to take a few minutes away from the kids to sit on the porch and smoke cigars. Throughout our marriage, this has been our little ritual, and our best ideas often come to us in these moments, when we step outside of our current reality and clear our heads to think.

Out on the porch, we agreed that it seemed ridiculous to be taking sick kids into the rain. Not one single family member, Kami and I included, had enjoyed the past four days. At this point, the coaching we were doing seemed completely hollow.

But a piece of advice we'd heard in all our trail research filtered back in to our discussions.

Never quit on a bad day.

We agreed that the advice was sound. How could we know how great the experience could become, how much the trail could have to offer us, if we left it when we were in a low?

The problem was, we didn't see any good days on the horizon. It seemed like going back home would solve our problem, which was, very simply, that life on the trail was too different from life at home. We couldn't enjoy the forest and togetherness when we spent all our energy staying dry or thinking about how badly our feet hurt. The bland winter landscape wasn't exactly helping; there were no leaves on the trees and everything was brown. All of our energy was spent trying to stay warm. We weren't even talking much to each other. Our warm, happy, close family had turned into a nearly silent, shuffling, frigid mass focused only on the crucial task of putting one foot in front of the other.

After a few moments, I said, "I don't think this is going to be sustainable."

We knew a certain degree of discomfort was inevitable, and we could handle that. We didn't mind pushing our kids, but we didn't want to *break* them. Currently, the morale-to-pain ratio was way off. Our kids were on track to hate hiking, and possibly end up hating us.

Then an idea hit like lightning.

The biggest sacrifice the kids had made for the A.T. was their summer vacation. It was a tradition for our family to go to our old home state of Washington in the summer, and the kids always looked forward to a summer camp there called Lakeside Bible Camp—a camp Kami and I had both grown up at, and where we actually met as teenagers. It was a religious summer camp, and although Kami and I had transitioned away from our super-religious upbringings and many of our beliefs had shifted, Lakeside was still a place that represented the relationships and memories that we cared about most. Our entire extended family descended on Lakeside every summer, and the kids and all their cousins had a blast. It was fun, it was nostalgic, and it was a time to connect with the people we felt safest with. This year, they'd given up Lakeside because six months of hiking meant it was absolutely impossible to do both. Every day we hiked in the cold was a reminder of that cost.

Now, knowing the kids needed a boost to keep going, Kami and I asked new questions: What if it were possible to still go to Washington? What if we could make it to Lakeside?

We quickly did the math. If we wanted to finish the A.T. and still make it to Lakeside, we would have to finish by August 9. That was 156 days away, just over five months, instead of the six months we had planned. If we accepted this goal, the math said we would have to average fourteen miles a day *every single day* for the next 156 days. We had already taken a zero day and only traveled thirty miles on our entire trip so far, averaging just six miles a day. We would have to hike more than twice as many miles per day, which assumed no more days off. Any more zero days would only make the fourteen miles per day average increase.

We briefly considered the option of heading to Lakeside even if we didn't complete the trail, then coming back to the trail after vacation to finish the hike. Just as quickly, we nixed it as a possibility—that would be *way* too expensive.

That left us with two options. The first was the more relaxed option of taking six months to finish the trail, with no deadline, but also no Lakeside reunion with cousins.

The second option was to go for the seemingly impossible, and try to finish the trail in time to make it to Lakeside. In the past, when we'd believed in a goal hard enough, and committed ourselves to it, our family had exceeded all expectations and accomplished what had seemed impossible—so we knew that with the right motivation, the *impossible* was actually within our reach.

We weighed the downsides. Kami's biggest fear was being rushed. "If we push the kids too hard just to make this goal, we won't stop and look around," she said. "We might miss everything the trail has to offer."

I heard her loud and clear, but my heart was telling me we should go for the Lakeside option. In our partnership, I've always been the one who has tended to push to go faster, focused on reaching distance or time goals. I'd seen what could happen when our kids were motivated and determined—they were unstoppable.

"We're not enjoying the trail as it is," I countered. "The priority here has to be improving their spirits, even if it means going faster. If they hate the whole experience, why did we even do this?"

Kami and I have learned as parents to see our often-different perspectives as an asset, not a liability. When the decision involves our kids, it's crucially important to combine our perspectives—making sure all possible paths are accounted for, and that we're both 100 percent bought in to the way forward.

And now, we both agreed that no matter the pros and cons of the Lakeside option, the inescapable reality of our current situation was clear: motivating the kids was the only way we even had a chance to finish the trail.

By the end of the conversation, we were both fully onboard. Pushing through to try to make it to Lakeside was the best option we had. Even though hitting the deadline of August 9 might kill us, it was the only way we could think of to tap into our kids' motivation. And doing so *had* to be our number-one priority.

If our kids were motivated, they could handle the cold. They could handle the fatigue. They could handle the discomfort. Fully motivated, they could handle *anything*.

But we also knew something else. If we were going to use this reward to motivate our kids, we had to hold up our end as parents. That meant following through on the trip to Lakeside whether we were able to finish the A.T. or not. If we couldn't make it by the deadline, so be it. It was a painful possibility to imagine—I pictured us hiking through wilderness for five months, walking almost all the way there, and missing the deadline by a week or mere days. To have to give up within steps of Katahdin. The moment we'd have to pull the plug would be the moment when we had the most to lose. If we actually did make it that far, proving that we could do it, could I walk away from the glory that actually came *from* doing it? It was going to be my job for the next five months to summon the strength to walk away, because it would be contrary to every competitive, determined bone in my body. But on the other hand, to require that much effort from our kids for four months and then rob them of their anticipated reward wasn't something Kami and I were comfortable with. We would have to hold up our end, no question.

In order to rally the motivation the kids so desperately needed, we were risking it all—risking our completion of the trail. We were also *definitely* sacrificing our original vision of our hike; instead of relaxed days taking swimming breaks and picnics, we were going to do nothing but hike.

Kami and I agreed it was worth it.

Decision made, we went into action mode. The only way to get into Lakeside at this point—which was already at capacity—was to see if we could help with the volunteer cooking at the camp, something our family usually did anyway. The first line of business was to make a couple of calls and find out if it was too late. There was no cell service or internet at the cabins, but we did manage to get a few texts out to my uncle who was running the cooking crew at Lakeside.

Soon, he texted back: "There's space for you guys! We can't wait to see you!"

It was game on.

Kami and I went back inside to the "sickbay." There was smelly hiking gear and frozen cheeseburger wrappers spread out all over the place. Six queasy, frowning faces looked up at us.

"Guys, we have an exciting announcement," I started. No one smiled. To be fair, they'd endured a lot of "exciting announcements" recently.

"Listen," Kami said. "We have a chance to finish the trail in time to make it to Lakeside in August. So your dad and I talked about it and worked out what we need to do. And if we do it, we'll all go to Washington at the end."

Right away, Memory, our skeptic, said, "But what if we *don't* finish the trail?"

Kami and I looked at each other. "As long as you give it your all," I said, "we'll still go to Lakeside. Whether we finish or not."

Instantly, we knew we'd made the right call. Their faces lit up. This was the best news the kids had heard in five days. As Dove said later in one of our videos, "That lit a frickin' *fire* in our hearts!"

Dove and Eden retreated up to the attic where they were sleeping and started making excited plans in hushed tones. Seven and Memory got chatting about their cousins. Instantly, the focus shifted from the rain that was still pouring down outside to the dream of spending a week at Lakeside.

We knew from the start that the kids weren't going to be as motivated to finish the trail as Kami and I were. We knew they were piggybacking on our motivation. Katahdin had always been much more our goal than theirs, and if our goal was all they had to push themselves, they might have resented us at the end. By giving them their own motivation, an incentive they truly valued, we gave them something to fight for. For the first time, they were motivated all on their own.

We could also see that, even though it was hard, it wasn't the hiking the kids had a problem with. It was the vision. Our kids were more like us than we thought; they could put up with perpetual discomfort for something they believed in, but it would be our job to help them find that belief.

It was going to cost eight plane tickets to Washington, and probably our goal of finishing the trail. But it would show our kids that we recognized their efforts and would deliver on our promise, whether or not we made it to that A-frame sign at the end.

Most importantly, we all now had an end date in mind. In 156 days, we would be finished with our hike, no matter what. It felt like our suffering now had a purpose—it felt a thousand times more endurable knowing it would definitely end at a concrete point in the future. It was a totally unintended benefit, but that end date would be one of the biggest contributors to our morale and speed.

Now with an ending date in mind, we started to enjoy the cabin as a launching point for our newly invigorated adventure. We took advantage of our first chance to brush our teeth, take showers, and sleep in real beds. We blasted the heat as high as it would go, something we never would have done at home, where we prefer to save energy and wear layers. We enjoyed the running water, took turns heating up our frozen burgers in the microwave, and took the opportunity to catch up on journaling. We even recorded a voiceover intro that would be used for the rest of our trail vlogs.

MONDAY Day#5 march 5th 2081

Everyone threw up last night. Thank goodness we're in a cabin and not a tent oh my gosh. Memory o Filia. Then Seven. Both Eden and Moma don't feel good. Dada thinks we're going to stay in the cabin for another day. Fox Cabin. Breakfast is cooking. Tofu breakfast burritos. num mmmmm. Its almost 10:00.

What a relaxing day. We went up to the main cabin and tried to upload the vlog again. The most it got up to today was 30%. We went up to the mountain store got some food, still wouldn't upload any faster. MoD smoked cigars on the porch and the kids watched Mr. & Mrs. Smith in the Cabin. Fun. AFTER DINNER MOMA AND DADA MADE THE LBC ANNOUNCMENT!!! WE HAVE 5 MONTHS AND 2,160 MILES PEOPLE LETS GO!!!

Dove's (16) journal. We learned early on that the kids
needed their own goals to stay motivated.

On Day 6, the sickness had passed; the kids all woke up well enough to get back on their feet. We left the cabin and walked back into the rain, everyone more motivated than ever.

CHAPTER THREE

The Towns, Our Salvation

"Truth, being limitless, unconditioned, unapproachable by any path whatsoever, cannot be organized; nor should any organization be formed to lead or to coerce people along any particular path."

—J. Krishnamurti

O ur newfound motivation was like a warm blanket around our shoulders as we got back on the trail. But by the end of Day 6, the misery of the freezing cold and our heavy, sore legs was starting to sneak under the warm blanket.

It occurred to us that the big-picture goal of making it to Lakeside would be an effective long-term motivation, but we needed a second level of short-term motivation to counteract the immediate moment-to-moment discomfort of the hike. Kami and I soon discovered we could take the same concept of a motivating goal and break it up into smaller chunks. The younger kids especially needed smaller rewards over shorter time periods. Filia, who was only seven years old when we started the A.T., didn't understand how long a month was, let alone five months, and Rainier couldn't grasp numbers yet. His only metric of future time was "tomorrow"—which he also used to refer to anything in the past. So we began using gummy bears and granola bars as small rewards at regular time intervals, instead of just eating when we were hungry. This also helped with the nutrition deficit we were facing from burning so many calories. It's amazing how much joy and inspiration even one gummy bear can bring when you've walked for miles in the cold.

Our multi-level motivation system worked. On Day 6, we hiked the most miles we'd done yet: 11.5!

We still hadn't hit the magic number of fourteen miles per day, but we were in the double digits. On Day 7, it got so cold that we wrapped Rainier's limbs in hand warmers, but we kept moving, and we made it 13.4 miles.

We were getting closer and closer to the average we needed. Having something to look forward to, even something small, had made all the difference.

THE FIRST TOWN

Even though the gummy bears were nice, they only worked for about five minutes at a time. As we continued, we found that another short-term motivation helped us keep moving forward: the promise of going to town.

Contrary to popular perception, much of the A.T. is not in the remote wilderness. The trail crosses over regular roads and highways and brushes past tons of towns as it snakes its way north. It was

Dove (16).

often possible for us to leave the trail and head into town, stay in a hotel overnight, and pick up at the same spot on the trail the next morning.

Coming into a town felt like finding an oasis in the desert. After days of cold, fatigue, dirt, sweat, and bland trail food, the towns were like a shining beacon of hot food, clean sheets, bright lights, and warmth.

The first major town we hit on our hike was Hiawassee, Georgia. We'd reserved two hotel rooms and kept the kids moving for days with promises of the pool, hot showers, and a breakfast buffet. As we hiked, I'd overhear their plans for that breakfast buffet get more and more detailed and excited. It was hilarious to listen to a bunch of kids having delirious daydreams about something as simple as a hot meal...except that Kami and I were doing exactly the same thing.

We had arranged for a shuttle driver to pick us up and drive us to our hotel in Hiawassee. After spending a week essentially isolated in nature, civilization looked weirdly bright, loud, and intense as the shuttle drove us into town.

"Look!" Memory yelled as the shuttle whipped us through the streets. She was pointing at a billboard for Hardee's with a giant, juicy burger on it. Our stomachs all rumbled in unison.

And ten seconds later, Memory pointed again. "Can we go there too?"

It was a local coffee shop. I looked at Kami, who'd been in the throes of coffee withdrawal since our hike began. "I *need* to go there!" she said.

The hotel would have to wait.

This became our "town arrival" ritual. We'd hit as many food spots as we could. Fast food, then a café, then a grocery store to pick up supplies for the hotel room. In the grocery store, we walked up and down the aisles and just stared. The abundance was overwhelming; we had no idea where to start. There were so many people, so many options! We weren't sure how much to buy. We saw a few other hikers in the store; we could spot each other from a mile away. To the outside world, we looked like people to avoid—dirty clothes hanging off our obviously unwashed bodies and all—but among each other, we felt like part of an underground fraternity.

After the grocery store, we walked to the Holiday Inn Express. We had two rooms next door to each other, and we spread our gear over the entire space. Our insulation layers, jackets, and gloves were all wet. The wet wipes were frozen together. It felt good to be free of wet clothes and know everything would actually thaw out. For the first time, we didn't have to think about staying warm.

The sudden comfort and ease opened up our minds in a way we hadn't anticipated. We dropped the icy, tough emotional guards we'd all put up against the wind and rain on the trail, and actually started enjoying ourselves again.

We snuggled up to the fluffy hotel pillows, something we definitely didn't have in our tents. Dove charged her iPod, Eden organized her gear and tried to dry everything out, Seven turned on the television—even the commercials seemed interesting—Filia rolled around on the carpet, and Rainier ran around naked between the two rooms, jumping on the beds.

That night in Hiawassee, since all our clothes were drying, we walked around town in flip-flops, shorts, and rain jackets, with no bras or T-shirts even though it was forty degrees. We looked like extremely out-of-style homeless people, but we didn't care. Hikers affectionately refer to the aesthetic as "hiker trash."

For dinner, we went to Daniel's Steakhouse, a run-down, all-you-can-eat Southern buffet that did not serve steak. The restaurant was littered with Bibles and Gone with the Wind paraphernalia. To our family, it was exotic bordering on bizarre, but we didn't care. We just focused on the fried chicken, macaroni and cheese, mashed potatoes, and in what seemed like an odd, old-fashioned touch, tons and tons of margarine, which wound up being one of the hallmarks of a meal in Georgia. We stuffed ourselves to satisfaction with what felt like the best food we'd ever tasted.

The best part was that we'd arrived in Hiawassee on a Friday night, so it was Shabbat night. In our much more religious days, Kami and I had explored our roots and found answers to many of our questions in the ancient practices of Judaism. One of these practices was in the practice of Shabbat, or a rest day on Saturday. We'd brought it into our family, keeping it a special day of celebration where we abstained from work and most social activities to enjoy peace at home with good food and the company of each other.

Now, we celebrated the upcoming Sabbath by stuffing ourselves and letting each of the kids order their own soda, a rarity for us. Resting at the buffet in that small town in Georgia, so far from home, we were reminded of who we were back home.

TOWN LUXURIES

The towns made us realize how much we missed, but also reminded us of the life tasks we wanted to stay on top of. As it was the only time we had internet, being in town was our only opportunity to upload videos to YouTube.

Three years earlier, our family had started a YouTube channel called Fight For Together. Our goal was to share the importance of the most difficult relationships—family ones—by filming the normal, everyday parts of our lives. We recorded family meetings, fights, road trips, chores, and our struggle to figure out how to "do" family in the age of technology. It was a daily vlog format that we published five days a week.

As we quickly discovered, most people don't find our normal life that interesting. After three years, we only had seven thousand subscribers watching our videos. According to all the social media advice out there, that number should have been much higher for such a consistent and sustained effort. But although we were never paid for our videos, we treated their creation like a job; it was important to us to create the very best content we could, even if we weren't seeing the kind of ROI we'd expected.

It was also, however, a ton of work, the kind of work we couldn't really see happening alongside a thru-hike. So it seemed natural to put the channel on hold when we decided to hike the A.T. After all, part of the point of the hike was to get away from the distractions of the modern world.

But as our departure grew nearer, we started to see that sharing our time on the trail would be the best opportunity to share what we were the most passionate about. Three years of filming, editing, and uploading videos had been the perfect training for this event. We considered what it would take to capture every step of the journey. We would have to carry cameras, batteries, SD cards, cords, a drone, and a laptop for editing—heavy, cumbersome equipment, when the name of the game in thru-hiking is the lightest load possible. We had never heard of anyone hiking the A.T. with a laptop.

After a lot of back-and-forth, we decided that it was worth the hassle and extra weight to share our picture of what family togetherness could look like. A trail vlog just seemed like too cool an opportunity to pass up. As we hiked, we posted videos of our experience. Each video began with the introduction we'd recorded back in the cabin on Day 4: "We're the Crawfords. We have six kids and are hiking the Appalachian Trail—a 2,200-mile hike from Georgia to Maine. We don't know if we can finish it, but we are doing it together."

Seven and I bonded over editing the daily hiking vlogs. Seven had been editing our YouTube videos for more than a year as a modified version of homeschooling, so it was only natural that editing our video footage was his job out on the trail. It was Dove's job to create enticing titles and thumbnail pictures that would capture people's attention. We made it our goal to edit and publish five days a week out on the trail.

Publishing interesting content five days a week is challenging back in the real world. When all you're doing is walking for twelve hours a day complaining about the exact same things, it's even harder to make your content exciting. Seven and I came up with challenges and tried to catch unique angles with the different cameras we brought. We cracked each other up collaborating on funny ways to bring boring events to life.

In addition to the opportunity to edit and upload our videos, towns provided us with welcome and dependable cellphone coverage. We were able to plan for the next hostel, arrange transportation, and order more gear. We also took showers every time we went into a town. Because of the cold, we never took our shirts off on the trail, so it was a huge relief to let our skin breathe a little after wearing the same damp shirt for four days straight. We wanted everyone to enjoy their showers, but we had to start setting time limits because the process took so long. Once in the shower, it would take ten minutes to get past the initial bliss of the warm water. It felt like being in a spa—we were shocked by comfort. Nobody wanted to get out.

In hotels, we often walked around in towels, waiting for our turn to take a shower and for all the clothes to be washed. I walked around hotel rooms in my underwear, feeling happy and relaxed. It was quite a scene.

Kami and I got used to new rhythms in our relationship too. For the first three months of cold, the only time we had sex was in hotels. On the trail, it was too cold and too ridiculous to feel sexual in sleeping bags, especially since, often, Rainier was sleeping in the same tent as us.

Hotels became an important connection point for us. Part of it was the practicality of lighting, covers, and not being cold. The bigger part, though, was that the trail didn't feel like a place for recreation. We were pretty consistently stressed; when we weren't walking on a narrow strip of dirt all the way to Maine, we were either trying to make sure our toddler didn't walk off a cliff, or desperately trying to find ways to stay warm. Hotels became a place to breathe, let our hair down, think, smile...and play.

In the towns, we each indulged in our own special items. Mine was beer. I'm not a big drinker, but it somehow made me feel civilized and I needed the calories. Kami and the kids loved Cherry Coke. In the mornings, Kami and I sipped coffee with half-and-half. Even things like carpeted floors made us feel more human.

The only hard part about visiting towns so often was leaving a town to go back on the trail, especially when it was raining. We got through it knowing that all of us, no matter our age, were sharing the same experience, and it gave us something to commiserate about. There's something about seeing your kids go into literal shock with you that almost makes the experience worth it. I remember twice my body broke out in cold sweats from being so depleted from calories and shocked from the temperature that it paralyzed me. Both of those times, I looked over at Memory, whose teeth were rattling uncontrollably and audibly, and we would instantly start laughing. Pain is often feared; but we learned it was more the *isolation* around the pain that we feared. When shared, the pain felt almost funny. It felt like a rare opportunity to be finding these limits of our bodies together.

It helped, too, that we knew there was always another town coming up. Walking in the cold for weeks, the finish line seemed so far away. But knowing a town was only twenty or thirty miles away made those miles easier and seem to go by faster. They were small stepping stones on the road to the greater victory.

The more times we left towns to get back on the trail, we started to notice that the "detox" time was shrinking. The creature comforts we took advantage of in town became easier and easier to let go of the longer we hiked. We just didn't need them as much as before. Our sense of entitlement around pillows, showers, coffee, and electricity began to leave us. We found the pleasure we used to derive from our things just from looking into each other's faces and laughing at our common misery. It seemed we were now finding just as much pleasure from being miserable together as we were from being comfortable alone.

MOVING ON

After that first fantastic night in town, we woke up in the Holiday Inn Express and looked at the weather. It was the same as the day before: rain and below-freezing temperatures.

Being cold was hard. Being wet *and* cold was dangerous. The predicted weather was the most dangerous combination for us, and especially for Rainier, whose little body struggled to stay warm. It was a hard decision, but we ended up staying at the Holiday Inn for three nights—two zero days against our goal that we could never get back. Every morning when we looked at the weather report, we wondered if we were making the right choice. Being at the hotel felt like paradise, but it also made us feel lazy. It was hard to fully enjoy the amenities knowing we would have to pay for the lost miles later.

That didn't stop us from trying, though. We took full advantage of the waffle machines, yogurt, and sausage at the hotel's continental breakfast. There was a pool and a hot tub, so we spent the afternoons sitting and soaking with other hikers.

While being in towns was wonderful, it felt like we were selling out by leaving nature at all. Kami and I often wondered if this was how we should be doing the A.T. It seemed like there was a more "right" or "pure" way to thru-hike. Staying in towns felt a bit like cheating, and a twinge of guilt set in. We'd imagined hiking the trail "for real" meant staying in a tent and braving the elements, regardless of the weather. Were we still thru-hikers if we stayed in hotels sometimes? Would other hikers still view us as equals?

As we discovered, the questions we were asking ourselves were a common topic of conversation on the Appalachian Trail internet forum Whiteblaze. We'd already drawn attention there because of our YouTube channel, and forum users were chiming in with their opinions on our hike.

"It is quite irritating to see him market his family as 'thru-hikers' when in reality they are pretty much just day hikers. Nine out of ten nights they are off trail either being hosted by someone or staying in a hotel." —Penny1942

"Talk about clueless. They're not going to last much longer. It only gets harder. BTW, they posted a new vlog today." —Slo-go'en

"I don't knock them for giving this a try and having some fun, but if they cannot keep those kids safe I hope they are smart enough to pull the plug on this adventure." —imscotty

"Their gimmick has worked...I've subscribed just to watch the slow motion train wreck." —Zed

The criticism stung. It echoed our own doubts about our endeavor. What had we even brought our whole family out here for, if we weren't "real" thru-hikers? But when it came to these outside voices, we tried to remind ourselves that what they thought didn't matter. In my mind's eye, I pictured a bunch of angry, crusty old men sitting around in the comfort of their homes wearing pajamas. They'd turned themselves into some kind of "council of elders," and they'd turned the A.T. into a religion. Having spent long, painful years rejecting the authority structures we had once been made to submit to, this was a religion Kami and I had *no* interest in following.

At the Holiday Inn, we were burning time. Because we needed two rooms, we were also burning a lot of money. At home, weather makes decisions easy. If it's raining, you stay inside. But our family had a goal to accomplish, and even though we had months to do it, we knew if we kept avoiding bad weather, we'd never finish. We were only on Day 11 and we had taken three zeroes, putting our daily average at 4.75 miles a day. So, even though it was raining on Day 12, the temperature had risen just enough that we knew we couldn't wait anymore. We couldn't afford anymore zeroes, and we'd have to skip towns for a while to make up for the lost mileage.

When we started the climb out of the parking lot, snow began to fall. It was the first time we became really concerned about Rainier and the cold. The snow was sticking to the ground, and that night, it was so stormy we slept in a ditch. It was the only protection we could find from the cold, harsh wind.

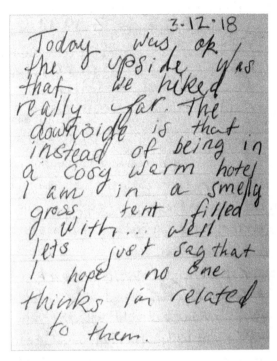

Eden (15) writing about what it's like to share one four-man tent with six people.

On Day 14, we sat in our tents eating our frozen Pop-Tarts for breakfast. We didn't want to leave. The weather report said it would be the coldest day yet. There was snow on the ground. Kami had just started her period. Could things get any worse?

The silver lining was that we were steadily increasing our mileage day by day. One day we managed twelve miles, and soon after, we had our longest day ever, at 15.8 miles. That was a long way in the snow, but we were still so far behind.

At the state line of Georgia and North Carolina, we celebrated our first major milestone; we had walked to a different state! We stopped to take a picture, but the cold wind was blowing so hard that it was hard to enjoy it, and the good feelings didn't last long.

The physical suffering was at times overwhelming. Our shoulders ached from our packs, our feet hurt from walking, and most of the time, we could not feel our fingers from the cold. Kami was lagging behind and seemed on the verge of tears most of the time. The pressure of our new goal placed a mental toll on her that the rest of us didn't feel; she hated being rushed. She liked taking it easy. These were feelings that she would have to put aside for the next five months.

We planned to pitch our tent again as usual, but judging by the plunging morale, I felt the crew could use a little something—Kami in particular. Her body had taken a huge toll from the cold and carrying Rainier for the first couple weeks of the hike until we reached Hiawassee, when I'd taken over. She wasn't complaining because she knew the effect it would have on the kids. We couldn't afford that. But I knew if there was any way I could help her, I should.

As we continued walking, I fumbled with the guide books in my thin winter gloves, trying to figure out how to get to a town. This was easier said than done. We had no phone service, and internet was non-existent. I've always been the most budget-conscious member between the two of us, and towns equaled money, but I decided at this point that money needed to be spent. If we could find a way to get to a town, we would.

Eventually, thankfully, we hit a sign indicating that a place called Winding Stair Gap was three miles ahead, and that a road from there would lead to Franklin, North Carolina. We didn't know anything about the town, or how we would get there, but we knew the road would take us someplace warm, and warm was what mattered at that moment.

Kami had stopped at the sign and begun to change Rainier's diaper on the super-thin foam pad we used as a serviceable diaper station. It was freezing, with the cold wind howling over Rainier's exposed skin. Kami struggled with the diaper fasteners, her fingers likely numb. I could tell she was at the end of her rope.

I asked Kami, "How would you like it if I tried and got somebody to bring us into town?"

She looked up at me with wide eyes and said, with tears in her voice, "Are you kidding? That would be *amazing*."

Kami was my biggest priority, and I needed to look out for her. If she wasn't in a good place, she couldn't help me keep the kids motivated and in a good place. Even though we had stayed at a hotel only two days before, I decided I was more than willing to spend more so that Kami could have a hot cup of coffee—something the budget-conscious part of me never would have done back home. Hotel rooms only ran us about $200–300 a night, but in that moment, I would have paid thousands.

The kids had hiked up ahead of us. We shouted to them about the new plan. By the looks on their faces, we knew we had made the right choice. Now it was just a matter of figuring out our ride. Shuttles, which you donate to or pay for, are the go-to transportation options along the A.T., but they require cell service, and we had none. Our fate and safety depended on the kindness of strangers. For most hikers on the A.T., hitchhiking is no big deal. Many locals passing by are glad to pick up hikers. It's a little different when you're a family of eight, though. Transportation isn't quite so easy.

"The road to town is just three miles up ahead, but we have no idea if we can find a ride," I told the kids, so they wouldn't get their hopes up. Our only option was to hitchhike.

None of them had ever hitchhiked, but they were all game to learn. We did a quick ground-rules session.

Put your thumb out.

Look for nice people.

Don't get in anyone's car until we catch up to you.

Dove instantly ran up ahead to stand by the road, her thumb out and a huge grin on her face. The other kids ran ahead to look for any cars that might help us out.

The A.T. runs across a lot of tiny roads, and we knew it wasn't likely that someone would stop, let alone be able to carry eight people. However, being in the woods does crazy things to you. Back home, we would have never even considered hitchhiking. We have two cars, we could always call a friend in a pinch, and Uber or Lyft seemed like reasonable options. Out here on the A.T., desperation made all sorts of previously questionable decisions seem normal.

MEETING ARNIE

We walked up to a parking lot about fifteen minutes behind the older kids, who'd run far ahead of the rest of us. Dove pointed out an old white van pulled over nearby. It was the only vehicle in the lot. We immediately ruled it out because it had no windows and was likely broken down, since there was a man underneath trying to fix it.

One of the kids said they had already talked to the couple at the van. The man, who was underneath, later introduced himself as just "G." He was tall with a bit of a beer belly. He wore a ball cap and his scraggly gray hair stuck out the sides. There was also a woman—a lady in her late sixties—wearing headphones, a red jacket, and a beanie. She called herself "Arnie-1-Mile."

Arnie-1-Mile said, "If you can't find a ride, we could probably help. There aren't any seats, much less a car seat—just a mattress in the back."

Kami and I looked at the van and hesitated. It looked like a mix between a church van and the kind of windowless van you see on

To Catch a Predator. By their names, these people seemed like they might be hikers, but that didn't fit with the fact that they had a van. *This cannot be a good idea*, I thought.

Arnie said, "Look, if we can get this van fixed, we'll definitely take you to town."

We decided that whoever she was, if she was willing to take us into town, it didn't matter. Some situations are worth the kidnapping.

Sure enough, within minutes, G fixed the van, and soon we all found ourselves crammed into the back on the mattress along with our seven backpacks—each of which took up the space of a whole person. It felt like we'd crammed seventeen people in one tiny room.

Back home, riding on a mattress in the back of a stranger's van with no seatbelts would have would be an obviously *terrible* idea. But when you've been walking for weeks, and that van is delivering you from the freezing temperatures of the woods to a bed with electricity and warm water, it feels like a stroke of genius.

Throughout the fifteen-minute drive, the van sounded like it was going to fall apart. It was so loud, we couldn't hear each other talking.

We didn't care. We were going to town.

BEING CARED FOR

We had never met anyone like Arnie. She was a sixty-six-year-old woman who had been sick and confined to a recliner for six years. A year and a half prior to meeting us, she'd decided to walk the A.T., and she'd been hiking the trail in sections ever since. She carried a ratty-looking white stuffed bear named ChaJulEv that sat on her shoulder and that she talked to constantly. She said she was taking it slow and had started the trail in early February, almost a month before us. Her appearance and walking style was unlike anyone we had seen so far. She was being supported by "G" in the van; she referred to their group as "the three of us" (including ChaJulEv). She was doing some sections northbound, some sections southbound, and skipping some sections when the van needed work, only to come back and walk them later.

When we all climbed wearily out of the van, even though we had known Arnie for less than half an hour, we exchanged hugs. Then she included us in a little ritual: she had all of us tap our chests three times and say, "God bless you."

Arnie knew everything there was to know about the town of Franklin. She was like a private tour guide. She pointed out all the best hotels and restaurants; she even knew the manager at the front desk of a hotel, and negotiated the cheapest rate possible for us.

"God bless you guys," she said to us. "You're living life your own way. That is so important." Then she added, "I'm sure you guys will hang in there and make sure you hike your own hike."

It wasn't the first time we'd heard of the phrase "hike your own hike," but Arnie-1-Mile was the first time we'd seen it in action. The basic gist of the saying is that there's no wrong way to hike the trail. Some people do it ten miles at a time. Others do the whole thing at once. Some do it over the course of fifty years. There are hikers in expensive waterproof gear, and others literally wearing garbage bags to keep the rain off their backs. Because the A.T. spans so many states, with so many different cultures, and has impacted many generations of people, "HYOH" makes it clear: there is no one style, culture, or purpose for hiking that trumps another.

Arnie had created her own category of hiker. She was truly doing the hike her way and not allowing any of the cultural norms or expectations from the hiking community to dictate her mission.

We thought a bonus of a town stay would be the opportunity to do laundry. Sadly, the hotel didn't have public laundry facilities. But when the lady behind the front desk heard we were "friends" with Arnie, she offered to do our laundry for us.

Kami started crying, overwhelmed with gratitude. We felt so taken care of.

Arnie and G were exactly what we needed, and they showed up exactly when we needed them. We wondered if they were angels put in that parking lot by God. We had signed up for the A.T. to deepen the closeness and intimacy of our family, but we had no idea how much putting ourselves through the experience would open us up to simply receiving care from others.

We had always heard *not* to accept help from strangers or get into weird vans. But these two strangers, and getting into their weird van, changed the course of our night, brought us to tears, and gave us a story to tell for years. And we never even knew their real names.

HIKE YOUR OWN HIKE

After seeing how much towns improved our morale, we felt like we needed to make stops like this a part of our routine. We hadn't considered ourselves *attached* to conveniences like electricity and hot water, but now that we didn't have them, we loved the feelings those things produced and appreciated their presence more than we ever had at home. They let us feel rested, human, and safe.

When we knew there was a town coming up in two or three days, we started making plans to go in. We'd say to the kids, "We have a hotel tonight!" Everyone would cheer, knowing what that meant. It would change the pace of the entire day and the last mile we'd all run to the road thinking about how good a bed would feel. It went a long way toward shifting the morale of our increasingly ragged crew; it turned a daunting, epic journey with no end into a series of four-day trips from town to town.

We started to notice energy levels rising among the kids. Memory and Filia were especially energetic, always wanting to explore a little farther and check out side trails. When the rest of us would hit a clearing or meadow and lay down to take a rest in the sun or eat snacks, Memory and Filia would take the camera and run up hills to film the view at the top. It felt easier to expend more energy on "unnecessary" side adventures knowing it was only a matter of days until we'd be able to recharge with a warm bed and hot food.

We thought about what Arnie had told us: "Hike your own hike." Having a framework of freedom and uniqueness was important because we were constantly surrounded by hikers from all over the world who were all hiking completely differently. Early on in the hike, we saw at least twenty other hikers on the trail a day, and sometimes many more. Loads of people started on March 1, the same day as us, which created a hiker-bubble. We'd start the day with a group of other hikers, spread out as we walked, run into them again at breaks, and see most of them at camp that night.

But soon, we started to see the hikers who had started with us fade away from the trail. Due to injuries, the difficulty, or the cold, they were giving up on the A.T.

Historically, the percentage of people who quit the trail each year before finishing varies between 75 and 90 percent. This means in the best years, only one in four people you meet on the trail will make it to the end. The year we hiked, we started with 3,862 hikers registered at Springer Mountain hoping to take their picture with the A-frame sign at the top of Mount Katahdin. Only 764 would report finishing. That's less than one in five.

For our family, the odds were obviously even slimmer. Most hiker groups formed loosely, meaning that if someone had to quit, the rest of the group would keep going. But because we were a family, committed to staying together, any sickness, injury, or major life event for any one of us meant all eight of us were done. It decreased the probability of all eight of us making it from one in five to one in 390,000. Those were very long odds.

Deep down, though, we all knew faces were disappearing fast. It was a common conversation around our warm food. "Have you seen Steve?" "Did you hear about Black Beard?" Hiker news was the common currency. We'd look across the restaurant at other hikers and wonder if this was the last time we'd see them.

No doubt, they were wondering the same thing about our family. We'd even heard there was a line drawn in Vegas and people had placed some very low odds to bet on our failure.

It wasn't our first time coming up against the critics when we attempted a physical feat. One thing our family has always done together is running; we run daily for exercise, and we run races, all the way up to marathons, for fun. Our kids run with us. Over the years, we'd had lots of people tell us we were running marathons "wrong." They'd say our version didn't count because we'd walk for a few stretches, and take breaks for our kids. As though there was some unwritten rule that "running a marathon" means doing it completely unbroken, and a tenth of a mile worth of walking would negate 26.2 miles of running. We didn't listen. We ran our own marathon. We made the marathon work for our family, so that we could all do it together. The only rule we set for ourselves was that to say they had "finished," each of our children had to move their bodies from the start line to the finish line without physical assistance. Besides that rule, we ran it our way. This meant taking beer and champagne when it was offered, stopping for Popsicle breaks when it was hot, stopping to hang out with Halmonee and Papa, and even stopping for Kami to breastfeed Rainier when he was an infant. At one point, we passed a park and took a break for Filia to play on the playground. Our family has always come in close to last place, but we've always finished together. Nothing else matters to us.

Arnie's message to us had made our priorities clear. The internet critics and the people betting against us in Vegas weren't in our shoes, and didn't have our goals—so to listen to their moral code for how they thought our days should go would mean disaster for all of us.

At the end of the hike, there's no panel of judges with scorecards waiting for you at Katahdin. To *hike your own hike* meant that to judge another person's experience, or even your own, is to totally miss the point of the trail.

To succeed on the trail, we would have to apply the same principle. In order to have any chance at succeeding, we would have to find a way to tune out the voices from outsiders and focus on what we thought was best for our family.

Ignoring other voices did not just pertain to people on the internet—it meant other hikers too. As the weeks ticked away, and the number of hikers dwindled, we started to recognize more and more of the hikers who remained. There was a sense of familiarity and camaraderie as we all experienced the cold and aches and pains together. When we made it to a town and saw other hikers at the store or in a restaurant, we shared our mutual appreciation for the amenities. We'd give each other glances across the restaurant, overtop our beers, like, *Nice, we made it this far. Haven't quit yet.*

This created a false sense of loyalty that had a large potential for danger. Because we so wanted the other hikers' company, and to be accepted by them, it would be so easy to ignore our own unique needs as a group in order to hike with them and try and stick together. Eventually, we had to recognize that while we may be able to get away with that a day at a time, it was not going to work for five months. No matter what, our top priority had to be our own needs and the abilities of our family team. We'd hike with our new hiker friends when it made sense, but we'd split off when it didn't.

We were starting to learn that that's what HYOH really means. Ignore the outside voices telling you you're doing it wrong; there is no "wrong." But also, watch out for wanting to fit in so badly that you start hiking someone else's hike.

Even though we were bolstered by the HYOH motto, there were still times when sticking to it proved difficult. It seemed like some of the hikers that were having the most fun were hiking in groups and making decisions to stay together. Early on, we met a group of three hikers, a group of college-aged kids who had become increasingly friendly. After seeing them several times, we started to exchange updates and conversations every time we passed each other. One of them, named Fun Facts, loved to stop and talk to the kids whenever she ran across them. She was a college student who was unlike anyone our relatively sheltered Kentucky-raised kids had come across in life: she was bisexual, had type 1 diabetes, and seemed to have a fun fact for all things geological, historical, zoological, and botanical. She carried a pack of Haribo Frogs gummy candy, which she'd have to stop and eat if the insulin pump on her arm beeped. In our first interaction with her, she taught the kids about a certain type of wintergreen leaf that's edible and tastes like bubblegum. With no internet, TV, or radio, one fact from Fun Facts could keep the kids entertained for hours as they walked along picking leaves to chew on.

Fun Facts was hiking with an Australian army vet who went by the name Nubs. He spoke with a thick accent and was hilariously sarcastic and cynical about everything.

Then there was an engineer from Iowa who called himself Culligan. He was raised on a farm and spent his summers competing in county fairs. Culligan was the fastest hiker we'd seen yet. He'd walk right past us with his headphones on, singing songs from *Mulan* and *The Lion King* at the top of his lungs.

This group traveled at a speed and with a style that seemed like *fun*. Kami and I, in our tent at night, occasionally imagined being independent of the kids and joining the group on fast, long days in which we didn't have to deal with a toddler and keep our eyes on five other kids needing our guidance.

It helped to remember that the "grass is always greener" and that our unique hike would have unique pros and cons that were different from everyone else's. We had to remember that we weren't on the A.T. to please other hikers, internet observers, or some fictitious panel of judges grading our purity. All that mattered was hiking the hike that worked for our family.

CHAPTER FOUR

Pushed to Our Limits

"Surely what a man does when he is taken off his guard is the best evidence for what sort of a man he is? Surely what pops out before the man has time to put on a disguise is the truth? If there are rats in the cellar you are most likely to see them if you go in very suddenly. But the suddenness does not create the rats: it only prevents them from hiding."

—C. S. Lewis

That first month on the trail, there were several constants. It was cold. It was hard. We were tired.

And Rainier cried.

With six kids, Kami and I were no strangers to toddlers and temper tantrums. When I was first learning how to be a parent, I had all sorts of ideas about why kids threw tantrums, and how to "discipline" the tantrums out of them. Then, about a decade ago, I got some parenting advice from an unlikely source: my twelve-step sponsor, William. He asked me a question I hadn't considered before:

"What if, when your kids cry, you just hold them?"

His advice was to simply be there for the kids—not to try to stop them when they cried or threw tantrums, but to simply hold them, to be comfortable in accepting exactly where they were at in all their messiness. It forced me to ask myself what I was trying to *solve* by disciplining them when they cried. What if the tantrum wasn't good or bad, but just an expression of the child's emotions—emotions that they're not equipped or motivated to hide yet, like us adults?

It was the first time I'd considered anything like it. I followed his advice, and began simply holding the children when they erupted with emotion. To say it wasn't easy would be an understatement. In fact, it was one of the most painful exercises I've done in my adult life. But it was also revolutionary. It completely changed how I viewed my kids' expressions of their feelings as well as my own issues that came up being around them in these states that I had just previously deemed as "unacceptable."

Heading onto the trail, I felt as well "trained" as I could be in being there for my kids in the full extent of what they were thinking and feeling. So it was a rude awakening when I found myself twitchy, anxious, even impatient when Rainier cried in his backpack. I just wanted him to stop.

His crying wasn't just a typical toddler tantrum. He had those too—if we broke a granola bar when he wanted the whole thing, or if he wanted to hold the milk himself—but the crying while hiking was different. It was freezing cold, and he was essentially immobilized in a carrier. He was deeply uncomfortable and didn't know any other way to express it. Just like us, his day-to-day existence had completely changed, but unlike us, he had no idea why. It was hard to see him unhappy, and even harder knowing it was largely due to the cold. It broke our hearts.

In Georgia, we traveled through land features called "gaps." There was Gooch Gap, Woody Gap, Neel Gap, Hogpen Gap, Low Gap, Deep Gap, and twenty more. Gaps are encountered when you descend one mountain and are getting ready to climb another, creating a low point that essentially acts as a wind tunnel—with the *coldest* wind. Picture walking into a giant Costco refrigerator, but instead of a refrigerator, it was a freezer. It was two or three times as cold as that.

The cold was a big trigger for Rainier, and through several of the gaps, he cried continuously. To him, the wind was a random, cruel enemy, and he had no idea when it would stop. As much as we felt sorry for him, his crying made what was already a miserable walk become unbearable—especially for me, carrying him. When he cried, his mouth was about four inches from my ear. Coming down off a hill, we wanted nothing more than to rest before heading up the other side, but the sub-freezing wind made stopping impossible. If we stayed still, we would literally freeze to death. The wind chill easily subtracted twenty degrees, which, when the initial temperature is twenty-five degrees, is dangerously cold.

Rainier's crying hit Kami hard. She'd ask, "What are we doing? Should we be exposing our baby to this? Is this worth it? Is he being traumatized?"

We'd taken flak from all directions for taking a baby out on the trail. "Why bring Rainier? He won't even remember it!" was the common refrain.

It wasn't just that we wanted our youngest child with us. Kami and I genuinely believed that the trip would be valuable for Rainier, himself, as a person. We believed he would learn and grow in ways that couldn't be matched at home. Especially in such a rapid-growth period of his life, the trail would make a lasting impression on his development. At least, that's what we told ourselves before we started—and we did see flashes of this instinct being validated throughout our hike. Rainier seemed to pick up words and motor skills incredibly quickly, and other hikers constantly mentioned how smart he was, how well he could speak for his age.

But all that being true, he was still a two-year-old sitting still in a backpack for hours each day, in freezing temperatures and unable to move or stretch. He was chilled-out and happy a lot of the time, but when it became too much for him, where the rest of us could complain and swear, all he could do was cry. And in those moments, we felt our confidence that we had made the best decision for our toddler drain away.

On one particular day, the piercing, merciless wind pummeled Rainier as we walked through a gap in the mountains. We felt helpless. There was nothing we could do but watch him suffer. This made Kami, in particular, feel like a terrible parent. At one point, it overwhelmed her. Everything felt out of control in this freezing, windy place. She started to melt down along with Rainier.

I'd already been feeling guilty and uncertain of our choices, and seeing Kami crack sent me deeper into a wave of self-doubt. *What are we doing? What have I gotten everyone into?*

Rainier was crying and he just wanted the cold and wind to stop, but for me, his crying was an unrelenting reminder of the fatigue and guilt I was feeling.

I lost my cool. Just for a moment. Rainier wouldn't stop crying. He wasn't in a full-scale tantrum, but he'd been whimpering all morning, and weakened by the cold and exertion and mental exhaustion, I just wanted him to be quiet.

So, after pleading with him numerous times, I reached around my shoulder and flicked Rainier's lip with my gloved hand.

But Rainier didn't stop crying. I had made it worse.

We kept walking. I could feel Kami staring at me. I played the scene through my head again and again. At first I justified it; what else was I supposed to do? We were all at the end of our ropes. How was I supposed to lead? I needed to keep our group moving to be safe, and I couldn't do my job with a toddler screaming in my ear. Was the cold just too much? Was it a mistake to bring him?

But the more I thought about what had happened, I realized I could never take it back. I felt sick to my stomach.

As the wind died down and the minutes wore on, I realized that I'd made a huge mistake. Rainier *couldn't* stop crying. I had failed him, I had failed myself, and I had failed my sponsor William. That was an opportunity for me to hold Rainier, try and understand him, and just accept him. He wasn't throwing just another temper tantrum; he was at the end of his rope, like all of us, and crying was the only way he could express his emotions and I didn't have the capacity to accept his emotions, so instead of accepting them or trying to help him, I tried to stop him in the only way I knew how—through force and violence. And now I had lost his trust. Maybe we *should* have left him at home. Maybe we *all* should have stayed home.

Many times during the trip, we were all near the ends of our ropes. Half of the mornings on the trail, I was yelling at Seven to get up, and there were some mornings where I'd have to pull Seven out of the tent and sleeping bag by his legs because no amount of shaking or talking would wake him up. He also hiked at his own, slower pace and paid little attention to the people he was hiking with. We would give him a very specific direction, like, "Seven, can you hand me that granola bar?" And he'd look back and simply respond, "Huh?"

The trail had thrown us into a situation the modern world had actively been shielding us from our whole lives. It's only natural—we had architected our lives to avoid discomfort and friction. I had often felt like being a successful parent was synonymous with never losing my cool, never being put in a position to owe my children an apology.

Kami and I wondered: What if success in relationships is better defined as working through the tough moments, being able to ask forgiveness, and accepting each other for who we really are? After all, our closest friends are not the people we go to to *avoid* hard times; they're the ones who've been with us *through* the hard times. They're the ones who have seen us at our worst and still stuck around. If our goal is to always perform well or never lose our temper in front of others, it means that when we find ourselves in the vulnerable moments, we're alone. If our goal is to be truly known by others, or even ourselves, we have to leave our comfort zone—in front of the very people we're afraid of hurting. This is scary. Kami and I didn't want to avoid it anymore.

These beliefs had been part of the calculus that brought us to the trail. But now, I wasn't so sure about those beliefs. Now I was wondering if I had gone too far.

On the trail, for better or worse, we were with each other 24/7. We'd come out to the trail to pursue this closeness, but now that we didn't have any other choice, we wondered—did we really want this? We could see the tensions mounting everywhere. Each member of the family expressed their frustrations and discomfort differently. Dove incessantly wondered aloud about her friends back home. Eden kept a loud verbal tally of how dirty her clothes were and how long it had been since her last shower. Filia often just laid down in the middle of the path, tired and totally done.

Filia (7) had not learned to read yet and used her journal to practice the alphabet and draw pictures as she was on her way to become the youngest female thru-hiker in history.

At nights, the tension we were all going through was the most evident. To save weight, we carried two tents: one for the adults, one for the kids. The adults slept in a two-man tent, and all six kids slept in a four-man tent, the largest backpacking tent on the market. The floor was eight feet by seven feet—only a little bit bigger than one king-sized bed, which was not much space for six kids and five large packs. The edges of the tent got cold and wet, so everyone tried to cram into the middle. The walls were paper thin and we heard the fighting before bed, sometimes for up to thirty minutes. "Seven, stop pushing me!" "Whose foot is this?" "Memory, scoot over!"

The kids would constantly complain about how much it sucked to be in the tent together every night. Most of the time, it was edged with laughter, but when the tension mounted, the laughter diminished. If we were camping on a hill, all night they'd slide around. Sticks and rocks would poke through the tent floor, making it so they would have to rearrange often in less space than the tent even had.

At the start of the trip, in the cold, the three kids sharing the down quilt were always in a war to make sure they were the most covered up and didn't have any exposed skin. During the end of the trip, when it was getting warmer, they were in a constant battle to make sure the quilt was nowhere near them. There was constantly condensation that would drip down to the tent floor edges, soaking any sleeping bag or person that was near the edges.

The kids would give us non-stop crap the whole length of the trail for the sleeping arrangements, telling us how good we had it and how we had no right, as parents, to complain.

Kami would say, "I'm hungry," and Eden would say, "Well, at least you don't have to sleep with five smelly rats and get poked in the face all night."

We knew there was nothing we could realistically do about the situation, and while the kids were always fighting with each other, they banded together in their misery to make fun of how spoiled us parents were to have our own tent. It was the one thing on which they always had each other's backs.

And now, walking away steadily from the moment when I'd lost control with my youngest son, I knew that although Rainier had fallen asleep, he might remember this moment. He might end up hating the Appalachian Trail forever. I had lost my temper with Rainier. I'd seen Rainier crying in a way that reminded me of how uncomfortable we all were, and I didn't want to face that. And when the voice in my head I didn't want to hear wouldn't shut up or go away, I lost control and I crossed a line. It was a wakeup call.

I didn't know what it meant about my parenting, and I didn't know what it meant for my relationship with Rainier. My old fears at the start of the trip came roaring back. *Am I going to be able to stop myself from bending everyone to my will? Am I going to be able to let go and let the kids make their own choices?*

The answers eluded me. In their absence, I did the only thing I could think to do: that night, in the tent, I apologized to Rainier for flicking his lip.

"Rainier, Dada sorry. I shouldn't have done that," I said. I looked over at Kami; she had tears in her eyes.

"Owie?" said Rainier.

"I know. I'm sorry. I won't do that again, okay?"

"Okay."

It didn't fix the situation, but at the moment, I felt a little better. I knew there was nothing else I could do but take it day by day. And Rainier seemed to understand.

The internet, however, did not.

THE OUTSIDE PERSPECTIVE

Our YouTube channel connected us to the online world in both positive and negative ways. On the one hand, friends and family—and internet strangers—could cheer us on by watching our progress through our trail vlogs. On the other hand, it was around this time on the hike that the negativity surged from another, very distinct, type of internet stranger. Naysayers criticized us on YouTube, in the Whiteblaze forum, and on other social media sites and blogs.

Some people said matter-of-factly that we were idiots. They insinuated that it was child abuse to force a baby to do something like this. They said we should have at least left Rainier home with Halmonee and Papa.

"You can call me a coddling parent or whatever, but I do think kids need more comfort then hiking miles through snow in freezing temperatures day after day." —Smackbork

"Apparently they don't believe in birth control, so she'll probably be pregnant with #7 soon. Anyway, if they expect to get very far they

will have to send the two youngest to foster care or go home for a while and wait for the weather to improve." —Slo-go'en

"To be clear, in the latest video the father did flick the two-year-old in the mouth (hard enough to break skin) because the toddler wouldn't stop crying. That's abuse. They had the toddler's pant legs tied off to try and keep the child's feet warm, causing the pants to fill with moisture while walking all morning in the rain. A two-year-old can't express pain or exhaustion properly, and hypothermic reaction just looks like a sleepy baby to these people. Then, when the trail is too much for the kid to handle, crying leads to being punished in a painful way. That's endangerment. I ever see someone treat a two-year-old child the way these people are, and I'm going to lose my cool real quick." —Richard

We could understand some of the frustration and backlash that was coming. And although we agreed that the actions I had taken toward Rainier were harmful, we've never bought into the belief that underpinned some of these comments: that because bad things like this could happen, the entire situation should be avoided. We had hoped that through the ups and downs of the trail, we would all learn together— adults just as much as kids. Extreme weather held lessons for us all.

There were a few other underlying cultural beliefs that ran through the comment threads. One was that if you're not giving your kids the most comfortable life you can afford, you're a bad parent. Regardless of how present or caring you are, you're not loving your kids if they aren't as comfortable as modern conveniences allow. Another was that kids should only do "age appropriate" activities.

But the biggest one was the reaction to our decision to share about what happened on our vlog, and that it's a mistake to talk about making mistakes. It's a concept that Kami and I completely reject. How can our kids be confident in any action or decision if we hide from them what it looks like to take risks, mess up—and if necessary, apologize?

When we apologize, it gives our kids permission to take risks. When we let them see our successes and failures, our strengths and flaws, it helps them feel less alone when they have doubts, difficulties, and regrets.

We hold hands and walk next to our children. We don't want to walk ahead of them, where they can't see us in our entirety; we don't want to represent vague principles for them to aspire to. We want to show our kids equal footing as partners in our family, and say, "I will not leave you in the difficult times." But we had found that true intimacy is not just about being a hero to our kids. It's about making mistakes and being willing to clean up from them afterward.

To us, in a way, the whole point of going out to the trail was not to find ways to succeed; it was to find the ways that we would fail.

But while all of these principles had felt right at home, I still felt like I had gone too far with Rainier. Especially now that the outside world's voice was so unified against us, and becoming louder and louder.

To them it was simple: we should have never started the trail, and we should quit before things got worse. Our confidence was shaken. We didn't know anymore if we could truly handle the ups and downs of the experience.

Little did we know that our biggest test was just ahead.

CHAPTER FIVE

Into the Blizzard

"In the end no one really cares—you do it for yourself. Everyone must decide for him or herself how much risk he or she wants to take. Risk is not measurable and is always dependent on the individual. You need to know that it is impossible to indefinitely push your limits: higher, faster, better."
—Steve House, *Training for the New Alpinism: A Manual for the Climber as Athlete*

In some ways, walking all day long made the online criticism harder to deal with. In other ways, it was easier.

On the one hand, I had ample time alone with my thoughts, which spun around and around in my head. *What's wrong with me? Why did I flick Rainier? What if we hadn't posted about it? Was this whole trip a mistake? Am I going to mess up the kids one by one?*

But on the other hand, I simply couldn't afford the mental energy to dive into processing any of my runaway thinking. None of us could. We had sacrificed too much to reassess everything for any singular incident. Every ounce of effort needed to be allocated toward getting the family to put one foot in front of the other, and staying warm.

I'd have the rest of my life to reassess our priorities and do all the soul-searching that I needed to. But in this place, all I could do was a quick calculus: assess my actions, evaluate my path forward, and move on.

We pressed forward on the trail, pushing our limits in every way. We finished off our second week by doing 11.7 miles, 13.4 miles, 15.2 miles, and 15.8 miles. We reached Fontana Dam, where hikers have their last opportunity to resupply before the seventy-mile stretch of Smoky Mountain National Park. This stretch includes the highest mountains on the trail—several of which are more than six thousand feet above sea level. It's exposed and challenging terrain, so hikers at Fontana Dam review the weather report and decide if they should press forward or wait for safer conditions. When we got there, the weather report for the next two days looked daunting.

Tuesday: Areas of fog, showers, and thunderstorms then patchy fog, rain, and snow showers. Cloudy, with a low around twenty. West-northwest wind at fifteen to twenty-four mph, with gusts as high as thirty-nine mph. Chance of precipitation is 80 percent. New snow accumulation of three to five inches possible.

Wednesday: Snow showers. Cloudy, with a high near twenty-two. West-northwest wind around twenty-five mph, with gusts as high as forty-one mph. Chance of precipitation is 80 percent. New snow accumulation of three to seven inches possible.

These would be the hardest conditions we'd faced on our entire trip. Most people were opting to stay behind and wait out the storm. Meanwhile, online, those who were claiming superior knowledge and expertise of hiking the trail were making clear what their opinion was.

> *"They have inadequate knowledge of their situation and surround-ings and [are] inadequately geared for being there. It is a recipe for disaster...I mean, seriously, if some of you can't see the complete lack of common sense and judgement, I don't know what to tell you."* —Mugthumper

> *"Well, today and tonight may make or break 'em. Snow and frigid temps in the Smokies today and tonight. I hope they handle it okay, especially the kids."* —Traffic Jam

We knew that walking into a snowstorm with kids would look bad to the online crowd. But risk is not a black or white metric; it's a complicated and dynamic variable that varies from person to person and needs to be evaluated relative to potential reward. I had been a part of numerous expeditions above the tree line on glaciers, and our family had hiked more than five hundred miles together over the years—including our distance on trail so far—so I was confident we had what it took. We also knew we had considerable experience in the snow. We had bought a case of hand warmers for Rainer and the younger kids, an upgraded and warmer quilt for the younger kids, and trekking poles for three of our kids that wanted them and we were confident we could keep everyone's core warm, which meant as long as we could keep moving, we'd be safe.

Also, my parents had agreed to pick us up in the middle of the park, and we already had reservations at a hotel and water park for

Wednesday night. If we sat around waiting for a clear-weather window, we could be stuck for weeks. So, on Day 19, we left Fontana Dam.

Online, commenters speculated the worst:

"Just my 2c, but looks more like a determined dad who is going to push through anything, regardless of the circumstances or risk... and that worries me. I hope they've also budgeted for a med-evac." —Pastor Bryon

"If someone takes a risk with their kids and things go bad, not only do they have possible legal implications but they will have to live with their bad decisions for the rest of their lives." —greentick

"Wait it out. People (like the Crawfords) have to be rescued every year because the wrong person, the Crawfords of our world, didn't know when to pump the brakes and give it a break. The trail isn't going anywhere. I realize that not all rescues can be avoided; obviously, there are going to be the broken legs, heart attacks; even as we've seen in previous years, bear attacks. But this was just pure ignorance to Smokies weather...high East Coast altitude weather anywhere. Which IMO isn't acceptable at the risk of children. You wanna go stumble around in waist-high snow drifts? Have at it, bud, but leave the children at home." —Gambit McCrae

The Smokies, as the locals call it, was one of two national parks we would go through. Most of the A.T. has very few rules, but the Smokies had additional permits, fees, and rules about where and when you could camp. This limited our plans and created an aura of intimidation. The increased elevation created harsher weather and intense remoteness. It would be the most challenging section of the southern trail. It felt like we were approaching the final boss in a video game.

Within an hour of entering the park, we met an Appalachian Trail ridgerunner. Ridgerunners are employed by various trail clubs to maintain the trail and educate hikers. The man sternly told us that our kids should not be running ahead. He said bears were common: "Just the other year, there was a decapitation, so practice extra caution."

He warned we should keep our children within eyesight at all times. "Everything will probably be okay," he told us. Very reassuring.

In the Smokies, staying at the shelters, rather than camping in the wild, was mandatory. Amongst hikers on the trail, rumors circulated that the reason was so park rangers could more easily find and evacuate people if there was life-threatening wind, which apparently was a normal occurrence.

On our first day in the Smokies, we stopped at Silers Bald Shelter to have a snack and get out of the rain. We expected to spend ten minutes there, but as we prepared to leave, freezing rain started coming down. We were officially in emergency mode. Others at the shelter were talking about the nor'easter—a particularly violent type of storm—that had been predicted and now was rumored to be headed right for us with a ton of snow. Everyone was abandoning their plans to push on and opting instead to hole up overnight or longer, and so the shelter was already filled to capacity.

We didn't know what to do, especially because Halmonee and Papa were planning to meet us the next day at Newfound Gap. We were planning to do two more miles that day, which would leave us with ten the next day. Now, we weren't sure if we could make it. We felt the pressure to move forward, especially since the shelter was already full. We were pretty sure we could make it, but looking out into the freezing rain, staying put started to seem more prudent.

The voices we had heard over the years about kids and large families echoed in my head. It's every parent's worst nightmare to be in a situation where your kid is the screaming disruption making everyone else's life hell—the classic "throwing a fit on a plane" scenario. I worried about that now, in the crowded shelter. After all, our kids were kids. Rainier would laugh, shriek, and sometimes cry. The smaller kids would run around collecting pine cones, playing games, and erupting in loud conversations. What would people in a dire situation, in an already packed-to-capacity shelter, think of a family optionally hiking with six kids (one a "screaming" toddler) barging in and disturbing their peace?

The internet echoed our fears.

"No offense to this family, but after a long, hard day of hiking, the last thing I would want to run into at a shelter is this group of people. It seems to me to be too many headaches, both for them and other hikers." —double d

"Yikes. They fill up a shelter. Folks who arrive after them will not be pleased." —Wayne

"Groups suck. Don't matter whether it's a group of old people, kids, or...thru-hikers. They monopolize space and disturb others. Out of the above, the old people would likely disturb others the least, though." —MuddyWaters

"When I think about the people who will bitch endlessly because I choose to hike with my well behaved dog, then think that these people are hiking with six kids, some of whom are not old enough to use their inside voices and the fact that they are also apparently traveling with a drone really frosts me..." —sketcher709

Some people even said that they would plan their entire trip to avoid children and families. Rolling up on the shelter with six kids in tow, Kami and I felt conspicuous to say the least, and prepared ourselves for dirty looks.

We were then left speechless by the reality of what happened.

"There's plenty of room!" one hiker said.

"We'll scoot over. There's space for two kids here," said another.

"I'll add more wood to the fire."

"You guys don't have to go out there, there's space in here!"

The kind welcome came from all directions. Hikers in the shelter weren't grumbling about our kids "not using their inside voices"—quite the opposite. They were happy to meet us and excited to make room.

One college-aged kid stood and introduced himself, then shook my hand. "I'll go pitch my tent outside. Really. You guys can have my spot."

The shelter's capacity was twelve people, but we counted twenty-two of us in there that night. It was cramped, especially because everyone had heightened emotions.

As we lay in bed that night, we felt the burden of keeping our kids safe. We were also struck by the offers of help that came from nowhere, from strangers—from people who should hate us, in a time when it was the most difficult to reach out to strangers. It seemed like people genuinely wanted to help, like they were looking for ways to sacrifice their comfort for the sake of another. It was as if that was part of why they were out on the trail to begin with.

On Day 21, we woke up early with our deadline in mind. Sure enough, all we could see was white. It had snowed about eight inches, and it was still coming down. It made it almost impossible to see the trail. As we packed up to leave, we had to thaw out our shoes; they were literally frozen solid from being wet the night before, and wouldn't bend. Strangers started helping us to get our feet into them. Several people said, "Are you sure you want to leave? This snow is crazy." It seemed like the common strategy was to wait out the storm. But we wanted to continue, not only because we had our goal in mind, but because we believed it was safer—physically and psychologically—to keep moving. My experience in the mountains, and from reading alpine adventures, had taught me one thing: one of the worst things you can do for morale and mental safety is to remain sedentary. As long as we could see the trail, we needed to keep moving.

In an innovative stroke, we wrapped Rainier in our down quilt in addition to his waterproof rain gear, hand warmers, and foot warmers, adding forty degrees to his outfit. The quilt was not waterproof, but this would be okay as long as the temperature remained below freezing. Plus, we knew as long as it kept him warm during the day, we could dry it out at the hotel that night. We said goodbye to everyone who had helped us and headed out into the blizzard.

In the snow, the white blazes painted on trees to mark the trail were useless. One or two people had gone before us, though, helpfully leaving boot tracks to follow. It snowed the entire day. At times, the kids were almost waist-deep in the snow. We became hyper-aware of our proximity to each other and tried to stay as close together as possible. If one person got off track, we might not be able to find them.

> It was the first time we understood, truly, that it was possible to die out on the trail. We'd known it intellectually, but now we believed it deep in our hearts. This was serious, and we couldn't afford a single second of not acting like it.

A few hours of snow-hiking later, we came across the shelter we had planned to reach the night before. Everyone was holed up in their sleeping bags, huddled around the fire. No one had left from there that day, and they invited us to come in. We planned to melt water since the temperature had not risen above freezing and our bottles were strapped to the outside of our packs and had frozen solid. Instantly, people started giving us their water, letting us know they could melt more snow later. Someone else offered us a chocolate bar. Back home, a chocolate bar was a one-dollar commodity we tried to avoid due to the calories. That day, it was a love letter. It told us we were not alone, and people had our backs. It warmed us from the inside out.

It was amazing how simple gestures like this made such a difference as we walked through the blizzard. It was like a pit stop. While Kami used the break from the wind provided by the shelter to change Rainier's diaper, everyone gathered around us to get news from the previous shelter, cheer us on, and support us in any way they could. Some people warned that the road ahead was probably closed. A few encouraged us to stay and offered to make space for us in the shelter.

Looking around, we didn't feel it was smart to stay stationary in the shelter. The shelters only had three walls, with a tarp acting as the fourth wall. Everyone was in their sleeping bags, and they were burning fuel for a fire. There was no way to stay warm by moving. This wasn't any closer to real safety.

To make matters worse, there was no outhouse, and people were literally shitting everywhere.

Even though it seemed like a long shot, the possibility of the road being open and our motivation to keep moving made us continue on. As we left, someone mentioned a heated bathroom at our final destination—Newfound Gap—that could be used as an emergency shelter. We didn't think much of it as we said "thank you" and "good-bye" before turning back into the blizzard.

At 11:00 a.m., we came to Clingmans Dome. It's famous for being the highest point of the entire trail at 6,644 feet in elevation. To get to the amazing view, you have to take a two-hundred-foot side trail. We were so miserable and the visibility was so low that we just kept moving and skipped the detour. We did take a moment to capture a picture at the sign and check on Rainier in his carrier. He was totally warm, cozy, and asleep. We were proud of our innovative use of the quilt and happy to see him so comfortable.

Going through the blizzard was the riskiest part of the whole trip, but not backing down from the fear and moving forward through it in a calculated way reaped massive rewards. It felt like we were in the middle of the ultimate outdoorsmanship challenge. Even though people thought we were making the wrong choice, our kids were motivated the whole way and had great attitudes. Many days on the trail, at least one of the kids would cry. Not on this day. Hiking through the snowstorm had been a unanimous decision—everyone was level-10 motivated by the promise of the hotel and water park with grandparents that came at the end.

Kami and I have never been more impressed and proud as we were when hiking behind our kids' little boot prints that day, which plowed through the snow with greater speed and efficiency than anything we had seen to date. It was as if they knew what the stakes were and were ready to rise to the occasion. It felt like we were collectively a well-oiled machine. For the first time, instead of having to motivate and coach, Kami and I were just members of the team. Challenges don't only bring out the worst in you; they also bring out the best. That day, from my wife to my teenage girls and down to my two-year-old son, I saw our family as a bunch of badasses.

That day, we needed to hike 12.5 miles in the blizzard. Our deadline to reach Newfound Gap was 4:00 p.m. We arrived at 4:15. The road was, indeed, closed. We thought we saw Halmonee and Papa in the parking lot near the road, but it was just a random van. We started searching for the heated bathroom the other hiker had mentioned, which sounded like a safer and certainly warmer option than being out in the blizzard.

SAFETY SECOND

"Safety First" is the mantra that best describes American parenting. Safety is how parents evaluate success and failure. It goes beyond parenting too—it's a permanent fixture in our culture. "Safety First" is the most common sign posted on job sites. It determines our purchases and it's the last thing we say when we say goodbye: "Stay safe."

Before leaving for the A.T., if we asked ourselves if what we were doing was safe, we would have come up with long lists of dangers. Any of us could fall off a cliff, get mauled by a bear, or even get catastrophically injured doing something so benign as tripping on a tree root. We had seen these possibilities prevent many people from going to the woods to begin with.

We had found that with a safety first mindset we were never able to leave home. So we started to adopt a *"Safety Also"* mindset, instead of "Safety First."

The problem isn't that safety is *bad*—the problem is that we prioritize it in a way that the fear monopolizes our minds and keeps us from considering other values and goals. Like the values and goals we had for setting out to hike the A.T.:

- We wanted to get away from distractions.

- We wanted to see the country from Georgia to Maine.
- We wanted to detach from standard comforts we felt entitled to.
- We wanted to grow as individuals and as a team.
- We wanted to spend quality time with each other.

You'll notice that *safety* is not on that list. That's because for us, safety is not a goal in and of itself. And it's not just us; when's the last time you heard *safety* mentioned as a virtue at someone's funeral? Safety isn't something people are remembered for.

We have a different ideology.

Safety Second.

Instead of thinking of safety as a goal, we think of it as a tool. A goal is something you shoot for. A tool is something you use to help you accomplish a goal.

The irony also is that often by not putting safety first, I felt like we were actually able to make safer choices for our family.

What's more safe?

Walking in the woods through the elements, armed with GPS and Gore-Tex? Or eating Cheetos while watching TV, never leaving your couch?

Each year, obesity kills 300,000 Americans. Heart attacks kill 647,000. Car accidents kill 38,000.

Bear attacks kill 1.25 people per year. That's right—the number is so low that it's barely a full integer.

That night, our family slept in a heated bathroom while dozens of fellow hikers who had prioritized "safety" were spending their second night on unprotected mountain ridges during a storm with temperatures dipping into single digits. They were not alone, and they had the comfort of being in the masses, but out in their sleeping

bags, burning fuel and calories, with no end in sight to the storm—
were they really safer?

As we walked, Kami and I made hundreds, sometimes thousands, of decisions that assessed and protected our children's safety. We evaluated how many layers to wear, the best way to cross a stream, proper hydration and caloric intake. Making decisions was our job on the trail, second only to coaching the kids through.

But we evaluated safety during our adventure, not before it as part of the decision to go. Safety was never going to be the deciding factor in our lives. Safety makes a great passenger, but a terrible leader.

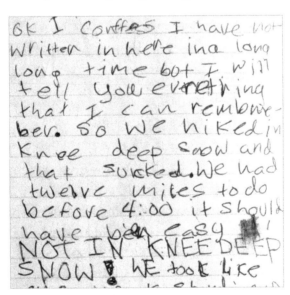

Memory (11) venting about the snow, but her disappointment was mostly about the road being closed and being stranded in a bathroom.

SURVIVING THE BLIZZARD

That night, we shacked up in the women's bathroom, completely spent. We met two men who were sleeping in the men's bathroom.

One of them, Buckeye, had reception on his phone and was kind enough to let us make a call. We phoned the park ranger to inquire about the road conditions. Our conversation was short. We confirmed we'd found shelter. He said the access road was closed due to the weather but offered to pick us up by helicopter if it was an emergency. We told him, "No, we're fine, thank you."

We didn't know if the road would open tomorrow, or the next day, or if we'd be in the bathroom for a week. The small room had a concrete floor—no paper towels, no electricity, and no sink. All it had was a drippy faucet that made the floor perpetually wet. It was like a barely-heated prison.

We stacked all the backpacks on top of the one garbage can to prevent the mice from chewing through them. We didn't know what was ahead, but we would take a little warmth and toilets for now and be grateful. Not for the last time either—we all agree now that gratitude was one of the trail's greatest gifts.

We later heard some people in the shelters suffered hypothermia and frostbite. One or two had to be rescued by the Smoky Mountains National Park rangers in helicopters.

Even so, our family took a lot of flak for our choice to hike through the blizzard. Rumors circulated online and among other hikers that we had to be rescued by the rangers. The rumor started after someone at one of the shelters wrote a blog post about us requesting that people "pray for the Crawfords." The author thought we'd been picked up by Park Services. A few people on the Whiteblaze forum saw the misinformation and blew it up.

"Their poor judgment and bad behavior may impact regulations for future hiking families. Hard to litigate common sense." —kestral

"They sure didn't wait long to post a video after getting their rescue. Priorities. Gotta get them clicks." —Mugthumper

Through our YouTube channel, we knew what it was like to engage with an online community, but until this point, we'd only engaged with people who were familiar with our lifestyle. Now, with rumors spreading rapidly online, we had a social-media shitstorm to deal with. People who knew nothing about our family were up in arms about our choice to hike through the snow or even be on the trail at all.

Another family had previously achieved prominence for breaking a record on the A.T. They also had a large social media following. The mom, who had once befriended us, now wrote a post slamming us and shared it with their twenty thousand followers. Although it didn't mention any names, everyone in the hiking communities knew exactly who she was talking about.

"Just because we were thru-hikers didn't give us an excuse to have a lack of judgment. Our first priority was our child's safety. Knowing when to get off trail isn't a sign of weakness or lack of courage; rather, it is a sign of experience, wisdom, and good judgment skills."

Kami and I were being publicly called out for reckless and negligent parenting—the worst crimes you can commit in American culture. With all this drama, there were more eyes on us than ever, and we knew that meant the stakes would only get higher.

Here's the truth: while we don't regret our decision to push through the blizzard, we would *never* defend it as being the safest option. It was a calculated risk, but it was still a risk. You don't get off the couch, go outside, and start a 2,200-mile walk in the elements because it's *safe*. You do it for other reasons. You do it because it's worth it.

For years, we'd constantly hear parents refer to their kids as lame-ass consumers, saying they just used up electricity and bandwidth, always stuck to their phones. That day in the blizzard, we saw our kids as heroes. It was a gift for us as parents. Maybe if parents could see what their kids were capable of, they'd be blown away too. Maybe the lack of opportunities today's kids are presented with to prove their courage is the real reason parents have such a low opinion of their own children's bravery and abilities. Maybe it's the safe environments and goals parents, ourselves included, have created that's the problem, not the kids themselves.

A lot of people think being pushed to your limits is a bad thing. Our experience on the trail solidified our belief that it's valuable for families to do difficult things together—that you can put safety second. In fact, we've come to believe it's necessary to building strong relationships and inner confidence. Adventure is one of the best tools to build relationships—and whatever your definition of safety is, in order to find adventure, you need to leave safety behind.

Sure, the blizzard was a bit scarier than other parts of the adventure. But, in the big picture, it was just another day on the trail. Once we accomplished that day, we felt like it would all be downhill from there. We thought, *If we can do this, we can do anything.*

Of course, for us, *anything* was now restricted to the floor of the women's restroom.

CHAPTER SIX

Child Protective Services

"If parents wish to preserve childhood for their own children, they must conceive of parenting as an act of rebellion against culture."

—Neil Postman

On Day 22, we woke up on a bathroom floor to find that the sun had come up, but the temperature outside was still just sixteen degrees, well below freezing.

We melted some snow to drink and did an inventory of our remaining food. We had split the final two ounces of salmon jerky the previous evening, so we only had two single servings of oatmeal and six ounces of nuts left. Even though the food situation was bleak, we weren't too nervous. We were warm enough wearing all our layers and conserving energy, and we'd be able to restock our food supplies when we met up with my parents. The real killer would be boredom.

Sitting huddled on our piece of Tyvek—a piece of waterproof construction material used to wrap houses that we used as a lightweight tarp—in the corner of the cement bathroom, there was literally nothing to do but wait.

Buckeye, our neighbor in the men's restroom, shared the weather forecast. The temperature wasn't supposed to get above freezing the entire day. This made us uneasy; we wondered if the roads were going to thaw enough to allow traffic and when my parents would be able to make it up to us.

At 8:00 a.m., we heard plows on the road a couple of hundred feet downhill, but everything around us was still covered in snow and ice. Everyone's shoes were soaked, so I walked out on the ice in my flip-flops to get to the road.

The parking lots were plowed. The guys driving the plows said there was no guarantee the road would open that day. But the National Park Service is notorious for not updating its employees, so we held out hope.

Buckeye and his hiker friend, who'd both slept in the men's bathroom, were so stir crazy they decided to go for it and hike the fifteen-mile closed road into town. After they left, we had no cellphone to connect with the park service, my parents, or the hotel—where we'd already missed our reservation. Because the parking lot was located in a high-elevation gap with crazy wind, it was unbearable to be outside for more than a few minutes. Still, Rainier wanted to walk around and play in the snow. We couldn't blame him. It was hell to be stuck in that bathroom. The boredom was insufferable, especially when we knew that just a short fifteen miles away there were pancakes, warm beds, and wireless internet.

Kami used the time to clean up the constant dripping from the windows with toilet paper—the one thing we had plenty of. She started at one window, went down the line, and by the time she finished, the first one was wet again. It gave her something to do.

Thankfully, we weren't alone for long. More road crews showed up to plow and shovel the sidewalks. At one point, someone poked their head into the bathroom and asked if we needed help. Since emergency vehicles could make it through, we wondered if they might offer to take us into town. We walked out to talk to them and took Rainier, thinking that having a baby might tug at their hearts and increase our chances.

The burly, bearded guy in a National Park uniform squinted at our baby and asked, "You guys okay?"

"Yeah, we're good," I responded. "Any idea when the roads are going to open up?"

"Nope. They don't tell us anything. We heard about you guys, though." *This can't be good.* "Bunch of people called in and said you're in trouble." *Where the hell did that come from?* "Also, heard your parents are in the Park Ranger's office waiting for the roads to open." *Finally, some good news!*

I could tell that he wasn't going to respond to my hints that we'd love a ride into town, and I didn't want him calling in help and making a federal case out of us. Doing this would trigger emergency procedures, a huge waste of resources—not to mention a massive fuss and even more negative attention online. Our boredom wasn't an actual emergency, it just felt that way. I started to back away with a wave. "Thanks for the help. We're great, we'll just wait."

"You sure? Cause I can call in, and they can send help."

"No, we're fine and don't mind waiting," I reassured him, and he nodded and walked away.

Finally, at about 2:00 p.m., we heard the road was going to open.

The kids cheered, and Rainier repeated, "Yay, out!" again and again.

We made our way out and hoped the first car to drive by would be Halmonee and Papa. But instead of my parents, a long string of cars climbed up the hill and pulled into the parking lot. One hour earlier, this had been a survival zone. Now, tourists were getting out of their SUVs, and kids were throwing snowballs and running around while their parents sat drinking Starbucks on heated seats. We had no idea this was a popular tourist spot; after all, it had taken us three days to walk here, part of it through a snowstorm. Now we could see that it was a popular spot right off a major highway in a national park on the Tennessee and North Carolina state line. The dissonance of watching clean, warm kids dressed for a day hike mess around in the snow while my kids sat in dirty, damp hiking gear on a piece of Tyvek in a women's bathroom was nothing short of jarring. In contrast to our survival situation, everything felt ridiculous.

MEETING CHILD PROTECTIVE SERVICES

After just a couple minutes standing alongside the road, three official-looking government employees approached and asked to speak with us. We assumed they'd been sent by the park service to see if we were okay.

"Are you the Crawfords?" they asked. We responded that we were.

"We work for Child Protective Services," one of them said, indicating himself and the woman next to him. The other man wore a sheriff's uniform with a gold star.

We froze. People who live non-traditionally like us—homeschoolers, for instance—think more about CPS than the average American family, because we often run up against the heat of other people's criticism and discomfort with us not following the "rules." American society is not set up to be accepting of variety in child-rearing styles.

That said, in our seventeen years of raising a family, we'd never actually had to deal with CPS. It was our worst nightmare—not walking in a blizzard or sleeping on a bathroom floor, but being separated from our kids. It was hard for our minds not to leap straight to imagining the worst-case scenario.

Any encounter with CPS is difficult, but it was made all the more harrowing by the fact we had just emerged from the single most physically taxing day of our lives, along with the worst *sounding* sleeping conditions we'd ever had. After enduring a night on the hard, cold, contaminated concrete floor of a women's public restroom, we thought we were finally free to enjoy a fun break in town. But now, we felt in more danger than at any other time in the entire trip.

The CPS officials immediately separated Kami and I from our kids. One of the agents stayed with us; the other went with our kids. The sheriff stood by to make sure no one caused any trouble, prepared to take our children away from us depending on how we all answered the questions and how the CPS agents assessed the situation. Standing in the cold and wind, we could see the kids being interviewed across the parking lot. We had no idea what they were being asked or how they would respond. We'd never prepped them for this type of situation.

One of the agents pulled out a clipboard that said North Carolina Safety Assessment across the top. She started asking questions and checking boxes as we answered. We could see some of the questions.

- Caretaker caused/allowed serious physical harm to the child. (Yes/No)
- Caretaker is aware of the potential harm *and* unwilling *or* unable to protect the child from serious harm. (Yes/No)

- Caretaker fails to provide supervision to protect child from potentially serious harm. (Yes/No)
- Caretaker does not meet child's immediate needs for food or clothing. (Yes/No)
- Physical living conditions are hazardous and immediately threatening to the health and/or safety of the child. (Yes/No)

The agent ran through these questions. She paused then asked where we were sleeping. We pointed at the cement structure up the hill and said, "Over in that heated building." We were careful to avoid the word *bathroom*. She looked back at the paper, made a check mark, and moved on.

- Domestic violence exists in the household and poses imminent danger of serious physical harm and/or emotional harm to the child. (Yes/No)

There was another pause.

"We got a call saying you flicked a baby, and the baby was bleeding," she said. My heart plummeted.

"He was never bleeding," I said. At this point, she walked over to Rainier and looked at his mouth. Rainier smiled back at her and laughed. She walked back to us.

"He looks fine to me," she said with a shrug. *Whew*. Then she checked something off on the paper and asked us another question.

- Current circumstances combined with information the caretaker has or may have previously mistreated a child in their care suggest the child's safety may be of immediate concern. (Yes/No)

Finally, she asked if we had any witnesses that had observed us being good parents. We both drew a blank.

It seemed so strange to have to defend your
parenting to the government and wonder
who had your back. Every person we had
met or befriended in the past two months
suddenly became a potential witness.

Thankfully, at that moment, my parents pulled up in our twelve-passenger van, the van we had left in the rain 207 miles earlier. Before any hugs were exchanged, the CPS workers asked Halmonee and Papa to answer a few questions.

It was humiliating. My parents were totally confused; they had no idea what was going on. And even though I knew they had been exposed to my and Kami's parenting for the past sixteen years, it still felt like I'd been caught doing something wrong, and was getting busted in front of my parents.

When the CPS workers were done, they had us initial every page of their report. That was when we saw what they had concluded. Both officials had given us the okay on every single question. It seemed clear to them we weren't the type of family they were looking for. They agreed everyone was safe, and the kids weren't doing the hike against their will. As they turned to leave, the agents mentioned they'd actually enjoyed watching some of our videos, and it was just required protocol to follow up when a report was filed.

We climbed in the van excited to drive away from our prison cell from the night before. That morning all we could think about was pancakes and a soft bed, and now we were just thankful to still have our kids. As we left that frozen parking lot, the thing we appreciated most was having our family healthy and intact, without any of our kids having been taken away. We were still together.

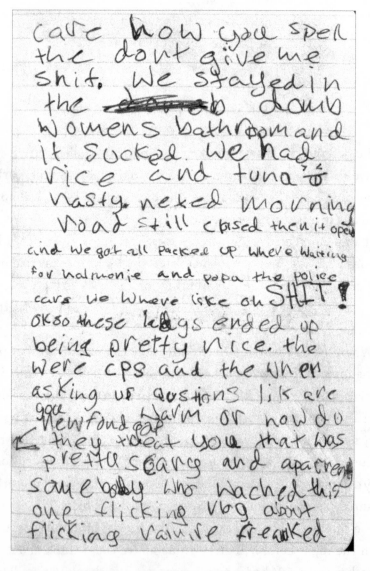

care how you spell the dont give me shit. We stayed in the ~~don't~~ donw womens bathroom and it sucked. We had rice and tuna to nasty. neked morning road still closed then it open and we got all packed up where waiting for halmonie and papa the police cars we where like oh SHIT! ok so these ladys ended up being pretty nice. the were cps and the when asking us qostions lik are you newfound warm or how do they treat you that was pretty searey and apacrent samebody who wached this one flicking vbg about flicking vaivie freaked

Memory (11) processing her time being interviewed by CPS. As you can see, we do not censor our kids' language, and they can get pretty colorful.

A BREAK IN GATLINBURG

The tiny, carnival-like town of Gatlinburg came along at the perfect time.

We ate all-you-can-eat pancakes for dinner. And then again for breakfast. We slept in beds with pillows and looked at the snowy mountains through the windows of our climate-controlled rooms. We strolled down Main Street like tourists and bought saltwater taffy and coffee and celebrated being halfway done with the Smokies. The hot tub felt so nice that we momentarily forgot about the whole CPS scare.

It was also nice to simply step off the trail for a while and feel like a part of civilization again. As a couple, this was my and Kami's first chance to step away from the kids completely since we began this journey twenty-two days ago. We took a few hours to smoke cigars and relax together while Halmonee and Papa babysat.

After a lot of searching, we finally found a bar in town that allowed cigars. It felt like a frat party was raging inside, and we realized that Gatlinburg was a tourist destination and a bunch of college kids were here on spring break. Five weeks earlier, spending spring break in a kitschy carnival town like Gatlinburg would have sounded like hell. Now we were just thankful to be out of the mountains. We looked at each other and laughed, thinking, *How did we get here?*

Looking at the weather report, we took an extra zero day to take advantage of the time with the grandparents. It was our fifth zero day of the trip at only twenty-three days in.

Finally, the time came for us to be dropped back off at the bathroom parking lot on the trail, in the middle of the Smoky Mountains. Yet again, we shared tear-filled goodbyes with Halmonee and Papa. This time was harder because we knew what we were getting into, and part of us dreaded the cold and discomfort. It was still freezing cold outside, and the trail was covered in ankle-deep slush.

After saying goodbye to my parents, reality hit again. Hard. Slush filled our shoes, and it was obvious our mini-vacation was over. The weather was, once again, a force to be reckoned with, but we were used to that by now.

We weren't, however, prepared for attacks of a totally different nature.

CHAPTER SEVEN

The Internet
Hate Engine

*"The more important a call or action is to our soul's evolution,
the more Resistance we will feel toward pursuing it."*

—Steven Pressfield

The CPS scare had been shocking at first, but we were able to rebound from it quickly. It was an ordeal of a whole different nature that introduced us to a new enemy that was not as simple and would follow us for the rest of our journey: the internet hate engine.

Back on the trail, Kami and I had a sleepless night. Someone had sent us an Instagram message to let us know people were talking about us on Reddit. Since we already knew people had called CPS on us, it felt responsible to keep up with what was being said about us online. After all, it was our lives they were talking about. After what had happened with CPS, we didn't want to be blindsided again, and we figured we should know what dangers lay out there on the web.

Up to this point, many people had already added their two cents via YouTube comments and hiking forums. But we quickly discovered that this Reddit page was different, and much darker. There were hundreds of hateful comments completely detached from people familiar with our story or hiking in general. The page was titled "Crawford Trail Wreck: Will these dumbasses get pregnant, kill one of their kids, or have their kids taken away?" Here are a few of the comments from the page:

> "I've watched a lot of thru-hiker videos on the Appalachian and Pacific Crest Trails and recently stumbled on the videos of this family, 'Fight For Together.' I started watching, thinking watching a family of eight hike the A.T. would be interesting, and I have been shocked at what I've seen. The father, Ben, is the biggest narcissist alive."

> "You're an asshole, Ben Crawford! I hope your children get taken away from you soon, especially Eden, the child you made a point to say is 'hard for you to love' on her birthday video. You are one fucked-up narcissistic, abusive grifter."

> "IMO he's a misogynistic, controlling, egotistical individual who sees himself as their leader. Thank goodness none of the kids have gotten seriously ill from drinking non-filtered water. His wife is looking more haggard and old as she loses more weight. She does not look happy and really needs to stand up to this asshat and take charge of her life and not let him dictate to the family. It is beyond me how people admire this creep. He makes my skin crawl; his voice is grating and just plain annoying as hell. How people find this guy

*charming baffles me. The gray stringy hairs in his beard are so yucky
and unattractive. He said they really have to push now (the most
difficult and dangerous part of the trail) to make their deadline. I
still don't get why this annual spiritual get together is so freaking
important, other than they promised the kids they would be able to
go. Which seems pretty unlikely since he never puts the kids first.
Thanks for letting me vent."*

*"I hate this guy with the fire of a thousand suns. He's battered down
his wife; she's so hunched and dead-eyed in her appearances. I hope
his kids kick his bloviating ass to the curb as soon as they're old
enough to do so."*

The more we went down the rabbit hole of comments, the more overwhelmed Kami and I felt. That was the worst night on the trail. The
physical obstacles we faced were hard, but simple enough to overcome. This felt like we had stepped into an overflowing river that
could sweep us away to a dark place.

The irony of the Reddit comments painting me as the villain of
this story was that it was Kami, not I, who had ignited the idea of
doing the Appalachian Trail. Ten years earlier, our family had hiked
the Wonderland Trail in Washington. It's a ninety-five-mile loop
around Mount Rainier, the mountain we named our two-year-old
after. During that trip, Kami, who was not an outdoorsy person, saw
how much the hike brought our family together into a single unit.
From that point, she prioritized time spent outdoors, as a family.

We went on to hike the Wonderland four more times. On every occasion, the challenge of ninety-five miles through the rain and hills was
hard and something we couldn't do as individuals. The goal was bigger
than anything we could accomplish on our own. Faced with a situation

where we were forced to rely on one another, our appreciation, team-work, and intimacy skyrocketed. Our days on the Wonderland were the highest highs and lowest lows our family had ever seen.

In some ways, our first days on the Wonderland were more diffi-cult than anything on the A.T. Our first trip, our kids were two, four, six, and eight. We actually didn't know if they could walk that far, especially since it rained for nine days straight. We did it a couple of times while Kami was pregnant, once again, not sure if she could make it. After the first hike around Mount Rainier, a friend picked us up from the trail and commented that we seemed different as a family. That it was hard to explain. We felt like soldiers returning from war. A very, very wet war. We were attached to each other in a deeper way than before we started the hike. We had made it, and we had only done it because of each other.

Those trips showed us another way to live life, but we always came back to the "real" world. We tried all of the typical things to re-create that connection at home. Our kids took dance classes and tennis les-sons and joined baseball leagues. We even tried rock climbing. Each of these activities scratched an itch, making us feel like good par-ents, but the kids never seemed to come out of them with the same sense of joint accomplishment that our hikes gave them. Even when they did, we found teams and sports actually competed with what we wanted to build. Eventually, we got bored and wondered if there was another way to experience the bonding and lessons we had learned on the Wonderland but a long- distance thru-hike seemed out of the question for us. We were a large group with small kids, and Kami did not see herself as the type of person that could handle an undertak-ing that large.

Then one day while surfing on YouTube, Kami found a woman named Dixie. Dixie was a blonde woman in her late twenties from

Alabama who was an engineer. She quit her job to thru-hike the A.T. by herself in 2015. She had never been on a backpacking trip before. Dixie posted videos on YouTube chronicling her entire journey. And Kami watched every video, transfixed. She cried as she saw Dixie touch the sign at the end. She started to imagine a trip of our own.

A GRAIN OF SALT

With our lifestyle, we'd become accustomed to disagreements, or people who make different choices than how we choose to live. But these Reddit comments were different. They weren't just expressing an opinion. There was so much energy, so much hate; they wanted to bring us down. They wanted to destroy our reputation, our trip, our story. We knew the people hating us were probably those who needed the most compassion; that there was probably a reason they were exuding so much nastiness. People vent to feel better about themselves, so it's important to be careful about how much weight you give what they say. But in our state, we were in no condition to be dishing out compassion. We were hurt. We felt defensive.

> After all, we thought, when the world sees walking in the woods with your kids as controversial, something's gone wrong somewhere in the culture.

Frankly, five years earlier, we would have judged others the same way as the Reddit commenters: applying one golden standard of parenting that is based upon our culture and own abilities and assuming that everyone else who didn't live up to it was irresponsible. Since then, though, we'd come to realize life isn't so simple or binary. We'd made the error of mis-categorizing people for the sake of our own security in the past, and now, we were on the receiving end of the same treatment. It made us realize anew how wrong we'd been to judge others.

The hardest thing about the comments was that even the worst ones contained bits of truth we had wrestled with and pondered at some point ourselves:

Emotionally abusive? On the trail, we had seen all of our kids cry and pushed them in ways that made us wonder what was abusive and how far was too far.

Was I controlling? Not compared to our early years of marriage, but it was something I'd battled with for a long time. It was hard for me to let go of projects I cared about, and I tended to micromanage people in the details and felt like a perfectionist with the kids.

And egotistical? Well, with all we had accomplished as a family in business and in physical feats, some of it did go to our head, and it was easy to think of ourselves as exceptional and "different."

"She deserves to be away from these people and to get a good education." Were we giving our kids a good enough education, even though we didn't make them go to public school and didn't force structured education at home?

"Gray stringy hairs in his beard are so yucky and unattractive." Rude, but true, I could laughingly admit to myself. Sometimes Kami didn't even like them, although most of the time, she said she did. Maybe she was lying.

"Normal families aren't like this." People in our spiritual communities had told us the same thing in the past using much more charged language, and we felt guilty of this for a long time. Our very presence seemed to make any normal family feel uncomfortable, and it was impossible to not blame ourselves for this discomfort. We constantly wondered if we were just trying to be different or make some sort of statement. Could we be normal even if we tried?

And finally, the worst: *"I hope his kids kick his bloviating ass to the curb as soon as they're old enough to do so."* This was the worst because it was my worst fear. Would our kids leave as soon as they were able? Did we really trick ourselves and pull some emotionally manipulative and controlling stunts to make them think they wanted to do this, and really, they would resent us for it someday? We had created so many safeguards in our life to prevent this from happening: apologizing to our kids regularly, going to therapy and counseling and encouraging our kids to do the same, having weekly meetings with our kids as individuals and as a group so they could speak to our parenting and household and regularly air all grievances. But still, I have such a strong personality that maybe it wasn't enough. Maybe we had drunk our own Kool-Aid, and these online sleuths could see through all of our bullshit for who we really were and the real effects we were having on our kids. The thought was paralyzing.

We could spend hours mulling these thoughts over in our heads, wondering if they were true and then wondering how we could respond online. But time spent thinking about online comments was time spent ignoring our kids' needs and even our own. Time that we could spend figuring out new ways to keep warm or planning breaks to boost morale.

So moving forward, we needed a strategy to deal with online dissent just to stay sane. Our strategy was twofold:

1. We asked, "Are these commenters even in the game?" We would listen to hikers—no one from the audience. Listening to a faceless "they" and "them" was worthless. If you had hiked through the snow, if you were heading to the next town, or if we were sleeping in the same shelter, you could

tell us anything you wanted about parenting, the trail, or gear. We would listen, we would discuss, and we would offer feedback when asked.

2. We asked, "Are the comments helpful?" This led us to our most helpful conclusion:

> Just because something is true does not mean it is helpful. And if it's not helpful to us in the moment, it's irrelevant.

Not everything we read was negative. For as much hate as we got online, we had tons of people reach out to us and share that they could relate. This matched our real-life experience with friends who made real-time mistakes and had regrets in parenting, just like us. What parents don't have stories of losing their temper or going too far in their frustration and anger?

It was helpful for us to see everything happening online as make-believe. And we were make-believe to them. We were just a story to provide fuel for their conversation, hate, and insecurity. Tomorrow, we would probably be replaced by someone else. These people didn't know us and didn't actually care about us. We were characters in a story to them, just like Darth Vader was a character to me. Their critique of our lifestyle wasn't real. *The trail* was real. Food, water, moving forward, and staying safe together were what mattered. Through the brightly lit phone screen, we saw an online world filled with passion and anger and so many opinions—but the second we turned off the screen, all we could see was a dirt path winding its way between trees and rocks. The people we met on the trail cared about us deeply. There was such a stark contrast between the online world and the trail—our real world.

Conflict has a way of either tearing people apart or bringing them together. If Kami and I knew anything, it was that if we were crazy, at least we were fine being crazy together. We saw what our relationship was made of, and knew the negativity we faced would only serve to pull us closer together. Kami and I developed a new dynamic that dark night in the tent with Reddit. We came together as a couple and as parents to say, "You don't know us."

We agreed to hold each other accountable to ignore the internet comments from then on. It was like we were each other's protectors. It became another piece of armor we forged together on the trail.

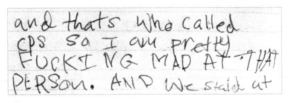

Memory's (11) thoughts after the CPS incident. Even though we had never trained our kids on how to deal with CPS, they felt the severity of the situation and felt violated by how confident outsiders could have a direct impact upon our family.

TRAIL FRIENDS

Early on in the Smokies, we'd met a man called Bill who went by the trail name Hops because of his love for home-brewing beer. Hops had a similar look to the other older male hikers we'd met: bearded, with scraggly gray hair. He hiked in a pair of green cargo shorts, which were instantly recognizable out on the trail.

When he was eleven years old, Hops had stepped onto the Appalachian Trail, and his scout leader pointed in one direction and said, "If you walk eleven hundred miles that way, you'll end up in Georgia. And if you walk eleven hundred miles the other way, you'll end up in Maine." Hops said that ever since that moment, he knew he would hike the trail. He'd always planned on hiking with his wife, but she'd had hip surgery that year and, being sixty-eight now, Hops knew he couldn't wait. He considered the A.T. sacred ground and hiked with a reverence and appreciation of history that we didn't have at all.

Twice, we came into shelters late at night. On both these occasions, we heard Hops had pitched his tent in the slush and saved spots for our whole family in the shelter. Hops said he missed his wife and grandchildren, and being around our kids reminded him of his own family.

In the second half of the Smokies, we ran into fewer and fewer hikers. It seemed many had quit, and quite a few were still recovering in Gatlinburg from the blizzard. On Day 26, we emerged from Smoky Mountain National Park tired, but together, and closer than ever. We walked into a hostel to celebrate with some ice cream, and Rainier got some chocolate milk. Hops was there. He had just pulled a pizza out of the oven and offered some to each of our kids.

"I heard what happened to you guys with CPS," he said. "I've been watching you guys hike. I was a district executive for the Boy Scouts for seventeen years, as well as the senior director for the National Aquarium for twenty years, so if you ever need someone to vouch for you, send them my way!"

As our kids devoured the rest of Hops's frozen pizza, it felt good to know that we had a friend out here.

As soon as we got back on the trail, two young women passed us. They were dragging their feet and appeared to be in an argument. They didn't look very excited to be on the trail; the Smokies had clearly been rough on them. We introduced ourselves. Mama Kish was the shorter of the two and had a ponytail of dirty blonde hair.

Her trail name was based on her last name, and she was the parent figure of the two. Not Dead was tall and thin, with disheveled brown hair. She chose her name because "not dead" was a phrase she used in her work as an ambulance driver, and she felt it most accurately described her state on the trail.

The two of them were best friends, and Mama Kish had somehow talked Not Dead into hiking the trail. In the words of Not Dead, "She forced me."

Not Dead wanted to stop for pizza and ice cream, but Mama Kish wasn't having it. She said there would be no stopping until the next town. The problem was that the next town, Hot Springs, wasn't for another thirty-five miles.

Spiritually arm-in-arm with some new real-life friends who knew what we were going through, and who were sharing the same struggle, we all headed that way together.

CHAPTER EIGHT

Clearing Our Heads

"When you accept somebody's offer for help, whether it's in the form of food, crash space, money, or love, you have to trust the help offered. You can't accept things halfway and walk through the door with your guard up. When you openly, radically trust people, they not only take care of you, they become your allies, your family."

—Amanda Palmer, *The Art of Asking; or, How I Learned to Stop Worrying and Let People Help*

The A.T. goes right through the center of the town of Hot Springs, North Carolina. As we entered the town, our first site was the Hiker's Ridge Ministry Center. It had a sign on the sidewalk that said, "Welcome Home Hikers!" The house was ten feet off the main street and right off the trail, and as soon as we stepped inside, a middle-aged woman who was volunteering there eagerly gave our kids all kinds of junk food, including juice boxes, moon pies, and cookies. For a moment we hesitated, wondering whether we should eat all this unhealthy free food. It seemed like we should create limitations of some sort. But the hesitation didn't last long. The opportunity for foods we couldn't access on the trail, along with someone waiting on us hand and foot, was too tempting to resist. Some places on the trail see hikers as a nuisance. Their smell and wild appearance can be a turn-off for many. It's not uncommon to see signs that say, "Hikers allowed. Keep packs outside." At some hotels, we had to sign special forms for hikers promising that we would keep our boots outside or be careful with mud and leaves. These places combined with the nuisance we felt like we were online made us feel unwelcome. But this place was different—not only did it allow hikers, but it was *built* for us. Here, we felt like we were being honored. We were seen and appreciated for what we were doing.

After about thirty minutes there, we crossed over a small bridge and went to a tavern for our second meal. There were hikers seated everywhere. Once we sat down, we were greeted by Buckeye, the hiker who had spent the night in the men's restroom and loaned us his phone. We exchanged updates about Gatlinburg, and he said his wife had been asking about us because she had seen our YouTube videos. The waitress said she'd heard of us, and everyone gave us a nod or a wave. It felt like the stories from the Smokies had spread, with fording the blizzard, spending the night in the bathroom, the false rumors, and deflecting CPS. Overnight, we had become legends on the trail.

After we ate appetizers, we headed across the street to a back-packer gear shop. This was one of only four businesses open in the entire town, and the whole place was set up for hikers. In the shop, we weighed our packs for the first time. In hiker world, the weight of your pack is a big deal, with packs ranging from sixty pounds for military and ex–Boy Scouts to eight pounds for the ultralight folks. So we were all eager to see how much we'd been carrying all this way.

Kami's pack had in it clothes for me, her, and Rainier; our sleeping gear, including two sleeping pads and a down quilt; and diapers. It weighed thirty-three pounds. This wasn't bad, considering it was three people's stuff.

Dove's pack weighed twenty-seven pounds and included her clothes, sleeping bag, all our tent poles and stakes, all our dinners, and fuel.

Eden's pack carried the cooking pot and stove, clothes, her sleeping bag, and all the lunch supplies, and also weighed in at twenty-seven pounds, but she was quick to point out that it was normally heavier because we had just come off the trail and had eaten all of her lunch supplies.

Seven's pack weighed twenty-eight pounds and held the computer, camera equipment, and both tents.

Memory's pack weighed seventeen pounds and held the drone, all breakfast and snack supplies, and clothes.

Our seven-year-old Filia's pack weighed twelve pounds and had her sleeping bag, clothes, and trash, including dirty diapers wrapped in garbage bags.

Finally, we weighed the child carrier with Rainier in his pack, and it came in the heaviest, at forty-four pounds. Now we could see why Kami had struggled the first week and why I'd been lagging ever since I took over carrying Rainier. Our other packs got lighter as we ditched gear and got more efficient—but Rainier's "pack" only got heavier, day after day, as Rainier grew. Rainier's pack had also begun taking on a different kind of weight: we'd started appeasing him by giving him sticks to carry so that he could be like everyone else carrying trekking poles. Each time he got into his pack, he'd go scout for his sticks first. It was often a negotiation limiting him to two sticks, but once he had them picked out, he'd happily climb into his perch.

It was common to hear of people starting the trail with heavier packs. In our years of backpacking, we had seen people carrying lawn chairs strapped to the outside of their packs, canned food (which is a big no-no because of all the water weight)—and we'd even back-packed with a friend who was planning on bringing four books and two journals with him before we told him it was a terrible idea. Simply put, the people with the heaviest packs and the most super-fluous equipment were the ones who probably wouldn't make it very far. They couldn't let go of their attachments and surrender to the trail. They say that on the trail you "carry your fears." In the end, those attachments and fears drag people down.

After weighing our packs, we sauntered over to an ice cream place and enjoyed multiple scoops of ice cream and coffee. Sitting there stuffed, we laughed about the fact that we'd hit up every place in the entire town in a few hours and had no idea how much money we'd spent.

The town is called Hot Springs for an obvious reason. That after-noon, Kami and I took our parenting hats off for a bit and went alone to the hot springs, which are essentially private hot tubs.

We spent an hour there, naked together, feeling human again. It was a total luxury, and *exactly* what we needed.

When we returned to the tavern for dinner that night, someone had anonymously paid twenty-five dollars of our bill. Once again, we felt so supported.

On Reddit, we were villains. But in the town of Hot Springs, we were rock stars. Everyone in town saw us as serious hikers and respected us for it.

3/25/18 Seven day 25 Mile 13

today we woke up at 830am ate
granula for breakfast and got out
at 9-10 am. I dried off all my socks
and they were nice and warm, but thrue
all that slush they got utterelly soake
d! so that was frusterating, but 5
miles in it was 12:45pm and we hit
a shelter and ate tuna wheat thins
cheese and awesome moon pies for
lunch. And hiked the whole time. The
snow and slush slowly went away
as we got further down the trail.
and we talked a lot and hit a sighn
at 5:30pm that was our destination
so we hiked down there and Dove
started dinner and there was lots of
room for us because nice people reser
ved a spot for us and camped outside
so we ate dinner and I Edited a wh
ole vlog using 17% Battery! YEAH!

In addition to hiking and setting up camp, Seven (13) maintained the
responsibility of editing vlog episodes five days a week, which was not
an easy chore on a laptop, in a tent, with limited battery life.

STATS AND A TRAIL NAME

At this point on the trail, we hit a few important highlights.

On Day 30, we celebrated three hundred miles, which felt like a huge accomplishment. Even so, we weren't as elated as we could have been. It meant that we'd averaged ten miles a day, which was well below our required average. We'd been trying for weeks to increase our daily mileage, and it just didn't seem to be improving no matter what tweaks we made to our gear or our schedule.

We heard some news in Hot Springs that consoled us, though. According to the gear shop owner, this was the worst March anyone could remember on the trail, and this year had the highest rate of hiker drop-off in history, which was impossible to prove, but encouraging nonetheless.

We took this to mean we should celebrate making it this far, and we hoped it would only get better.

That same day, we also celebrated our top mileage day so far: 17.3 miles, which we accomplished in rain and hail. And the biggest highlight was that we now had our trail name: *The Family.*

As I mentioned earlier, it's A.T. tradition to be given your trail name by other hikers. We didn't initially like this tradition because people often come up with *incredibly strange* trail names, and we didn't want to be stuck with something weird. One guy was called Loner Boner. Another was No Name. You could literally be named after the ramen you burned the night before.

We value our kids' names tremendously. Kami and I had waited weeks and even months to name some of our kids after they were born, searching for meaning and a name that felt right. We didn't want to change those names just because someone burned some ramen. We also didn't want the trail to feel like an escape from reality.

We wanted it to be an extension of how we approach life, keeping our identity true throughout.

But as much as we avoided trail names, the majority of people who came up to us on the trail recognized us and asked, "Are you The Family?" Finally, we accepted that "The Family" would be a good trail name for us. It was totally accurate, after all. It reflected why we were doing the A.T. And it was only one name to remember, not eight, which would have been a pain.

The name was confirmed as we continued. At one point almost three months in, a group of guys came up and said they had been chasing us for months. They said they viewed different parts of the trail like levels in a video game. Mount Katahdin was the final boss, and they said that finding The Family was the ultimate side quest.

We laughed about this for days after. We were someone's ultimate side quest! For those hikers, The Family had become a mascot, a motivator, and even one of the highlights of their trip. This sweet, supportive attention and "trail fame" stood in stark contrast to our online infamy and helped with perspective and motivation—something we were in constant need of as our miles continued to increase.

If we could stay focused on the people in real life, instead of everyone who had an opinion in the rest of the world, maybe we'd be fine.

EASTER ON THE FARM

Before starting the trail, we received two invitations to stay at people's houses from people who had seen us preparing for the trail on YouTube. One of those invitations came from a couple named John and Nicole, who owned a farm where they helped rehabilitate war veterans. This would be our first night in a home since starting, thirty-one days earlier.

We reached John and Nicole's town on March 31, which was Easter weekend. The couple drove an hour to us and an hour back to their house in two separate cars. When we arrived, we took our shoes off outside and saw a giant table covered with all our favorite creature comforts.

The kids gasped.

Rainer saw the juice boxes. "Pop!" he yelled.

Seven started opening the cookies. "I'm gonna eat them all."

"These are all our favorite cereals!" Dove said. "How did you know?"

"I watched the video where you each said your favorite," Nicole explained. "I couldn't find Blueberry Morning for you, Ben. I'm not sure if they make it anymore. I just got Golden Grahams instead. But—John spent all of his allowance on some cigars!"

I was blown away.

Kami was too. "They brought a French press!" she said, smiling wider than I'd seen in days.

This was a special treat and such a great way to celebrate our first month on trail, and once again, we felt honored. It felt incredible to unpack our bags in someone else's home, do laundry, and be cared for in this way. It reminded me of that feeling I got when I came home from college for the weekend and my mom prepared all of my favorite meals and took care of me. We could relax.

It was also awkward to receive so much from strangers with no easy way to repay them. We worried we were taking advantage of them, but they made it clear they wanted to do this. Nicole told us that she'd watched the YouTube video we'd made of Rainier's birth, which Kami did at home in a birthing tub, myself and all our kids surrounding her. Since watching that video, Nicole had wanted to meet us—"I've always thought we should be friends," she told us.

So, we had to learn to simply receive, enjoy the time as a gift, and trust that this family knew what they were getting into.

With some space to unwind on the farm, we finally had a chance to talk to the kids and hear their thoughts about what we experienced with CPS ten days earlier. Of all the kids, Eden had been particularly frustrated by the whole thing. She's typically our quiet one. She doesn't complain or vocalize much. As such, we were surprised when she told us she wanted to make a video about how angry she was with the incident. We supported her wholeheartedly.

In the video, she talked about how upset she was that people she'd never met thought they knew what was best for her, or that she and her brothers and sisters didn't have a choice in all this. Here's some of what the kids said that video:

Eden: I was mostly annoyed. If anyone should be telling our parents that they're doing something wrong, it should be us, and there's six of us. They're always asking us how we're feeling, and we're not afraid to tell them.

Dove: I felt really, really scared. My mind went to the worst-case scenario. We might get taken away. I was angry that whoever reported us would think it would be better that we are taken away from our family than allowed to walk in the woods.

Eden: I don't usually want to read the comments on the video, but for *these* people, I want to reply to every one. It seems like some of these people have a lot of time on their hands. I don't normally like to talk on camera, but I feel like it's important that the people who are watching this know that they have no idea what's going on.

Dove: On the comments, it feels like people are turning it into a human rights thing, saying we have the right to be comfortable, but that's not how it is on the trail. We're not always thinking about how we have a right to comfort. Wishing for comfort does not help you survive.

Memory: I was really frustrated. The people who are really negative online, you can watch our videos but you don't get to see the behind-the-scenes stuff, and you feel like you know everything, but you don't.

Dove: We weren't really excited to go on the trail, but we trust our parents enough that we could see that even though some parts suck, we would learn a lot and that there would be amazing moments.

It felt good to hear the kids were forming opinions on their own, especially since those online were hellbent on painting our kids as helpless victims. They hadn't heard Kami and I venting to each other as we walked. It offered us hope that maybe we weren't making a complete mistake.

We later found out we were reported by someone from the Whiteblaze hiker forum, who had also warned the Smoky Mountains National Park rangers about us. He wrote a post sharing his actions, which he ended by stating, "Now I am able to sleep soundly." With a statement this straightforward, it was crystal clear why people were intervening. Their primary concern was for *their own* conscience and peace of mind. The best interests of our children were secondary, at best. This created an interesting dynamic. People with limited information but a lot of passion could interfere with our family's success all while trying to take credit for being a good person. We were suddenly happy our videos were delayed until we could get to towns and upload—people online would have more difficulty locating us that way.

The one benefit from the wealth of outside opinions was they helped us clarify whose voices we should listen to. It's easy to pay attention to the loudest voices, especially when they come with the authority of the masses and apparent concern for our children. But this made it clearer than ever: these people online did not have all the context, and they did not really care about our children. They were using our story and even our kids for their entertainment and comfort.

So, whose voices *should* we listen to?

The answer was clear to Kami and me. We believed the most important group to hear from was our children.

To many in the online community, our kids were one mass—one homogenous representation of what they considered "typical" childhood wants and needs. They didn't see our kids as we saw them, as six individuals with different perspectives, goals, and capabilities, who might agree and disagree seemingly at random. To these people, simplifying our kids' autonomy into a single generalized box was easier than imagining that kids could ever have the kind of self-determination that would lead them to choose short-term discomfort for a long-term benefit.

When Eden asked to address the critics online, it further confirmed to us that our kids had voices and weren't afraid to speak their truths. Even though we weren't sure if her video would help us or just add more fuel to the fire—we knew we were setting ourselves up for ridiculous "Stockholm Syndrome!!" and "They're brainwashed!" comments—we thought it was important to encourage our kids to express their opinions, even if someday, they might be expressing their opinions against *us*. If the choice before Kami and I was to make the online crowd happy, or to bet on our relationship with our kids, we knew which side we were on. Our stance was unpopular—but just because our way was different didn't make it wrong. Doing what we viewed as the best job we could as parents was worth the criticism. Doing what was popular would be selling our kids short, and we wanted to send a message to ourselves and to them that our relationship was worth standing up to the masses for.

After all, our relationship with our kids would last the rest of our lives. In ten years, the internet hate engine would be nothing more than a memory.

CHAPTER NINE

Our Allies

"I have learned that to be with those I like is enough."
—Walt Whitman

On Day 42, we set a new mileage record, covering 19.1 miles. At camp, our feet were in pain, but our spirits were high. We were less than a day away from Damascus, the most famous trail town on the A.T. It's the home of Trail Days, a huge A.T. festival held in early summer, to which thousands make the pilgrimage each year. Damascus is a destination for hikers, and many try and do the thirty miles preceding it in one single day, calling it the Damascus Dash. Earlier that day, we passed Fun Facts, Culligan, and Nubs, who were going to bed before sunset with the hopes of starting the Damascus Dash around 2:00 a.m. A huge part of me wanted to join them, but I knew that it just wouldn't be feasible for our family; Kami wouldn't be up for it, and I had to prioritize the needs of our kids.

As much as I hated to admit it, it did feel like I was missing out on a special trail experience. I'd already felt like I was also missing out on "choosing" trail family—finding other hikers who you formed a bond with. My trail family was already set.

We woke up earlier than usual, though Fun Facts, Culligan, and Nubs had long passed us while we were sleeping. It was Kami's birthday, and we were in a hurry to get to Damascus and celebrate; while the sun rose, we crossed the Tennessee border into Virginia, our fourth state. As we walked, Kami munched on a birthday present from Seven: dehydrated cheesecake, which was like bizarre astronaut-style crunchy cheesecake-flavored puffs. Seven had found it weeks earlier in a store on one of our stops, and we laughed about what a sweet but strange gift it was.

Along the trail that day, I dropped my headlamp. I hadn't shut the zipper on my pack properly. When I realized it was missing, I had to run back, find it, and then run to catch up again, adding an extra four miles to my hike. This was demoralizing, but it also led to a revelation. Without my pack, running felt easy. As I made my way back to my family, I thought about the upcoming marathon in Cincinnati, the Flying Pig, which took place five minutes from our home in Kentucky. We had run it together with the kids for the past four years.

We'd assumed we'd have to give up the tradition that year for the A.T. Quitting the A.T. to run a marathon seemed ridiculous, especially now that we had a deadline. Plus, we hadn't run in almost two months, so we weren't anywhere near properly trained. But as I was running back with my headlamp, feeling great, I questioned that assumption. *What if we could still participate?*

WHERE IT ALL STARTED

Damascus wasn't just a trail milestone for us; the town represented a nostalgic moment from our past.

Seventeen years ago, before we heard of the A.T., Kami and I were living in Seattle and were struggling to pay for Kami's nursing school, stay out of debt, and raise our one-year-old daughter, Dove. We lived in a tiny apartment attached to the college and had a car that we had to push-start every morning down the hill. I worked lunches waiting tables, and we made ends meet with the help of government assistance vouchers for free cheese and peanut butter. We'd just found out we were pregnant with number two. We were living under the poverty line, but we were happy; we'd decided early on in our marriage that we'd rather live with a little inconvenience than spend our effort accumulating creature comforts.

I had wanted to take a particular trip for a while: ride bikes across America. I was scared of settling down, and so was Kami. Now that we were having kids, we thought our adventure days may be over— everyone was warning us that the fun days were done. I was desperate to fit in one last adventure that scratched the itch of feeling wild and undomesticated by our society.

Having saved up $2,000, I quit my job; we flew to the Atlantic Ocean with two mountain bikes and our government peanut butter and planned to bike back. Four hundred miles and many tears into our cross-country trip, we slept in someone's garage with a bunch of hikers sleeping on bales of hay. We started talking with two women: Penguin, who was sixty-two, and T-Time, who was fifty-eight. They explained they were hiking this thing called the Appalachian Trail that went right through this very town. We were captivated late into the night by their stories of the trail. We didn't know what a thru-hike was and had never tried backpacking, but a dream was born that night.

Back then, I'd wanted to hike the A.T. right away, the year after our bike ride. With Kami expecting Eden at that point, I thought having more kids would eliminate the possibility of a thru-hike because we could soon be outnumbered. We began to make plans for a thru-hike, but Kami hated the idea and the plans quickly fell through, and I eventually gave up the dream. We'd never heard of anyone doing it with kids; the A.T. is commonly populated by young people (pre-kids) and retired people (post-kids). Sixteen years passed until Kami stumbled on Dixie's YouTube videos, reignited my dream, and began to dream of it for herself.

Now, on the trail, waiting so long seemed like the best thing that could have happened. I wondered for the first time if we were actually having a *better* experience out on the trail with six kids than our twenty-two-year-old selves or even some solo hikers.

That garage where we first heard of the trail was in Damascus. We had arrived there on bikes, and now we had arrived on foot. A woman named Tonya had offered to meet us at a park in the center of the city. She'd been following us online for a while and, like Nicole, she knew exactly what we liked. When she found out it was Kami's birthday, she brought us cheeseburgers, candy, miniature boxes of our favorite cereal, and gourmet cupcakes. She even brought us lattes from Starbucks, freshly made in paper to-go cups. This was a huge step up from the Starbucks powdered drink we were mixing in Gatorade bottles with unfiltered, freezing stream water. It was an emotional experience—it's hard to articulate the amount of care we felt coming out of the woods to a perfectly tailored list of our favorite creature comforts from a stranger in a park, with no ability to reciprocate. Not only was her hospitality meaningful, but her mere presence meant everything. We felt perfectly at home in the public park that sat in the center of this small town that didn't even have cell reception.

Full from the burgers, cupcakes, and drinks, we mentioned the idea of the marathon to the kids. We had no idea how they'd respond to making the long drive home to run a 26.2-mile race with no training, then driving all the way back to continue the A.T.

"What do you guys think?" I asked. "It's just an idea, but anyone want to take a detour...to run a race?"

Dove's enthusiasm practically exploded out her, despite how tired she was. "Yeah! Very much yes. I really, really, really, really want to run."

Every other kid gave a resounding yes right away. Although running a marathon was a grueling activity, it was one the kids were familiar with. It felt "normal" to them. Also, the opportunity to go home to someplace familiar was exciting. Every night for the last five weeks, we'd had no idea what type of weather we were going to face or where we were going to lay our head each night. The kids were homesick.

We spent a few hours eating and laughing, and Tonya drove the older kids to do their resupply at the store while we relaxed with our lattes in the grass, watching Rainier and Filia playing at the playground.

As we lay there, Kami shared her reservations about the marathon. The thought of our schedule was tough enough on her. She was already resistant to the idea of finishing in 161 days, and now we were taking three days off to run twenty-six miles that weren't toward our goal. We still weren't making our daily mileage goal, despite constant attempts to tweak our hiking to save time and get more miles in. Taking another zero day was not a relaxing thought for Kami when we were so behind. While these types of challenges and interruptions gave some members of the family more energy, that wasn't true for Kami. She valued planning, predictability, and relaxation.

"Look, we don't even know if we can still register for the marathon," I told her. "Let's just enjoy your birthday tonight. We can worry about the marathon later."

KAMI'S BIRTHDAY CAKE

Besides John and Nicole, the couple we'd spent Easter with, one other couple reached out to us before we began our hike, offering a place to stay. Their names were Mike and Claudia, and their house was less than a block from the park. They had a bunch of rooms they'd made up for us and had gift packages for each of the kids full of treats and new socks. Claudia even bought "loaner clothes" from the thrift store for all the kids to wear while our laundry dried on clotheslines hanging in the front yard.

Claudia helped organize the delivery of a cake for Kami's birthday. She drove more than an hour to a famed specialty bakery in Virginia. When I ordered the cake, I wasn't paying much attention. On the small phone they all looked the same. I just knew I wanted red velvet cake with buttercream frosting, which was Kami's favorite, and I ordered the largest, at fifteen inches. What I couldn't see from the small picture was the cake was more than eight inches high!

It ended up costing one hundred dollars, weighed twelve pounds, and had forty-five servings.

As per my request, it had "Embrace the suck" written across it in script lettering, which is a famous phrase Kami wore on a patch on her pack.

We ate as much of the cake as we could, but were already stuffed from our meetup with Tonya at the park. We gave part of the cake to a nearby hiker hostel and packed out the remaining eight pounds for the next day.

As the laundry was drying on the clothesline and we were all walking around in our loaner clothes, I looked up registration information for the Flying Pig Marathon back in Cincinnati. The race happened in three weeks, and it was completely sold out. *Crap.*

However, there was one possibility: we had a special connection with the race director. Years before, when we first decided to run a marathon as a family, we saw the minimum age was eighteen. So I registered, and the four older kids joined me unofficially, running the entire course. After 26.2 miles, we all crossed the finish line together, and the officiant gave everyone a medal, even though the kids weren't registered. When another officiant found out what we'd done, she took the medals away from the kids, even though there were plenty to spare. The kids went home heartbroken at how close they were to getting a medal, so they decided to make their own. Within a week, the director of the race, a woman named Iris, heard about our kids and their homemade medals. She came by our house and put medals on each of the kids' necks. She told us to contact her if we ever needed help running again.

Now in Damascus, I contacted her right away. She told us to put our names on the waiting list, and she would see what she could do.

That night, we went on a walk through Damascus and told the kids about the significance this town played in our story. When we'd first fallen in love with the idea of backpacking, we never would have imagined hiking with six children. It was amazing how quickly that time had passed, and how easy it would be for another sixteen years to fly by.

TO DO:
~~Throw away trash~~
~~wash dishes~~
~~empty pack~~
~~resupply snacks/TP~~
journal
~~play piano~~
~~stretches~~
brush teeth
~~shower~~
repack
~~wash treking poles~~

Towns were an opportunity to catch up on many tasks that were
not possible in the woods. Eden (15) used her lists to maintain
sanity in a world that had been flipped upside down.

THE DEGENERATES

The next morning, we had breakfast at the only cafe in town. Sitting in the restaurant were three of our friends: Fun Facts, Culligan, and Nubs.

They told us they'd been so hung over from hiking, alcohol, and sleep they didn't think the thirty miles was worth it. Also sitting with them were the two women we had seen stumbling out of the Smokies: Mama Kish and Not Dead. They were fiddling with some new conch-shell necklaces they had shipped there, blowing them and making a funny sound like a cross between a horn and whistle. They were taking turns blowing and laughing as they responded to each other with the conch. On the trail, it's common for hikers to form up in groups and travel in packs, affectionately called "tramilies"—trail families. This group of five had decided to hike together and, as was common on the trail, adopt a group name. Given the fact they had slept in for more than half the day due to their thirty-mile bender, they appropriately called themselves The Degenerates.

During breakfast, we got an email from Iris, the race director. Not only was she able to get all seven of us registered (Rainier wouldn't join us for this one), but she registered all the kids for free! Kami and I looked at each other; we knew it was crazy and that we should be saving our zero days for rest and weather. But we knew what going home and participating in one of our kids' favorite events would do for morale. It was too good an opportunity to pass up. It was final: we'd be running the marathon in May.

We called my parents and made arrangements. They'd pick us up from wherever we happened to be on the trail at the time. Of course, we could only estimate our location, but we did know one thing: Virginia was the longest state on the entire A.T. We'd need two days for the marathon, one to prepare and one to run, plus two partial days of hiking in which we'd also have to get in eight hours of driving. We'd have to get as many miles on the trail as possible until then.

We left The Degenerates at the cafe and hit the trail, walking straight uphill for most of the day. Due to our slow speed, we were passed at lunch by all five of them. It was kind of depressing how much faster they seemed to go with so much less effort. We exchanged nods and a few quick words about how difficult the hill and heat were. We struggled with the heat for the rest of the day, and when we were a couple miles short of our goal for the day, we heard a familiar sound. It was the conch-shell necklace. The Degenerates were camping by a stream. Exhausted from our hike, we took a vote as a family. The vote, mostly led by the kids, was to stop short of our goal and spend the night by the stream with our friends.

This was a big moment for us: it was the first time we prioritized hanging out with people over reaching our goal. When we first started the A.T., all the kids could think about was the friends they'd left behind. They never considered they'd make new friends like The Degenerates, who we never would have met if not for the trail.

When we smelled their fire and thought of the eight pounds of cake we had in our pack, it seemed like a no-brainer to stop and share. Before we knew it, we were sitting around the fire, smoking cigars, and using plastic sporks to eat one-hundred-dollar red velvet cake straight out of Ziploc bags. The cake was totally mashed by this point. It had no effect on the flavor.

Most hikers fit into two categories. Some are young and full of energy; they're often on the trail to find themselves (with a little partying on the side). Others are older, retired, and finally completing a bucket-list item. The Degenerates were in the younger category, and were laid-back and friendly. We later realized we'd actually met Culligan on the first day of our hike.

We really enjoyed being around the group, but we were still trying to hold friendships loosely. We hadn't considered forming friendships with hikers because most were so focused on the practical aspects of the trail and didn't seem that interested in talking to kids. But The Degenerates seemed genuinely interested.

"We've been watching your family for a while," Culligan said to the kids as we all finished off the birthday cake. "I'm impressed. Not many adults could do what I've seen you guys do."

A lot of people start in Georgia with big talk about being a thru-hiker. They talk about what pose they'll strike when they get to the A-frame sign at the top of Mount Katahdin. You hear a lot of excuses when they quit. It's their knees and feet. It was the weather. One simply said, "We don't do the cold." Others had more nuanced explanations. "It wasn't what I expected." Or, "I already got what I wanted from the trail; I don't need to keep going."

By making it this far, we'd earned The Degenerates' respect, and in turn, they'd earned our trust.

RESONATING WITH OTHERS

Right before we hit Damascus, we met a few of the many people along the trail who would make a big impact on our family.

First, we met a woman who called herself Grace right on the heels of the comment attacks on Reddit. She was in her late fifties and wore a green hoodie.

Grace said, "I've heard so much about your remarkable family. I'm so impressed, and I've been hearing from all the other hikers that have spent nights with you in shelters how well behaved your children are. God's richest blessing on you! I've been praying for you, and I refer to you as 'The Family' when I talk to God. It made my day to be able to meet you."

Grace's words touched us deeply. She hugged all of us, and we walked away with a spring in our step.

Only an hour after meeting Grace, we met a group of older men who called themselves The Old Guys Hiking Club. Every single one of them was so encouraging and funny. They told stories of how they'd left the trail a few days earlier because of the cold, and how embarrassed they were because they knew "all of you were up in the mountains with the kids." They treated us like celebrities. They knew all the kids' names and took pictures with us, exclaiming, "We're amazed. We can't believe we ran into you!" It was like they were starstruck. They'd watched our YouTube videos, and dissected the miserable scenes of our start at Springer Mountain, Rainier's missing rain paints, and how we went back to the van as if recounting a scene from their favorite movie.

"Bless your hearts," one of them said. "We didn't think you guys were going to get one hundred feet after that start." As we left them, they pushed trail mix into our hands, and said, "We're with you all the way."

We met a hiker named Gnome. He was in his sixties and had a raspy voice and long gray beard, which gave him his name. He wore an orange rain jacket with a hood and looked like a character from *The Lord of the Rings* crossed with *Fiddler on the Roof*. When he heard we were near, he waited in the rain and fog on the top of a hill hoping to meet us. We approached, and he ran up and hugged us. He had tears in his eyes.

"I am so blown away by what you guys are doing, and so encouraged to see family pulling together. Just like the Jewish tradition, I want to lock arms and literally support each other. I'm walking *with you*. I love you guys." He said most of this in tears.

As he continued, tears welled up in our and the kids' eyes. Our journey was resonating with people. Hiking as a family struck a chord, and people knew something about it was right. There was a power in what we were doing that people could sense.

The kids loved when people assumed we were out there hiking for a weekend, but after talking to us for a minute, they were shocked to learn we were doing the whole thing. After a while, people usually said, "Oh, are you the family I've been hearing about?"

Because we often walked in a line spread out over a quarter mile, we didn't always hear everyone at the same time. Often we would pass strangers going the opposite direction and overhear them talking about our kids, not knowing we were the parents. "That's unbelievable!" "Did you see *that*?" "She was carrying a full pack!" After these meetings, our family would get together and regroup. The kids would repeat what they'd heard, trying to imitate the accents and excitement "I *saaaaw* you guys on *you*tuuuuube," "You guys are the famileeee from the compuuuter..." and we would all laugh.

Even on Whiteblaze, a few supportive voices had started to appear amidst the critiques and moralizing. Even a user who had previously criticized us had changed his tune:

"Well, I met the Crawfords this weekend at Devil's Fork Gap in between Hot Springs and Erwin. I came up on the kids first and kindly asked them all individually how their trip was going. They all had smiles and a tired expression of their thoughts on the hike. Overall they seemed pretty happy, and they were very well behaved and well spoken. Up and over the next hill I ran into the parents with the sweet little boy in the carrier. I have to say that these folks

are 100 percent different then they seem to be on their YouTube channel. They were easy to talk to, very polite, and I could see myself enjoying a fire and some beers with them. The two-year-old was a little shy, but I would talk to him and make funny faces and he would just smile and laugh. I spoke with them for about twenty minutes; I did not question them on anything controversial...I did ask how the Smokies treated them, and they said that they had a real tough time of it but ended up making it to Newfound Gap during the worst of the snow, and slept in a women's bathroom up there for the night along with several other hikers. They made it down to Gatlinburg the next morning via some sort of hitch I would assume by Gov employees (salt truck, park rangers etc.), and they holed up there for two-four days.

"I would like to personally restate my opinion on the matter, and that opinion is I don't really have a right to have an opinion. It's not my family, and I won't ever be lucky enough to have the experience, good or bad. Dad shouldn't flick his lip, correct. May have been more suitable to start in April, correct. But now it is April, all is well, and they are in high spirits. I hope they make it to Maine and if not, well, they had a great trip." —Gambit McCrae

For many of these people that we met, we made their day, and they made ours. Kami loved that many of our encouraging encounters were with older people. Having lived long enough to see their own priorities play out, they saw what we were doing was special. Many said they wished they'd done it with their kids or said we'd never regret this. We felt honored and emotionally uplifted from these encounters that eventually happened every day and then multiple times a day.

HIKING SHOES OR RUNNING SHOES?

Back in Damascus, I decided it was time for a new pair of shoes.

Shoes are the most important piece of equipment when you're hiking such long distances. Most people go through three to five pairs on one thru-hike. At this point, mine had holes on each side and needed replacing. At the local shoe store in Damascus, I tried on a pair from a shoe company named Altra. Right away, my feet felt radically different. These shoes were intended to be more natural, with a "zero-drop" design that meant the heel was not raised. It was more like the barefoot running shoes I used back home that were supposed to be better for your knees and back than traditional running shoes. These Altras also had a wide-open toe box, and I couldn't believe the difference on my first day wearing them. It felt like I was walking on clouds. I felt like I was cheating.

Within a day of hiking in them, I wanted to get Altra shoes for everybody, but at $150 per pair, it would be more than $1,000 to outfit the whole family. This would be a major expense upgrade from our earlier strategy of buying whatever was on clearance.

So we emailed the company with a video telling our story. To our excitement, they responded right away: "We'll mail you seven pairs. Just send us your shoe sizes!"

Telling your parents, co-workers, or friends that you're quitting work and life to go and walk in the woods can be a bit awkward. People just stare at you. But being a sponsored athlete was something that everyone in the real world understood. Altra's support made our journey feel legit.

As the weather gradually—*finally*—started to warm up day by day, our bodies and minds began to change as well. We were getting stronger physically, and it seemed like each day we were letting go of our attachments to creature comforts. But no matter how much we changed, and no matter how much more attuned and comfortable the trail started to feel, one thing never changed: the distance of each mile. We'd hiked almost five hundred miles at this point, but that still left 1,700 to go. And because of our zero days, the daily average we needed to hit had only increased.

We'd pushed ourselves to our max, but had still only averaged 10.9 miles a day. If we were going to run the marathon, we needed to raise our average to 14.8 miles a day. It seemed impossible—no matter how hard we tried, we just couldn't find a solution to our mileage problem. Was the marathon going to dig us a hole we couldn't get out of? By taking the time off, were we actually saying goodbye to Katahdin?

CHAPTER TEN

Trailer Park Friends

"The greatest reward and luxury of travel is to be able to experience everyday things as if for the first time, to be in a position in which almost nothing is so familiar it is taken for granted."
—Bill Bryson

During our first month on the trail, we were so focused on surviving the cold and getting used to the miles that we didn't have time to feel bored.

Now the reality of walking so long with no entertainment, no books, and nothing new to talk about started to set in. And, ironically, now that the days were getting warmer, the cold didn't focus our attention. Our minds wandered, idle.

Our new motivator became our timeline. We had three weeks until we left the trail for the marathon, and we were under pressure to do as many miles as possible before the race or we'd be punished for it afterward.

So far, we felt okay about our mileage. Knowing that we'd have "a break" at home soon, we were motivated to set daily goals. We set out to do sixty-five miles in four days. At more than sixteen miles a day, that was more than we'd ever accomplished four days in a row. We woke up at 5:30 a.m. and hiked until 8:00 p.m., only to start over again the next day. These goals were crazy. Back home, waking up at 5:30 a.m. seemed impossible, and walking for fifteen hours wasn't feasible or sustainable. But wanting to run the marathon gave us a purpose, something to shoot for. It felt like every mile and every calorie counted.

There was still some bickering, especially when it came time for the six kids to pile into the four-man tent. But now the bickering stood out as the exception, not the rule. Most of the daily fighting had been replaced by teamwork. During our waking hours, we were either walking or resting. The kids didn't have the energy to fight. This made us reinterpret our life back home. Fighting there was common, with kids arguing over who said what, who crossed whose boundary, who left stuff out, who took someone's Popsicle. Many of these fights were a byproduct of excess energy and time. We had solved this problem on the trail: we had a common goal that was more difficult than any of us thought we could accomplish on our own.

More than once, we overheard the following "discussion" between Eden and Filia.

"Good job, Filia."

"Good job, Eden."

"Good job, Filia."

"Good job, Eden."

"Good job, Filia."

"Good job, Eden."

On and on it would go, for thirty minutes or more. These types of games were how the kids passed their time on the trail—that, and belting out every song they knew. They'd also come up with the hilarious habit of leaving Kami and I notes spelled out in sticks, leaves, and gummy bears. Because we lagged behind with Rainier, we'd often spend hours with the only communication with our older kids being the words *hurry up* or *good job* arranged crudely on a rock, next to a little pile of gummy bears or Sour Patch Kids.

Kami had come up with a game of her own: a video series called *Rate That Privy*. Each outhouse we came across on the trail got a Yelp-style rating for cleanliness, privacy, and memorable features.

On one of those long days, we came across breakfast being served at a road crossing. Another hiker named Silver, who we'd been seeing for a while now, greeted us. He pointed over to the pancakes and coffee with a big smile on his face and bellowed, "The trail provides!"

We'd heard this phrase before, but the way Silver said it while holding the coffee and pancakes felt spiritual. Silver was a thirty-year-old Jewish lawyer from New York. We easily recognized him by his outfit: he wore a black kilt and a giant silver puffy jacket that made him look like a baked potato in tinfoil—hence his trail name. Silver had unsuccessfully attempted the trail the previous year. He kept his headlamp around his neck, day or night, so he wouldn't lose it—he was on his fourth one.

Silver pulled us aside and said, "Hey, I think it's really cool what you're doing with your family."

Because of all the flak we'd gotten online, we had started to wonder if deep down most of the

hikers still saw us as not "real" thru-hikers,
and it was such a boost every time a hiker said
something to us that validated our effort.

It was also a boost to watch our team mileage record continue to climb. We did 19.1 miles in one day, then 20.5 miles. On Day 48, we found out about a hostel called Quarter Way Inn. For the first five hundred miles, hotels had been nice because they kept us warm, but they were expensive and impersonal. Hostels were smaller, often operated by one person or a couple, and varied from trailer parks to vast Victorian mansions. Now that we had discovered hostels and felt like we had the ability to call ahead and negotiate custom rates for our group, it felt like we had a special tool in our tool belt. For Quarter Way Inn, the guidebook boasted "indoor bunk room with comfy mattress, pillow, shower, towel, extensive VHS collection, pizza, pop, and ice cream." And here was the kicker: it included a "gourmet breakfast with fresh roasted coffee." We read the description to the kids and drooled. There was only one catch: we had to do 21.5 miles in one day to get there.

We managed 11.5 miles before lunch then hauled ten more miles in the afternoon and into the evening, running the last mile to beat the sunset. We arrived at 8:15 p.m. to meet Tina, the inn's owner. Once again, we had redefined what we thought was possible for our family. We were proving to ourselves we could do anything we put our minds to as a family, and these mileage victories mattered more to us than the opinions of anonymous strangers on the internet. The trail was testing us, but it was also nurturing us, gifting us a confidence we couldn't have imagined before.

Quarter Way Inn (named for being a "quarter of the way in" to the A.T.) was a beautiful Victorian house in the Virginia countryside. It ended up being one of our favorite hostel experiences. It functioned more like a bed and breakfast, and we had the whole place to ourselves. Tina was a previous thru-hiker and had gotten tips from her favorite hostels on her trek. She cooked an amazing breakfast, with biscuits, cheese grits, scones, and freshly-ground coffee. In the midst of the most difficult physical challenge of our lives, crushing miles from sunrise to sunset, we ate like kings and queens in a Victorian bed and breakfast. This was the glory of thru-hiking.

The next morning, Tina posted a picture of our family in front of the house. The caption said, "What a joy to have the house filled with kids. This family was a well-oiled machine, and even after their longest day yet, everyone was in good spirits and health!"

Our confidence soared as we realized that people we met in real life actually liked us and our kids. It was a stark contrast to the distaste our virtual critics had dished out.

IN SPITE OF THE COLD

We were especially proud of our speed because of how hard the cold was hitting during this time. Seven weeks in, after a brief spate of slightly warmer weather, we were back to battling snow and hail. On Day 50, we made a video that we titled *Sick of the Cold*. After hiking through freezing rain that day, we gained some hope when we heard from hikers going the opposite direction that there was some trail magic up ahead. On this occasion, a man was supposedly giving out beef stroganoff. In the cold, any type of warm food, comfort, or luxury was extra valuable because it served as a distraction from the pain that came from just existing outside and could take over as the primary motivation to keep going.

Too cold to write. powder potatos and 14 miles.

After a full day of hiking and after getting all of our camp chores done,
journaling felt like a difficult task. Often we skipped it altogether, or like
Dove (16) here, simply scratched out a few lines to remember the day.

When we arrived at the road, we saw a zipped-up tent and an empty truck. It seemed the cook was hiding from us. It was a total letdown.

That night, we camped with The Degenerates; Hops, our friend from the Smokies; and our new acquaintance, Silver. As we sat around the fire, everyone shared stories of coming to the sealed tent and empty truck. Hops told of how he'd waited in the bitter cold for the trail magician to try and boil water to defrost the frozen stew, but he couldn't get it going. He ended up giving the lump of frozen gravy to his dog. He was so embarrassed, he hid in his tent hoping all the hikers would pass.

"There's trail magic," Hops said, "and then there's...trail *tragic*." And so a new phrase was added to everyone's vocabulary to describe those moments on trail when Murphy's Law seemed to be pulling the strings.

I made it worse by sharing that I'd tried to get pizzas and beer delivered for everyone, but it was too remote for any pizza company to deliver out here. We all commiserated as we ate our ramen, tuna, and dehydrated potatoes—food that we had eaten every day for almost two months.

But our individual misery was redeemed as we shared it with our traveling friends. The kids had gathered firewood, a task most hikers didn't have the energy to do. I built a fire. Everyone gathered around. Culligan passed out gin from his tent, and Hops pulled out his bourbon. Silver smoked a cigar with us as we exchanged stories of frozen extremities and took turns describing how good the pizza would have been. Dove, who was responsible for dinner, carried an extra bag of marshmallows with her. She pulled them out, and everyone gathered sticks and roasted them as we traded stories. Sharing felt natural to all of us. It was more fun to be smoking cigars together. Having limited resources added so much more value to the few resources we did have, and made it even more special when they were shared.

Sitting in these spartan conditions, we could see that, without the adversity, we wouldn't be forming such powerful bonds. For a few hours, in the warm glow of the campfire and camaraderie, we forgot about the cold.

A NEW APPRECIATION

One year before we started our hike, we were driving home from a beach vacation in North Carolina when we came across a sign that said *Appalachian Trail*. In a moment of spontaneity, we stopped to find a spot where we could step foot on the trail for the first time, snap a picture of a white blaze, and stretch our legs from the long drive. We were the day-hikers, the tourists.

The road crossing was in the middle of nowhere, and as we drove around trying to find the trailhead, we passed a little convenience store in a double-wide trailer home. It looked like a gas station without the gas pumps. A picnic table sat outside, and we laughed at the people standing outside wearing camouflage and overalls.

We found the trail. It was a sunny day, but we were still totally unprepared. Our dog ran off chasing a deer, then the kids ran off chasing the dog, and we stumbled after, tripping over our flip-flops.

We eventually found the dog and all our kids, took some pictures, and said, "Someday we'll be back."

Thankfully, a year later, our hiking skills had improved. But that wasn't all that changed.

On Day 51, our kids woke up at 6:00 a.m. We'd spent the night nice and dry in an abandoned church and were able to pack up in record time. The kids were excited. Word had it that up ahead was a restaurant called The Brushy Mountain Grill, and we might be able reach it in time for breakfast. After hearing this place had incredibly good milkshakes, everyone started moving at top speed. Our gear was packed in record time, and the kids were far ahead, skipping breaks for the reward that lay ahead.

Seven miles later, we arrived. It was 10:00 a.m., and we saw a stack of backpacks outside, which is always a friendly sight. When you're a hiker, you recognize your friends' packs just like you recognize their cars back home. And then we heard the conch shells, and knew for sure that The Degenerates and Hops were already there.

The Brushy Mountain Grill was an old convenience store that sold Pop-Tarts, knock-off Hostess pies, and neon shirts with confederate flags on them. It was one of those remote places only locals and hikers knew about. Once we arrived at the little makeshift restaurant, we realized it ran like the local outpost where everyone was friends and locals exchanged gossip. The owners sat there all day waiting for the usual customers and the few who might wander in from the trail.

Once inside, we received a warm welcome. There weren't enough chairs, so somebody went to get more right away. They were plastic lawn chairs; no one cared because any place to sit was such an amazing relief. They had power strips in the corner next to the neon sunglasses so everyone could charge their phones—the ultimate luxury for a hiker.

We sat down and took a look at their menu, which didn't take long. It was essentially a bullet point list of a few items. They had biscuits and gravy, eggs, hash browns, and coffee. The Degenerates had scarfed down the last of the French toast. Our family placed what was probably the biggest order this restaurant had ever received. The platter, which we all ordered, was four dollars. It included two eggs, two biscuits, gravy, two pieces of some kind of mystery meat, and coffee.

We didn't stop there, though. We ordered everything else they had—corn dogs, cheeseburgers, and more. For the first time in her life, Filia had a cheeseburger and a chocolate milkshake for breakfast.

I had very specific craving. "Do you guys have banana milkshakes?"

"Well, we got milkshakes. And we got bananas. Never thought o' that, but shouldn't be too tough!"

Five minutes later, I was gulping down the best banana milkshake of my life. The restaurant owner's eyes widened when he saw how fast I'd finished it.

"This is the best milkshake I've ever had," I told him. "I'll take another."

"You may be on to somethin'! May have to consider puttin' that on the menu!"

We ate all our food and then ordered more. For each order, the owner scratched frantically on a notepad then took the requests back to what reminded us of a tiny church kitchen, with a grill, a deep fryer, a freezer, and a fridge. It was a ridiculous scene, and by the end, we had ordered over one hundred dollars of this cheap food. There were no scraps left over.

As we were finishing up, Silver walked in wearing his puffy jacket. Even though we'd only hiked for a few weeks with Silver, we'd grown close to him in that short time. While we walked, we talked about religion, fancy watches, cigars, living in New York City, and his long-term goals of practicing law and joining the armed forces. Silver had a sporadic way of hiking. He was known for loading up on Starbucks energy drinks in town and carrying them for ten miles, drinking one every hour, and marching through the night. He'd cover incredible distances for long amounts of time. Then, depleted of motivation, he'd spend two days recovering. We called it "bipolar hiking." We'd constantly be surprised because we'd unknowingly pass Silver when he was passed out at a shelter, and then he'd catch up with us from behind.

Here were all of our favorite hikers in one place, sitting in chairs and out of the cold, laughing about what we'd been through to get here. It's hard to explain the energy and joy we felt as we enjoyed the simple pleasure of sitting in the equivalent of that double-wide trailer, the relief of not walking after focusing only on the next step for so long. There was something special about coming from the woods and enjoying this with others. It felt like the town hall. We caught up and let our hair down. We recharged. We laughed. We told stories. Dove said it felt like a reunion with The Degenerates, even though we had just seen them the night before.

It was hard to leave, but we had miles to do. As we walked away into the woods, Eden stopped dead suddenly and looked around, an inscrutable look on her face.

"Wait..." she said. "We've been here before!"

Shocked, we realized she was right—this was where we'd been tourists the year before, where the dog had run off and the kids had chased him. This was the convenience store we'd laughed at and swore we'd never stop at!

As hikers, we'd just spent two hours at that same store, and spent the best one hundred dollars of our lives. One year ago this location was the butt of our jokes, and now it stood as a monument of our journey reminding us of joy, provision, and friendship. The store was the same—we were the ones who had changed.

UNPREDICTABLE RELATIONSHIPS

On the trail, we could feel ourselves changing. We had fewer distractions; we created friendships with people we never would have appreciated back home. More importantly, the trail was helping us develop deeper friendships with our kids, and they were starting to see each other the same way. They spent time together making up games, joking, and telling each other stories. We all described our favorite meals and daydreamed out loud of heat when it was cold and air conditioning when it was hot.

The trail created a completely different environment for the children and brought out traits and characteristics in them we'd never seen before. It was immediately obvious to Kami and me that the simple laser-focus on their mission each day was making a big impact; they thrived having such a clear purpose, a job. "Memory, you're in charge of water." "Dove, you're in charge of dinner." "Seven, you're in charge of editing and tents."

Eden, in particular, was experiencing a whole different existence from the one she had at home. Eden had always been one to set far-reaching goals, and when she set herself to a task, she invariably got it done. This had led to Kami and I watching her closely to make sure she wasn't overextending herself, because she also tended to be pretty hard on herself for falling short of her own standards. At home, Eden had created tons of obligations for herself. She made long lists of activities every day, things she felt she *had* to accomplish:

1. Work out
2. Math with Halmonee
3. Study for two hours
4. Clean my room
5. Make my bed
6. Walk the dog
7. Edit podcast
8. Practice music
9. Learn Korean
10. Read for one hour
11. Do chores
12. Do laundry
13. Driving lesson

She constantly felt pressure to add things to the list while never feeling like there was enough time to complete it. Whereas on the trail, her list was simple:

1. Walk and eat
2. Walk and set up camp
3. Eat and sleep
4. Repeat

It was a whole new way of life for her.

On the trail, it was also easier for all of us to hang out together. Everything was carved out and planned. Purpose was built in. It radically changed our family dynamic. Back home, everything felt muddled; there was so much to choose from that it was hard to choose, and intentionality was a constant struggle. We all lived in the same house, but sometimes, it felt like the house was *all* we shared. It could be really difficult to connect with each family member equally. The varying age groups that lived in our house tended to gravitate toward different goals and activities: the parents wanted to read and talk over cigars, the older kids wanted to see movies, and the younger kids wanted to play video games. The trail leveled our interests and brought all the age groups together. Everyone was the same on the trail. We were all equal. The seven-year-old and seventeen-year-old could hike together, and they both were in charge of specific, equally important responsibilities that we all depended on. We all carried weight that benefitted the group, traveling to the same destination, feeling the same sense of accomplishment. We all needed each other. Not just sentimentally—*practically*. And in turn, the practicality created sentiment we had never seen.

The simplicity and challenge were bringing us together. On the trail, the seventeen-year-old and the seven-year-old woke up each day more the same than different.

We would need this unity as we picked up speed and headed into our toughest challenge yet—one we never could have anticipated, and that threatened our title as "thru-hikers."

1. Dove at one year old, meeting hikers on the A.T. in Damascus.

2. The night before we started.

3. At the top of Springer Mountain. My dad (top right) is not amused.

4. Our cigar session at the Blood Mountain Cabins, where we came up with the plan that would save us.

5. In the beginning, staying warm was a full-time job!

6. The nine of us crowded on the mattress in the back of Arnie-1-Mile's van.

7. Filia on Day 20. We faced waist-deep snow and frozen water bottles. It was impossible to see the white blazes on trees marking the trail.

8. Spending the night in the women's bathroom at Newfound Gap.

9. Arriving in Damascus on Kami's birthday, sixteen years after the first photo with baby Dove.

10. Eating eight pounds of Kami's leftover red velvet cake out of Ziploc bags.

11. Receiving some trail magic out of the back of a car with The Degenerates (left to right: Fun Facts, Not Dead, Culligan, and Nubs).

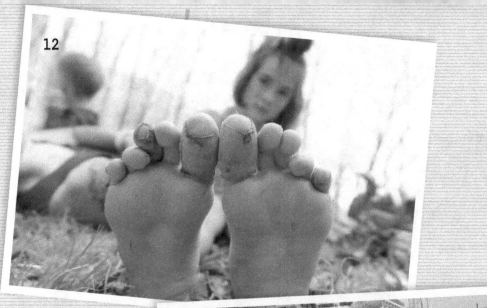

12

12. Filia's feet before we got Altras.

13. Stopping the hike to run the Cincinnati Flying Pig Marathon with our new shoes. This was at Mile 26 with 0.2 left. The most painful decision we ever made.

14. Eggs Benedict for Dove's seventeenth birthday. No easy feat when you have to secretly hike twenty-five miles with a dozen eggs!

13

14

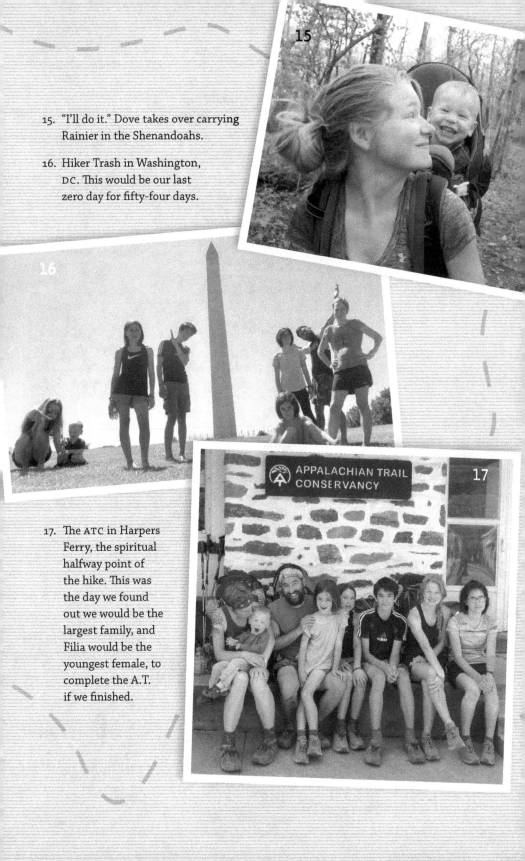

15. "I'll do it." Dove takes over carrying Rainier in the Shenandoahs.

16. Hiker Trash in Washington, DC. This would be our last zero day for fifty-four days.

17. The ATC in Harpers Ferry, the spiritual halfway point of the hike. This was the day we found out we would be the largest family, and Filia would be the youngest female, to complete the A.T. if we finished.

18. As the weather warmed up, we started to see more wildlife, like this black snake in Pennsylvania.

19. We all developed "trail legs" of steel and were stronger than we had ever been in our lives. Our first day slackpacking felt lighter than ever without our packs.

20. We took naps often. When you only have ten minutes, even the dirt will do.

21. The top of Mount Moosilauke on Ben's thirty-ninth birthday. This is where we took the picture that became the cover of this book!

22. The view from the Barron Ledges in the Hundred-Mile Wilderness—the most beautiful scenery on the trail. You can see how thin Kami had gotten by this point!

23. Mahoosuc Notch in Maine, the hardest mile of the A.T. Climbing and squeezing through a boulder field was tough with a two-year-old.

24. Crossing rivers in Maine required ferrying the littler kids across.

25. The first time any of the kids ever rode on a school bus! Odie from *The Hiker Yearbook* drove us around for four days.

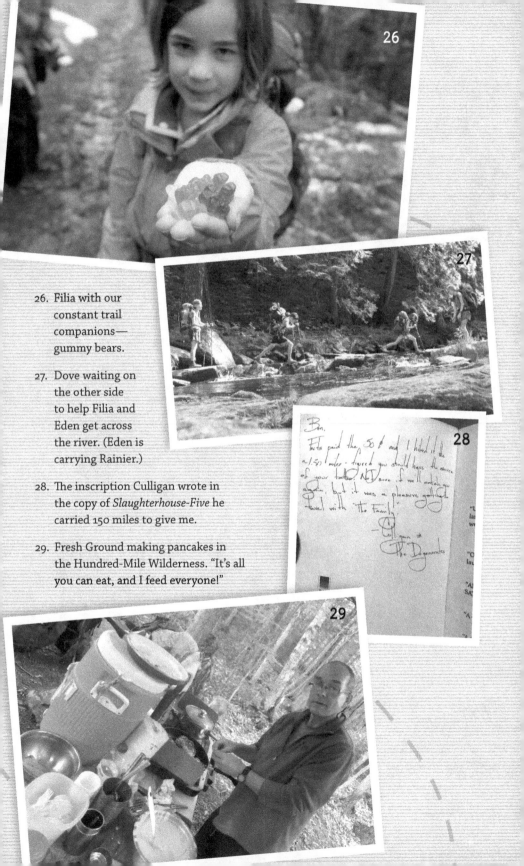

26. Filia with our constant trail companions—gummy bears.

27. Dove waiting on the other side to help Filia and Eden get across the river. (Eden is carrying Rainier.)

28. The inscription Culligan wrote in the copy of *Slaughterhouse-Five* he carried 150 miles to give me.

29. Fresh Ground making pancakes in the Hundred-Mile Wilderness. "It's all you can eat, and I feed everyone!"

30. We became the largest family (and youngest female) to complete the Appalachian Trail! Here's our finish, with all our friends who met us at our terminus at the tree line (Hudson on the far right).

31. The day we arrived in Washington to go to Lakeside Bible Camp. The only one who gained weight was Rainier.

CHAPTER ELEVEN

The Fire and the Big Questions

"'Would you tell me, please, which way I ought to go from here?'
'That depends a good deal on where you want to get to,'
said the Cat.'"

—Lewis Carroll, *Alice's Adventures in Wonderland*

Our newfound speed on the trail lasted until we reached Harrisonburg, Virginia.

Heading into town, we got a text out of the blue from Hops saying he wanted to introduce us to his friend, Jordan. Jordan and Hops picked us up in a church van filled with donuts and soda and drove us to a running-shoe store an hour away. Jordan had worked there for years, and when Hops told him we needed to get our feet sized for our new Altra shoes, he offered to help. Jordan functioned on a professional level both as a runner and as a gear outfitter. He ran hundreds of miles on the A.T. every year and had worn every model of Altra shoe the company offered. I couldn't have dreamed of someone better to help us determine sizes and models for the seven of us, and to be randomly introduced to someone like this by Hops seemed like a godsend.

While stuffing pancakes in his mouth, Silver had said, "The trail provides." We had seen that could be true about food, but now it seemed like the trail also provided the relationships we most needed, right when we most needed them.

We stayed the night with Jordan and his wife, Kristen, and liked the couple so much we stayed at their house an extra day with Hops.

Jordan knew everything about this section of the trail because he was an ultrarunner who competed in races one hundred to two hundred miles long. It was one of the most famous sections of the A.T.; it included destinations like the famed Dragon Tooth, Tinker Cliffs, and McAfee Knob. McAfee Knob is the second most iconic and photographed section of the entire trail, after the A-frame sign at the end. You can stand on an overhanging cliff there, and it appears nothing is beneath it. Every hiker gets a picture of themselves posing on the edge doing something silly, and the most dedicated show up at sunrise when it's the most picturesque.

When we woke up ready to go back to the trail and get our picture at McAfee Knob, things suddenly took a turn for the worse. It started with Eden, who didn't feel well the day before. She got sick. Then Hops got sick. After we'd all packed and sat down for breakfast, Rainier threw up all over the table.

Kami and I looked at each other and knew we weren't going anywhere. It's the most helpless feeling to watch your kids throw up, and it's hard to look up at a host you hadn't even met three days earlier and ask if your sick family can stay for another day. It felt like we were putting them in a situation where they couldn't say no. But

Jordan and Kristen were kind and accommodating, and we had no idea how much more helpful they'd be in the days to come.

We'd already done our laundry, our resupply, our video editing, and charged all our batteries, so taking an extra zero day seemed like a waste, but we knew we made the right choice when another wave of people went out of commission. Kami, Filia, and Dove all got sick, one after another. We spent the day hanging out with Hops and resting, which is a little strange when you're in someone else's house.

The next morning, we weren't feeling 100 percent, but when you're thru-hiking, you don't ask yourself if you feel your best. You simply ask, *Can I walk today?* Everyone decided they could, so Kristen drove us the hour back to the trail. When we arrived, there were fire trucks everywhere. The day before, we'd seen smoke from the nearby forest fire but heard it was contained. Now, roads were closed, and 325 acres of brush were on fire with little information about how dangerous it was on the trail. We sat in the parking lot trying to decide whether to chance it.

All our hopes for continuing came crumbling down when we met a young man with a white bandana wrapped around his nose and mouth. He had just returned from the trail up ahead and showed us a video of how close the fire was to the A.T. He said it actually crossed the trail at some points, and firefighters were telling people to evacuate. With no way to move forward, we didn't know what to do. Thru-hikers don't skip miles, and it seemed dangerous to wait in the parking lot. Kristen offered us a ride back to their place. We felt bad imposing on them for longer, but we were out of options. Back to Jordan and Kristen's house we went, another one-hour drive and another zero day. We tried to make the best of our time, and we enjoyed getting to know Hops, who was now stuck with us, a bit better. After spending three rest days in a row—not to mention the month of hiking 450 miles together—with Hops, he was the best friend on trail that we had.

At the Changs's, Hops pulled Kami and I aside.

"I have something to confess," he said. "Remember how, in the Smokies, I gave your family my spot in the shelter and slept out in my tent?"

"Yeah, we really appreciated that," said Kami.

"Well, I really like you guys, but I also *really* hated sleeping in shelters. So your family gave me an excuse to say the shelter was at capacity so I could sleep in my tent." We all laughed.

The next day, we heard the trail was open, so one more time, Kristen drove all of us back. When we arrived, our hearts sank. There was yellow fire tape across the trail entrance. Nineteen miles of the trail was closed due to the fire.

We faced a difficult choice: stay put until those nineteen miles reopened—and take more zero days, and keep imposing on Jordan and Kristen—or skip those miles?

Skipping miles is *not* something thru-hikers do. It just isn't. It defeats the entire purpose of thru-hiking.

> But taking more zero days meant that the mileage
> we had to make up was compounding fast. It felt
> like Katahdin was slipping away from us.

The clincher was that poor Kristen had spent so much time driving us around and hosting us that she was now sick. We simply could not go back.

It was one of the most difficult decisions of the entire hike, but we knew we had no choice. We decided to skip the nineteen miles of the trail that was closed by the fire, and rejoin the trail up in Daleville, the next town where there was access to the A.T. Kristen drove us there and dropped us off near a grocery store, where there was a barbecue restaurant and a Wendy's.

After three zero days and a heartbreaking section of skipped miles, Hops was anxious to hike. He said a quick goodbye and set off. We assumed we'd see him soon. We were wrong.

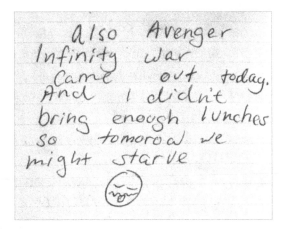

also Avenger Infinity War Came out today. And I didn't bring enough lunches so tomorow we might starve

By now we had split up many responsibilities, and Eden's (15) was to buy, pack, and serve lunches. We decided it was worth exposing ourselves to mistakes for the kids to learn.

THRU-HIKERS?

Sitting in the parking lot, the mood was glum and uncertain. We had skipped nineteen miles of the trail. It felt like we were collecting baseball cards and had the complete set except for one card. And the one card was sitting right in front of us, but we weren't allowed to touch it. So far, we had always known exactly what we needed to do: keep putting one foot in front of the other, and follow the white blazes. It was hard, but our course was clear. Now, for the first time in our journey, we didn't know what to do. We walked up and down the air conditioned aisles of the grocery store, not even sure how many days to resupply for. We walked across the street to Wendy's and ordered burgers for everyone and chicken nuggets for Rainier. Then we sat there eating chocolate Frosties. With each dejected bite we took, Hops got farther and farther ahead of us.

For the first time, we were faced with the question of whether we'd be considered thru-hikers not on a cultural level, but on a *technical* one. Wikipedia defines a thru-hiker as someone who hikes "an established end-to-end long-distance trail with continuous footsteps...completing it within a twelve-month period." Lots of people hike the A.T. every year. Very few of them are thru-hikers.

We'd skipped nineteen miles. Were we?

The impulse to optionally skip undesirable sections can be strong. Sometimes, buddies are getting a ride into town, and it's easier to just pick up your hike from there instead of paying to get a ride back just to hike the five miles you missed. With 2,200 miles of trail, there are hundreds of shortcuts that bypass dangerous overpasses, steep climbs, or ridiculous roundabouts. There's a class of hikers known for "yellow blazing"—skipping around in a car. To the thru-hiker community, they're seen as fakers, posers. They're generally not respected.

We'd been accused of secretly yellow blazing online in response to the videos we'd been posting. It seemed that some people out there just couldn't believe we were actually hiking every mile just like everyone else.

"Sooo Fake!!!! Lol...I am looking forward to meeting you all along the Appalachian Trail. (As I am the southern ridgerunner this year my (eighteenth year as a caretaker and ridgerunner for the Appalachian Trail as well as a three-time thru-hiker on the trail itself!!!...I heard from a fellow British thru-hiker who said that he

heard they yellow blazed a bunch of times because they had the means to from a support team? Friends or family? This is completely WRONG!!! I've been wondering all along if its staged somehow??" —The Great Greenman

Because of the rumor-mongering, we were more dedicated than ever to prove to the haters and ourselves that we were legit. But legit thru-hiking is not always back and white, and can actually be difficult to define. Some people are purists, and others understand the definition of thru-hiking a bit more loosely. Do you have to touch every white blaze that marks the trail? What happens if you get picked up to go into a town on one side of the road, and then get dropped off on the other? Purists would say that you have to actually backtrack across twenty feet of road, wasting both time and energy, to feel good about calling yourself a thru-hiker.

Even though we later discovered most people define thru-hiking as hiking every accessible mile of trail, and that forest fires are common deterrents from hiking long-distance trails, we felt on that day like we were cheating. That was hard. Something seemed incomplete, and we started making plans to go back and complete the nineteen miles of trail.

We made a video and posted it online asking people what they thought we should do. This was one of the few times we asked for advice from the online hiking community. Many people said we had to go back or we'd feel incomplete, especially since we missed the coveted photo op at McAfee Knob.

"Go back!! DO it. You're there!! If you don't, I can tell in your faces you'll regret it. You have gone through so many challenges to have that mark on your journey..." —Following Walkers World

"It appears in your faces you do not want to miss those miles, especially McAfee Knob! I say do it while you're there, IMO." —koegeb16

"If you don't do that section, trust me, you will never feel 'whole' about hiking it. Yes, it's closed, but trust me on this, you will never feel like you finished if you don't do that section." —RV Traveler

"I would do it at some point before you finish because you will want Mount Katahdin to be the end and be able to celebrate the whole trail." —James Parkins

"I would shuttle back ASAP to do that stretch. You may regret it later if you skip it. I personally would have not considered it a thru-hike if I skipped that part." —Joe Vanderkooi

On Instagram, user @iamerichubbard wrote a comment that stood out to us because of our religious background: "Legalism sucks. Carry on. Enjoy. Never look back."

Another commenter named "Donjojohannes" expanded on that thought:

"I realize that the sense of accomplishment is often measured in miles (or 'every' mile) and can seem to be an important objective. I personally would say that this goes counter to what any of the long-distance trails were actually established for. Taking an alternate that makes it a continuous journey from border to border even if it leaves the official route and included road walks for a bit makes more sense to me. But neither should be crucial. I understand. I did exactly that kind of thing when I started out and thought the whole thing was about proving something (to myself or others). Turns out

it isn't. I've done over twelve thousand miles of long distance walking now, and will be adding another 2,500 miles this summer. The things I take with me from the trail are the experiences and encounters and no amount of backtracking or going out of my way fill a gap (which I have done in the past) could add to it in a meaningful way. Enjoy the trail. Fight it if you must. Battle with yourself when necessary. But don't measure yourself by miles or by gaps. So many hikers quit the 'rat race' just to apply the same principles to the trail. If anyone feels 'less' for skipping miles of official trail (for any reason), I suggest he reevaluate why he is out there."

These and many other commenters encouraged us to do what we wanted, emphasizing that we didn't serve the trail—it served us. We had started to feel a compulsion to do every part of the trail, like an item on a to-do list feeling like we were on trial by a panel of judges. We thought about our decision back in Hiawassee, Georgia to stay in hotels when possible and do the best things for our family. We thought back to Arnie-1-Mile and her example and words and considered what it really meant to "hike your own hike."

Taking on the identity of thru-hiker had felt optional to me when we started our hike. But waking up at 6 a.m. and hiking for fourteen hours with a never-ending goal in mind had gradually changed me, and now, being a thru-hiker didn't feel optional. It felt like a job description we needed to live up to.

"Donjojohannes" was right. We didn't want to serve the trail. We weren't there to earn a title or check off a box. We were after an adventure, connection with our kids, and a valuable experience as a family. We didn't want to re-create the grind of life on the trail, just in a different way. We had given the title of "thru-hiker" too much importance. We saw how easy it could be to lose our focus and become indoctrinated with an artificial sense of duty at the cost of the thing we thought was most important to us: each other.

In this way, the fire re-centered us. We lost the chance to take our photo on McAfee Knob, but solidified our sense of why we were doing the trail and who we were doing it for. This was a gift. It reminded us that in the end, more than thru-hikers, we were people. This meant that if we had to choose, we would prioritize what was best for our relationship with our kids over the particulars of being a successful thru-hiker. Plus, the iconic picture at McAfee Knob wasn't really the picture that mattered most. As long as we could get our picture at the A-frame sign on Mount Katahdin, no one would remember the fact that we had to skip this section.

Now we were preparing to leave the trail for the marathon, and the real cost of the break was starting to set in. We had just completed our second full month of hiking. We'd improved from averaging 10.3 miles a day to thirteen miles a day, but we were still well below the average we needed. Taking more than two days off would only make that number go up.

And now, the marathon introduced another factor we had not considered. A break meant saying goodbye to our friends. The single hikers and groups with no kids were able to move much faster than us. They didn't have to deal with diapers, shuttles, nap time, and the slower pace of smaller legs. We had been able to compensate for this by leaving camp earlier, arriving later, and taking fewer breaks and rest days. The kids were resentful because The Degenerates had taken a whole day off just to go see *Avengers: Infinity War*, and still caught up to us with ease. They came back raving about how awesome the movie was. We had only been able to hang with our hiker bubble by the sheer amount of hours and effort we had put in. Taking two full days off could mean saying goodbye to our friends for good. This wasn't just emotionally difficult; it was a practical matter. The Degenerates had given us motivation on a day-to-day basis to push the extra miles so we could meet them at camp. And people like Hops had helped us with food, lodging, transportation, getting our shoes sized, and others things that were absolute game-changers on the trail.

But the trail offered no guarantees, and our group was complicated enough that we couldn't take the plans of others into account. We had to do what was best for us. We had to hike our own hike. So we said goodbye to our friends, knowing, just like so many other hikers, this would probably be the last we'd see of them.

CHAPTER TWELVE

Our Best Story

"I always take the same perspective with each new adventure. I put myself in the position of being at the end of my life looking back. Then I ask myself if what I am doing is important to me."

—Reinhold Messner

Initially, not all of us completely agreed on going back to Cincinnati to run the marathon. I'd thought it made sense because we must be in the best shape of our lives at that point. Kami's concern, though, was that running a marathon was a whole different beast from hiking, and the muscles we were using for hiking didn't really translate the same to long-distance running. If it had been solely her decision, we wouldn't have done the marathon. But it was important to the rest of the family to go home, and Kami was willing to compromise; she agreed that keeping morale high trumped any other concerns.

Once we decided to go for it, we looked forward to going home for a few days and taking a break from the trail. At one point, running a marathon was an ultimate, once-in-a-lifetime, bucket-list achievement. But now, as we thought about the physical effort required, it didn't feel like a big deal. Trail life made 26.2 miles without a pack seem completely doable. Most people run marathons in four or five hours, and four or five hours of doing anything didn't seem like much compared to the fourteen-hour days of hiking we had been doing, especially with the excruciating weather we'd endured at the beginning.

We had started to think about life differently years ago after reading Donald Miller's book *A Million Miles in a Thousand Years*. In it, he challenges the reader with a simple question: if we were to live our lives in a way that tells the best possible story, how would we live? What if we were to live the type of story people would want to read? People love to read stories where the main character is faced with defeat, and forced to make difficult decisions that result in them being uncomfortably changed. Movie studios and publishing houses don't usually finance stories about people who live comfortable lives, make comfortable choices, and never change. It's only through challenge and change that we see what a main character's potential is, what they're really made of, and what we could aspire to. It gave us a new way to think about big-picture decisions: every decision was in service of living a better story.

When we lived in Seattle and first started backpacking, we heard the same situation play out many times. Friends would hear our plans and say, "Oh, we tried camping ten years ago. It was pouring rain, we got soaked, and we've never gone back. It was a disaster." We felt like they were asking the wrong question; they'd based their evaluation on whether or not the weekend was comfortable. From that perspective, the poor weather and planning certainly made it a disaster. But if they were to instead ask themselves, Was this week-end a moment in our best story? Then the fact that they were still talking about the experience ten years later indicated that it had the type of disruptive potential that all good stories are made of.

In the course of a lifetime, a series of uncomfortable adventures that shape your character and give you stories to look back and laugh about isn't a disaster. A disaster is a series of unmemorable weeks, months, or years that leave you unchanged.

The question we asked as we approached the hike was the same question we used when considering the marathon. How can we live the type of story we want to read? It's led us to experience a lot of fun things together—and a lot of hard things together—and to keep pursuing experiences that will help us learn and grow. We've been called crazy, we've been called brave, but I think we've just constantly improved at knowing what question to ask.

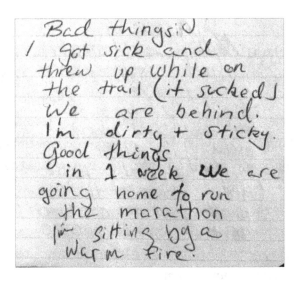

Pain is relative. Away from home and in the cold, going home
to run a full marathon sounded like a relief to Eden (15).

A FAMILY TRADITION: BUCKING TRADITION

Running a marathon is a common bucket-list item. It's one of those things many people want to accomplish at least once; it's momentous, it's challenging, and you get lifelong bragging rights. But most people's bucket-list items are centered around themselves—individual pursuits. Family and marriage are often seen as sacrifices that take us away from these pursuits; they're the ultimate freedom- and fun-killers. I knew this firsthand: I thrived off of adventure and challenge, and when I got married, it felt like that part of my life was over. I tried to convince myself that having kids was better than adventure, but I also had embarrassing daydreams of leaving Kami and our young toddler at home for months so that I could climb Everest.

We knew it had to be possible to have freedom and experience epic things with our family. We could never have predicted, though, that experiences together could actually be more enriching and epic than if we had pursued them individually.

Over the years, we've noticed a subtle dismissal of our family's accomplishments under the guise of admiration. Friends say, "I wish my family could be like yours" or "We could never do that." They comment that, "My kids would cry five minutes from the parking lot." By making our family out to be somehow extraordinary, they let their own "ordinary" family off the hook. They wanted to use their family as an excuse for why their life had to be boring.

My hope is that instead of comparing themselves to us, families ask a very simple question of their own lives: how can we live a better story? It's easy to put certain people on a pedestal, but that's just a way of abdicating our own stories. This isn't about comparison. It's not about running a marathon or hiking the A.T. Those are just events. More important are the questions we ask ourselves; anyone can engage in that level of reflection. It's about living your own best story—one you yourself would want to read.

Upon arriving home without a hitch, we found a big box of shoes from Altra waiting for us. They were all the same matching style and the kids had their own colors that they had picked out. It felt like we were a legitimate sports team with matching high-end uniforms. We tried them on the night before the marathon, and then we ran 26.2 miles in them the next day to break them in. They're technically trail shoes, but they worked great on the road.

This was the second marathon for Filia, our seven-year-old, and it was the fourth or fifth for the rest of our kids. It ended up being much harder than we expected. The first ten miles were fairly easy because our cardio was good. But around that point, our thighs started to scream, *Wait, this isn't hiking. This really hurts!*

For most of us, the final ten miles were excruciating. Filia was the exception. She sailed along happily with no problem at all. A bunch of older kids and adults telling a seven-year-old to slow down so we could keep up should have been demoralizing, but it was more hilarious than anything else.

We all crossed the finish line holding hands, on an emotional high. It only lasted a few seconds, though—we all limped to the grass and fell down, feeling awful. I laid down and fell asleep in the grass for an hour. I couldn't stand afterward; I thought I was going to throw up and pass out at the same time. Eden described it as the most painful experience of her life.

It was unanimous: the marathon had been a terrible idea.

But then we looked at each other and also agreed unanimously that we didn't regret it at all. We knew that, just like camping in the rain, it was miserable, but in ten years, we'd still be talking about that marathon.

When we set out to live the type of story we would want to hear, we constantly surprise ourselves.

Our rule for running marathons is simple. If we can't go any farther, stop. So far we've just never hit that point. We've been amazed by what we can accomplish when we focus on the very simple goal of taking one more step along our story. Those last ten miles were agonizing, but we could always take one more step.

Ironically enough, we finished the marathon in six hours and seventeen minutes—our family's fastest time ever, by forty minutes.

With all sorts of accusations and discussions about our hike going around online, taking a break to run a marathon was a reminder to ourselves—and a sign to the critics—that we weren't taking our thru-hike too seriously. We were hiking our own hike. And we were doing it for us, not for anyone else.

We also learned that flexibility was the name of the game. After the marathon, exhausted and so excited to be back at home, we surprised the kids: we added another zero day so we could all go see *Avengers: Infinity War*—the movie they had wanted to see with The Degenerates, who by now were miles and miles ahead of us. The kids were ecstatic. It was yet another important morale-boosting moment, weighed carefully against the cost of a zero day.

It would mean three days with no trail miles, which at the pace and intensity we had gone meant that unless something huge changed, our chance at seeing the sign at Katahdin was probably over.

For the first time, we didn't care. Our thru-hiker status didn't matter as much as our collective mood. We had a new perspective: we had fully bought in to hiking our own hike. Going home had been wonderful, and had reminded us of the comfort we could so easily have at our fingertips—the comfort we were rejecting back on the trail. It reminded us that the identity of being a thru-hiker was completely optional, something no one would notice if we didn't achieve, and something that would add nothing to the overall experience of our hike.

But being home had also reminded us that so much more awaited us on the A.T. The Degenerates were still trailing up the Eastern Seaboard. So were Hops and Silver. Our mission on the trail was not yet complete.

CHAPTER THIRTEEN

Sharing the Load

"You can't run alongside your grown children with sunscreen and ChapStick on their hero's journey. You have to release them. It's disrespectful not to."

—Anne Lamott

On May 8, it was time to head back to the trail. Halmonee and Papa drove us back to Virginia. We left home at 5:30 a.m. and drove for eight hours; before we knew it, we were all standing back on the familiar wooded dirt path we had left four days earlier. It was time to say goodbye yet again. This time it was easier. It had been nice visiting home, but now more than ever, it felt like we had purpose on the trail, and it was right where we needed to be.

Even though we were all sore from the marathon, we still got 9.1 miles in that day. This meant that over the past five days, we'd averaged 3.8 miles a day. The next morning, we woke up at 6:00 a.m. and hit the trail hard. We hiked until 9:30 p.m., arriving at camp well past dark. We clocked in a new high of 22.4 miles, and we could barely walk. Everything hurt.

But the kids were hell-bent on catching up with their friends. We did sixteen miles the next day, then nineteen miles. Our miles felt like a success—but we didn't think we could keep the pace up. Adrenaline only lasts so long.

I, especially, was struggling. I'd been carrying Rainier since Week 2, and the extra weight on my back was starting to take its toll. I'd lost thirty pounds in the first six weeks and I was constantly low on energy, even though I ate like crazy. Others who traveled ultralight had the option to ditch gear to lighten their load; I didn't.

Rainier was the only one of us who was still gaining weight! We started to joke about how much macaroni and cheese he ate and the path it traveled. First, Dove carried the mac and cheese in her pack. Then Rainier ate it, and I carried it while it was inside of him. Finally, it was pooped out, and Filia carried it while in the diaper until we reached a trash can. We laughed at these calculations and couldn't figure out if this made our group the most efficient or least efficient hikers on the trail.

With Rainier on my back, I was the weak link. I had to take a break every twenty minutes or so. The kid carrier was the best on the market, but I doubted it was meant to be used twelve hours a day for five straight months. My shoulders were rubbed raw from the backpack straps, and I'd started having hip problems. I tried not to complain because I didn't want anyone's sympathy and knew that there was nothing anyone could do to help, but my struggles were obvious. By this point, we just laughed at pain—but when my thigh started to go numb, Kami became concerned.

Not only was my physical health at risk, but so was our goal of summiting Katahdin, with only ninety-three days left to meet our deadline. Our entire "hiking workflow" had to be shifted and refocused. We had gotten more efficient as a group setting up and breaking down camp, so that helped. Our meals were always rushed, feeling like we spent half as much time as we wanted to to rest and enjoy not moving. We sent slower kids out earlier, so we weren't waiting for them. We rearranged packs with weight, so things were distributed in whatever way would make the group quicker. And walking, the thing that occupied the most of our time, was always done at 100 percent speed. But the few days we had hiked over our average came at a cost. Physically and emotionally, we were exhausted; we knew we couldn't sustain that pace. We were all getting stronger, but my weight loss showed that we were burning the candle at both ends. It didn't help to dwell, but if I sat and was honest, the math didn't add up. We were not going to be able to make up for the mileage we had already lost. We were probably not going to make it to Katahdin in time.

There's no way you can just will a group to walk faster. We were out of hacks; our strategy meetings had reached the limit of their effectiveness. We had tried everything.

Stubbornly, I just put my head down and kept walking. I napped multiple times a day. I'd set a timer for eight minutes, lay down on a rock or some leaves, and usually be asleep within a minute or two. That gave me some relief, but it was always temporary. I clocked our hiking by how long it would be until our next break. No matter how long we slept, I was always tired.

THE KIDS TAKE OVER

Four days after rejoining the A.T., we arrived in the Shenandoah National Park. That was when the kids decided they'd had enough of the slow speeds. They'd arrive at a road crossing or a fork in the trail and wait sometimes for thirty or forty minutes for the adults to catch up. Sitting in the rain, getting bitten by bugs, knowing they could be making progress, their frustration levels rose. At one point, they wanted to reach a rest stop with a little convenience store and a milkshake machine. As usual, Kami and I were running behind, and every step caused pain in my hip. All the kids could think about were the milkshakes up ahead.

When Kami and I finally caught up to them, waiting scowling for us, they gave us crap for how slow we were moving.

"What's taking you so long?" "We've been here for twenty-five minutes!" "I'm so bored!" "What have you guys been doing?"

"We've been hiking the whole time!" I shot back.

"Well, at this rate we've never going to get there," said Dove.

Out of frustration, I snapped, "Fine, if you think you're so fast, why don't you carry Rainier? See how fast you'll go then."

It was just one of those things you say as a parent to put kids in their place. It wasn't a challenge, and I didn't expect anyone to do anything about it.

But Dove squared her shoulders and said, "I'll do it."

Surprised, but smug in the assumption that Dove would change her mind soon, I handed the backpack with Rainier in it to her. Once she actually had to carry the extra forty-four pounds for more than a half-mile, I was sure she'd apologize for berating me and Kami.

But the apology never came.

Dove, our eldest, is a lot like me in that she lives for a challenge. She also isn't the type to broadcast her pain in the face of difficulty. If carrying Rainier was painful, she didn't show it. She proceeded to knock out four miles in record time with him on her back. She was way ahead of anyone else, and we couldn't believe it.

In a sudden bolt of understanding, I realized my mistake. For eight hundred miles, I'd struggled needlessly because I believed I was the only one who could carry Rainier. I had wanted to be the strong dad. I saw Dove as smaller and weaker. She was my kid. She was a girl. My prejudices has cost me. And now here she was, showing me up. I found it humbling, but also incredible—I was so proud of my daughter.

As I walked carrying Dove's lighter pack, the pain disappeared from my hips and back. I started to enjoy walking. I lifted my head and saw the trees and flowers blooming. For the first time, I realized why this was a national park. I saw beauty. I had energy for conversations.

> I'd definitely gotten a boost from feeling like I was stronger and more capable than my family—but it was nothing compared to the energy I got from being supported and cared for by my daughter, seeing myself as her peer rather than her superior.

It was beautiful to see Dove shine like this, and it revealed something far more glorious than sentimental pride in my child. This was the answer we had been looking for. The solution was right in front of me the whole time; I just had not been able to consider it because I'd assumed it wasn't possible for anyone else to carry Rainier. Also, I never wanted to put the burden on my kids. The thought never occurred to me that they would become so invested in the trail or in their own relationship with their brother that they would volunteer to take him. I had sold Dove, and all the kids, short.

If I didn't have to carry Rainier the whole time, we could go faster as a group. With all the previous effort and endless tweaks we'd made, we'd maybe gained a 10 percent increase in mileage. With help carrying Rainier, we might be able to increase our mileage by 25 percent each day. That was huge. It was a game-changer. Here it was, finally—a solution to our eight-hundred-mile problem, and a counterattack to the biggest threat to our goal.

That night, as Kami and I marveled at the power and strength of our teenage daughter, and I felt the relief of her support, I broke down and cried. It's empowering to be needed by your children. But just like we had learned with receiving trail magic from strangers, there's something magical about being in a place where you're vulnerable enough to need care from others. As a self-proclaimed strong dude, getting care from your teenage daughter is about as mind-bending as it gets when it comes to re-identifying family roles. I thought I had signed up for the A.T. to give my kids a new perspective on life. As it turned out, I was the one who was getting the new perspective. It was scary. But I loved it.

The next day, Eden offered to carry Rainier as well. Then Seven volunteered to join in. We started a rotation; now I was carrying Rainier only thirty minutes out of every two hours. With the extra help, I could essentially sprint those thirty minutes, then recover for an hour and a half. I didn't have to constantly conserve my energy for later on.

There was another added benefit of the older kids carrying Rainier: it was an opportunity to grow closer to him. I'd really enjoyed that aspect of carrying him, and I'd been enjoying it alone. They sang the same three songs together about the alphabet and the wheels on the bus going around, and they formed a special bond.

Later, we received hate comments from our internet peanut gallery, which was "appalled" that we "forced" our kids to carry their little brother, but nothing could have been further from the truth. The kids were volunteering to carry Rainier so we could finish the trail faster, and they enjoyed hanging out with their little brother. Rainier became the mascot of the family. He was the one that bonded us together tighter. It was difficult to have him along, but the difficulty was worth it.

For us, it's a metaphor for all of our parenting: it's difficult, but it's worth it. But the most valuable thing we learned about parenting that day was that sometimes, the most effective thing you can do is trust your kids and get out of the way. I had been trying to protect them from something that they were capable of. It was my stubbornness that was preventing them from growth. Not their attitudes or abilities. I wondered how many other areas of our life back home this was occurring in. Maybe our kids are capable of so much more but because of our own fears, we're not allowing them to shine.

Soon after we were back in the groove on the trail, with the older kids helping out with Rainier, we had another celebration to plan: Dove's seventeenth birthday.

As I put together what her surprise would be, there was no way to hide that I was planning something. I could tell Dove knew that I was packing out a special meal for her birthday, the same way we'd packed out Kami's red velvet cake.

But Dove was blown away when we all woke her up singing "Happy Birthday" and holding out a plate full of her favorite breakfast—eggs Benedict! It had been a risky move; I had to make sure twelve eggs survived a twenty-five-mile hike from the closest store, and I had to figure out a way to toast English muffins, poach eggs, and make hollandaise sauce all in one aluminum pot using only a spork.

"I figured you packed out doughnuts or something!" she cried happily, digging in to the meal. She later said she ate so much of it that she felt a little sick that morning on the trail.

Dove's birthday was perfect timing for us all. It felt like a small way to give back the enormous contribution that she had given me: the ability to enjoy hiking again.

Our newfound teamwork meant we were crushing more miles than ever. Our mileage woes seemed to drop away with each passing hour. Two days into Shenandoah National Park, we were sitting at a shelter having lunch, and who walked up behind us? Silver, who still had his headlamp hanging around his neck! This is the first person we had caught up to since our departure to run the marathon.

Silver did not like hiking in the rain, and he'd had a hard time leaving town. This, in addition to his sporadic hiking style, had slowed him down. We hiked together for three hours, just catching up. He talked about the gear he'd ordered, the beer he'd drank, and the food he'd enjoyed in town. We told him about the marathon. It felt good to be back together.

He noticed the kids were carrying Rainier and was impressed. He compared it to the scene in *The Lord of the Rings* when Samwise, the bigger hobbit, carries a load that's too heavy for Frodo because Frodo literally can't take another step with it. "I missed you guys. You're like no other family I've ever seen," he said.

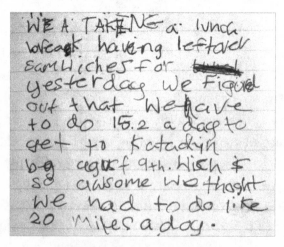

Memory (11) breaking up the full trek into weekly and daily goals gave the kids motivation and all of us a way to be encouraged by our progress.

HUMAN ACTIVITIES

When researching the A.T., we didn't see it as an adult activity. We saw it as a human activity. This perspective led to awkward conversations with other hikers. They'd ask us, "How did you decide to hike with six kids?" The answer was simple, but felt weird to say: we just wanted to hike the A.T. for all the same reasons every other hiker did. And we didn't want to leave our kids at home. Our angle was different; instead of asking how we could bring our kids, we asked, how could we not?

All we'd heard people claim for years was that the A.T. is an awesome, life-changing experience. If that was really true, how could we justify excluding our kids? We had found that kids, just like adults, value things like challenge, going beyond preconceived limits, and exciting adventures—when given the opportunity to participate. It's just that, most of the time, they're not given that opportunity. We'd learned to not shy away from giving our kids challenges. So our decision to hike with our kids was very natural for us—it didn't feel like it needed explanation.

It wasn't the first time we'd run up against not knowing how to answer a question about our kids. Since we'd become parents, Kami and I had noticed a "trap" that exists in modern parenting and that we, for a time, got sucked into. Kids' activities, like school, sports, dance, music, and every other extracurricular out there, are sold as conveniences to parents: get your kids out from underfoot for a while. But these optional children's activities became obligatory events that ended up running our lives and placed demands on our finances, schedule, and relational priorities. It was too easy to become trapped in the prison of convenience. For these reasons, Kami and I started to reexamine the limitations of the kids' activities that are sanctioned by our culture. We didn't believe in putting a wall up between "parent activities" and "kid activities." Because of this, our world had been opened up to a whole realm of possibilities that seem crazy, or downright impossible, to others—like running a marathon with our kids.

The kids themselves didn't see the A.T. as an adult activity. They didn't understand why some kids were told they weren't able or allowed to do it. They faced the same challenges that adults faced and had overcome many that adults had not.

On the trail, we saw our kids the same way we saw any other adult hiker. We delegated different jobs to everyone just as we would if we were on a high performance team of adults. People would tell us, "You guys are a well-oiled machine." This seemed important for them to point out, but we couldn't figure out why. What did they mean by "well-oiled machine"? Then one night, we saw it. When we got into camp, every person had their task, and they went about it automatically and efficiently, working together. Dove gathered water and boiled it. Eden set up the kids' tent. Memory found a water source and filled up everyone's bottles. Filia and Rainier gathered firewood. In towns, Eden would do laundry, Seven would edit videos, and Dove and Memory would resupply at the store for the coming days. It was amazing to watch and stood in stark contrast to people's expectations of a family arriving at camp. The common assumption was that the kids wouldn't be able to focus and would play or slack off while Mom and Dad did all the work. Our camp workflow even stood out among groups of adults, who hiked together yet accomplished their tasks and retained resources independently.

We certainly didn't start off on the trail as a well-oiled machine. As cautious parents, Kami and I intervened when needed on our kids' cooking or setting up while they were learning how to do it well. I cooked for our entire first week on the trail. It involved boiling half a gallon of water for our five boxes of mac and cheese. The pot balanced on a flaming red-hot wire contraption with three legs that usually had to be balanced on dirt and rocks—or even snow. There was no way we trusted our kids with the boiling water. We also had limited food, fuel, and time, so one wrong move could cause injuries and leave us with no dinner. But we soon discovered we simply couldn't boil water, set up tents, find firewood, and babysit six kids. We had to trust Dove to make the dinner. And she did it ably, never once spilling the water.

Okay, maybe once.

But it didn't matter. Allowing her to own that task was worth it for her to see what she was capable of without us micromanaging her life.

As we gave all the kids more autonomy, we realized we were the ones who'd held them back. They were capable of far more than we were initially comfortable with, and they were more interested in helping than we'd anticipated. Like many people, we had assumed kids prefer being consumers instead of producers, but we learned that they're actually just put into the role of consumers because we don't often entrust them with important jobs. Doing their jobs created value, and the kids loved adding value. Occasionally, it was hard to watch them not measure up to our adult standards, but that discomfort was our problem, not theirs.

We were a team, and a good team pushes its individual members to explore their capabilities and develop their talents.

Kami and I realized that instead of doing everything ourselves, our role as parents was better served by:

- Using our imagination to create a vision for the kids of what was possible, and then

- Communicating clearly a list of jobs that would need to be accomplished to accomplish the vision and asking for volunteers.

This created more free time, allowed each family member to focus on what they were good at, and invited the kids to take more owner-ship of our trip.

So when people heard there was a family hiking, they expected to roll up to a campsite and watch two parents (the producers) set up camp and cook for the six children (the consumers). Instead, they saw eight people working toward a common goal. This was what they meant when they called us a "well-oiled machine."

Some people couldn't imagine hiking with a group, but we couldn't imagine hiking alone.

RECIPROCAL HELP

With the kids pitching in, we were able to manage additional tasks unique to our group, such as editing footage, uploading videos, changing diapers, gathering firewood (something most hikers had no energy for after a long day of hiking), and responding to social-me-dia comments. Amongst all the negativity were wonderful people who saw our videos and offered us accommodations or meals along the route. One of these special people lived in the Shenandoahs, or "the Shennies," as Silver liked to call them.

The Shennies are known for bears, hills, and no good places to resupply. The week we were there, it rained nonstop. So it seemed like a gift from heaven when we got an email from a family offer-ing to drive an hour to pick us up and bring us back to their vaca-tion home—for free. One wet morning, we put on our cold, damp clothes, ate some Little Debbie Honey Buns, and told Silver he better meet us at the parking lot by 1:00 p.m. if he wanted to be included in a special surprise. It rained buckets, but we made it to the parking lot at exactly 1:00 p.m. Griffin and Claire came to pick us all up in two cars, and the eight of us and Silver piled in gratefully.

Griffin and Claire's vacation house was like a mansion. It had four bedrooms, plus a bunk room. The huge master bedroom had an en-suite bathroom with a huge tub. There was a hot tub, a pool, and a massive lawn. They had fully stocked the kitchen with many of our favorites in a huge walk-in pantry. The living room had a flat-screen television and big couches. They normally rented the place out for $800 a night, yet they gave us the whole thing entirely for free.

We loved being able to share the luxury with a friend. We couldn't use all the space, and we also knew others would appreciate it just as much as we did. For hikers, these types of places along the trail were like hidden treasures. Sharing them, we felt like a rock band offering friends a backstage pass. It was surreal. We stayed up late with Silver, who was still wearing his silver puffy jacket. We sat in rocking chairs on the huge wraparound porch, smoking cigars.

Silver smiled and said, not for the first or last time, "The trail provides!"

The next day, when it was still pouring, we looked at each other and knew what the other was thinking. The hot tub, the rocking chairs, the unlimited food. "Twist my arm," said Silver. We had to stay. We knew we had to be selective with our zero days, but we also saw this was a once-in-a-lifetime thing. Not only did Griffin and Claire say we could stay as long as we needed, but they also kept bringing us food. At first, we felt guilty accepting their hospitality, but we soon realized there's a mutual benefit in giving and receiving. It's a lost art in our society.

Claire opened up about her time in prison and how she dreamed of hiking the A.T. She asked us questions about gear and planning for an adventure of this magnitude. She was a researcher and we encouraged her by saying there was never a right time and there's no exact way to do it, so don't research it to death. It was so cool that we could help as we were being helped.

Our time with Griffin and Claire was a welcome respite, but, as Silver said, "The trail isn't going to hike itself." There were 1,400 miles between us and Mount Katahdin, and regardless of the weather, they had to be walked. It was a long road ahead of us—but now that we'd found the missing puzzle piece of the kids all trading off carrying Rainier, for the very first time, we thought maybe it was possible to hit our goal. Despite the challenges ahead, we felt more confident than ever.

CHAPTER FOURTEEN

Safety Second

"A ship in harbor is safe, but that is not what ships are built for."
—John Shedd

Between Shenandoah National Park and Harpers Ferry in West Virginia, we experienced several difficult obstacles that shook our confidence.

On Day 82, we entered into a fourteen-mile section of trail called the Rollercoaster. It's notorious for unending, grinding ups and downs, and takes most people two days to complete. There are fourteen peaks in a row, and when you finish descending one, you immediately start climbing another. While we never anticipated that we could possibly complain about it not being cold, we were finding the rising temperatures increasingly tough on our morale. It was downright hot. Climbing in the heat and bugs was taking a toll.

And we were facing a brand-new challenge: Filia had begun complaining of a toothache.

At just seven years old, Filia had walked the entire way carrying a pack that weighed about 25 percent of her body weight. If she finished the A.T., she would be the youngest female ever to have done so. Often, we'd hike from 7:00 a.m. to as late as 10:00 p.m. Back home, Filia had barely grown out of taking daily naps, and now here she was, hiking for up to fifteen hours a day. She's a tough kid. So when she expressed that she had pain in her mouth, we took note. Kami and I are no different than any other parents in that, when one of our kids is in pain, we feel the primal urge to comfort and care for them. The question immediately became clear: do we get off the trail and try to find a dentist, or do we keep moving and hope she'll be okay?

The ground was covered in mud, the heat made sweat drip into our eyes and our packs stick to our backs, and the endless ups and downs were starting to wear on us. To make matters worse, Rainer pooped through his shorts and peed through his pants, so his only clean clothes were his rain pants. All these tensions made normal decisions very difficult.

Back home, this kind of situation is a no-brainer. We could phone the dentist right away, schedule the next available appointment, and do anything needed to get rid of the pain. There would be no reason to wait it out. On the trail, it's not that easy. A stop like this affects everything, especially when you're hiking as a family. A trip to the dentist would take us anywhere from one to three days; it would involve finding a dentist, getting transportation, and getting accommodations for the eight of us while we waited on Filia's status. This didn't even take into account the forty-five miles we wouldn't be hiking on those three days. So we had to dig a level deeper and ask: is the pain dangerous, or is it just uncomfortable?

Filia (7) usually lived in the moment but expressed her fantasies through drawing our family van, in which my parents drove three times to meet us on the trail.

WHAT IS DANGEROUS?

The birth of our oldest child, Dove, really educated us on the difference between comfort and safety. It was assumed that we'd deliver her in a hospital, where it was safest. We were both born in hospitals, and our friends who'd had babies all delivered in hospitals. Hospitals were where we had the best access to doctors, life-saving machines, and drugs that would ease the process.

We signed up for a birthing class in a hospital and were exposed to all sorts of awkward situations. We had to practice breathing, watch graphic videos, and hang out with uncomfortable dads-to-be. We learned what an episiotomy is (don't google it) and the instructor drew a picture on the whiteboard of what happens when you get an epidural, the most popular method of pain relief during labor. She drew a string of lines that represented all the machines that would need to be hooked up to you because of that one decision. The intravenous line limited mobility, which lengthened the labor and increased the possibility a Caesarean section or other surgical procedure would be necessary. According to our research, this dramatically increased the risks, and the only benefit was temporary pain relief. The statistics at the time said more than 50 percent of women giving birth at hospitals end up with epidurals. We concluded the medical field was not necessarily there to promote safety. Sometimes, it prioritized comfort, and what's comfortable is not always safest.

And now, while we believed that Filia's comfort was important, in light of the cost we had to pay to achieve it, we needed to consider the decision through a different lens.

On Reddit, things were always painted in black and white. People talked about our parenting as if we were violating an absolute moral code that, online, everyone appeared to agree to.

"Why CPS *wasn't notified of their latest abhorrent behavior is beyond me. Anyone who has had a toothache that causes tears (yes, she was crying for a full day prior) knows that Advil would help more than Tylenol. Asshat dad says it's only a baby tooth, so they're not worried. Does this self-proclaimed know-it-all not think a baby tooth can be infected and painful as hell! Any other parent would get their stupid asses off the trail and bring that poor baby to a dentist. That the mom is allowing her child to suffer is beyond belief. I hope they read here and understand that they are terrible parents. Not even going to address the fact he now has the kids carrying the baby for portions of the day. He is an egotistical, arrogant, narcissistic idiot."* —52er

There seemed to be an unspoken dichotomy at work: kids are either in pain, or they're safe. Even if Kami and I had just given Filia Tylenol, we would have been seen as more responsible because we would have been taking away her pain—making her "safer." But it was a false dichotomy.

We asked ourselves, "Is Filia's toothache likely to threaten her long-term health?" As we weren't doctors or dentists, it was easy to feel unqualified to answer this. But we've learned to value our intuition and experience as parents. While a dentist will look at her teeth, he only looks at her teeth. We're the only one in Filia's life that have the ability to look at everything and everyone else. We were the only ones aware of Filia's emotional capacity. Would she feel cared for? Would she feel disregarded or ignored for the sake of the group? Filia had run two marathons by the age of seven and proved she could proactively communicate about her pain and her limits.

"Are you still able to walk?" we asked her.

"Yeah," Filia said.

"Are you okay if we keep on going?"

"Yeah."

"Can you please let us know if it gets worse?"

"Yeah, it feels okay now."

Our job as leaders was to evaluate Filia's physical and mental state, the other kids, the weather, the emotional pros and cons of being able to finish our trip, and how to cram an additional forty-five miles into an already impossible-feeling task. The same situation would come up with Rainier getting an eye infection, Eden getting stung by bees, and even Kami freaking out about thinking that her uterus was falling out—which sounds like hysteria, but it's a real thing, and with as many kids as Kami's had, the possibility was something she was always paranoid about. At one point she was so worried, she asked me to "check her" in a public restroom. Now we look back on it and laugh—it was exactly like what a pregnancy scare feels like, and on the trail, it was genuinely anxiety-inducing.

While we weren't always confident in our decisions, we did feel we were the most qualified to assess all the information available. We determined that the toothache wasn't a threat to Filia's long-term health. So, we decided we were comfortable waiting it out, giving Filia occasional doses of Children's Tylenol, and carefully watching for any new symptoms. We knew that if we were wrong about this, we'd be criticized by the public as well as our friends and family—but we didn't want to make our decisions based on avoiding criticism. We wanted to base our decisions on what was best for our family. And for now, the best decision was to stay on the trail.

Eden's job on the trail was to supply and prepare lunches, and every day, she'd announce our midday meal on camera like a chef at a fancy restaurant. "For lunch today, we have..." Even though the menu usually consisted of things like chips, hummus, Nutella tortillas, and honey sandwiches, it was still a high point in the day for morale. That day, we had guacamole, chips, hummus, and sugar snap peas, which was thankfully all relatively easy for Filia to chew with her painful tooth.

That day was Seven's first time taking a shift carrying Rainier. "It's not as heavy as I thought it would be," he said as he hoisted Rainier's carrier onto his back. "It's only a little heavier than my backpack."

"Just wait till you get up that hill, kid," Kami said, grinning.

But Seven was just fine, and did a double shift as we pressed through to our destination. Since we were staying at a hostel that night, and would therefore get a hot breakfast the next morning, Memory made the executive decision to eat our packed-out breakfast supplies early. She pulled out a bag of doughnuts late in the afternoon and eagerly bit into one. A gummy worm emerged from the giant pile of frosting on top. "It's a gummy worm doughnut!" she said happily.

"Can I have one?" Filia asked. It seemed her tooth was feeling a lot better.

When we arrived at the Bear's Den, which is a famous trail hostel, we discovered Silver waiting there for us. He said he had some pain in his foot and was taking it easy, which seemed like a normal thing for Silver to say. Filia's toothache had gone away, and although it would come and go for the next couple days, it appeared we'd made the correct choice.

Silver joined us in sitting around the hostel's community piano. The kids played us songs for the first time in months. Beautiful music filled the air as we sat eating pepperoni pizza, drinking Mountain Dew, indulging in Ben & Jerry's ice cream, and listening to the kids belt out two months' worth of suppressed musical expression. Afterward, we stayed up late smoking cigars with Silver on the porch, discussing the craziness of crossing another major milestone: the one-thousand-mile mark. We were all close to the halfway point now, but we knew we were still a long way from finishing.

The next day, we said goodbye to Silver. He wanted to give his foot a break and was going to spend the entire day watching the *The Lord of the Rings* extended editions from beginning to end. This was his pattern. He'd catch up to us later. "I'll see you guys soon," he said as we headed toward Harpers Ferry.

"HALFWAY" DONE

As we got closer to Harpers Ferry, the spiritual "halfway point" of the hike, we started to reminisce about the changes we had been through. Eighty-three days ago, we had left our van at Springer Mountain; now, we were almost done walking through our fourth state, Virginia, the longest state on the A.T. As Silver had said, the trail had provided. And our YouTube channel, which had started with just seven thousand subscribers, now had close to forty-five thousand after just three months of hiking.

We were used to hate comments at this point. But slowly, something different started to happen. More and more people contacted us after seeing our videos to offer us a place to stay. We'd get Instagram messages or emails saying, "This may sound kind of weird, but we've been watching your channel..." There was a two-week period in May when seven different families hosted us.

Kami and I started to feel like we weren't doing this trail alone. Back at the beginning, we thought we'd need to be little G.I. Joes and have the individual fortitude to keep going and keep everyone motivated. In reality, we were becoming more like facilitators. I could see that all of these wonderful meetings and offers would have never come to us at home. They only came because we left. We put our-selves out there and made ourselves vulnerable—and when people saw what we were doing, they wanted to be a part of it. We just had to get out of the way and let them help. Often, we had multiple offers of hosting. Instead of focusing on saving money and pushing every mile, I took on a more secretarial role of keeping track of offers and replying back with our schedule and needs and coordinating pick up points. I found it was helpful to be clear and straightforward about what would help us: "Meals, laundry, showers, and at least one pri-vate bedroom." Many people were eager to help and just needed to know how.

FRIENDSHIP AND HOSPITALITY

Our time on the A.T. gave us a unique perspective on traveling and meeting people in America—the country in which we had been born and raised. Before we started the trail, if a foreign tourist had come to America for one year and asked us, "What should I do to get the American experience?" we would have advised going to the big cit-ies like New York or Los Angeles and maybe a handful of national parks along the way. Now, we'd tell them to spend six months hiking the Appalachian Trail. Instead of the polished, corporate gift-shop experience, you get to meet people as they really are; people you'd be unlikely to meet any other way. Instead of sights and things to see, it was the relationships and the care that was having the biggest impact on us.

Our family enjoyed the hospitality of a number ex-cons, a doctor, a small-town hairdresser, and a family that made mascot costumes and traveled the country participating in contests. We were able to see that there were families everywhere that were inspired by our attempt to do something difficult together because they themselves struggled with separation in their own ways.

> The A.T. is really all about people. You could measure the trail through various lenses: miles, states, important mountain peaks. For us, we marked our progress and our memories primarily through the people we met along the way.

One of our favorite accommodations was a huge, award-winning brewery called The Devil's Backbone, in Virginia. The brewery and campsite were on a one-hundred-acre property with multiple restaurants, a cigar lounge, and concert venues, all surrounded by the Blue Ridge Mountains. We stayed there through a rainstorm and ate dinner at the restaurant. It was like an oasis in a difficult section of trail, and we loved that this company dedicated resources and amenities to hikers.

The next day, we needed a ride back to the trail, but the shuttle from The Devil's Backbone didn't leave until noon. We knew we had to get in nineteen miles that day, which would be impossible with such a late start. As we were eating breakfast in the coffee shop, someone overheard our dilemma and offered to give us a ride to the trailhead. Five of the kids got in the back of the man's pickup truck, and we got in the cab with Rainier. The man asked about our trip and couldn't believe what we'd accomplished so far. We asked if he worked at the brewery or if he was just visiting.

That's when he told us, "I started the brewery. I'm the CEO."

He managed hundreds of employees and made close to one hundred thousand barrels of beer a year. And here he was, driving our family so we could walk in the woods. On the drive, he told us that his original vision for the brewery was a place to gather people and live communally—beer was never really the original goal.

One of our most informative meetings was with a woman named Roberta, who dressed like a nun. She came to pick us up from the road so we could stay at her place, and she explained she was Mennonite. We didn't know what that was, so we learned a lot on that car ride. Roberta said Mennonites were essentially mellowed-out Amish people but didn't mind a little bit of technology—we were thankful she had a flip phone to get in touch with us. She drove like a maniac, and that car ride was probably the closest we came to death in all of Pennsylvania. But we loved staying with Roberta and her family. They served us a huge meal, and we stayed up late talking about homeschooling. We had a lot in common. She introduced our kids to an encyclopedia set they had on the bookshelf that she called the "Mennonite internet."

Before going on the A.T., our world was geographically huge. There were a thousand places we could go. But our perspectives were pretty small. The places we went—gas stations, restaurants, hotels—were all created by businesses and all felt the same. Although we had traveled all over the world, we hadn't created many relationships along the way.

On the trail, that all flipped. Our world became smaller, but our perspectives grew larger. Now we were being invited into people's homes. Many of these nights, Kami, who was more introverted, would go to the room early and rest for the next day while I would stay up late into the night answering questions about what it was really like out on the trail and exchanging stories. This was a privilege you can't buy.

The day after we left Silver, we stayed with a woman named Kate near Washington, DC. Her husband was serving abroad in the military, and she had three small kids. Kate picked us up in a twelve-passenger van that she had rented. We drove for thirty minutes back to her place with her kids screaming in the back. We were thankful for the ride but wondered for a minute if we'd made the right choice; it wasn't always easy to know what we were getting into when accepting help from strangers. We didn't have the luxury of screening people. If they offered us a place to sleep with electricity and running water, we were in.

Kami really ended up connecting with Kate and loved our time with her. Just for a little while, we didn't feel like crazy hiker people with a horde of kids. Kate made us feel normal. She'd lived internationally, so she had a different perspective on life. She was also really funny. We loved talking to her and her neighbor as we watched our kids play at the neighborhood playground. She was also generous. She bought coffee and beer just for us and even reworked her schedule to let us stay another night. We stayed up late talking with Kate about our videos, and she shared how much they'd encouraged her. We could tell she truly understood us, and we had a great conversation.

The next day, Kate dropped us off at the train station because the family voted to go sightseeing all over DC like typical tourists— except we were dressed in hiking clothes and flip-flops. We visited the Washington Monument, the Lincoln Memorial, the Smithsonian Natural History Museum, and walked down the National Mall. We went to Starbucks, and Kami ordered a cold Frappuccino and a hot Caramel Macchiato. She put the drinks in the cup holders of the luxury stroller Kate lent us and wandered around DC, pushing Rainier, feeling like a normal human being as she took turns sipping from the cold drink then the hot drink.

Filia's tooth was feeling better, and being away from our stuff, we didn't have to focus on resupplying, laundry, video editing, or trip planning. For just a day, we let go of our identity as hikers; it was one of the only days we felt like we truly got a break from the trail. Little did we know that we were about to head into the longest stretch of hiking we would encounter our entire trip. Our time off for the marathon had created a painful sense of feeling behind. In our next stretch, we would hike so much and so far that our zero day in DC would feel like a daydream.

HARPERS FERRY

It had been eighteen days since the marathon. We said goodbye to Kate and crossed into West Virginia. That day, we finally made it to Harpers Ferry.

As we walked into the town, Kami and I watched our kids in front of us crossing a bridge. We stopped for a moment just to look at them, and I thought, *Wow, we're doing this. It's crazy, but we're actually doing this.*

Two famous rivers, the Potomac and the Shenandoah, converge at Harpers Ferry, and the place has all sorts of historical significance—a former US armory, and the site of John Brown's abolitionist raid. Thomas Jefferson called the view "one of the most stupendous scenes in nature." Hops had really hyped it up for us, so we were looking forward to it. But in some ways, it was a letdown. We needed him here with his "the A.T. is sacred ground" perspective to help us appreciate it. All we knew was that it was hot, lunch was incredibly overpriced, and we waited what seemed like forever for our food.

Harpers Ferry is home to the Appalachian Trail Conservancy, the organization that manages the A.T. At the office, you can get your picture taken and logged in a book so other hikers can see when you passed by. It's the ATC that officially recognizes completed thru-hikes by awarding the thru-hiker with a "2000 Miler" certificate and a special patch.

We checked the book for our friends. Hops had been through two days earlier. The Degenerates had passed by so long ago it was hard to find their pictures. We felt like we'd never catch up to them. And then we saw Silver's picture. He was wearing his black kilt and had his headlamp hanging around his neck. He had gotten ahead of us because of our day in Washington, DC, and had checked in that morning.

The young man behind the desk knew who we were right away, before we even said anything. "Oh, Becky is going to want to meet you!" he said, bustling off to find her.

Several people came out from the offices, said hello, and shook hands with our kids. "We don't have a record of any family of your size finishing the trail," one of the ladies said. It was the first we'd heard that if we finished, we might actually set the world record for the largest family to have ever hiked the A.T.

As the most competitive member of the family, I'd totally been drawn to records like "first ascent" of a mountain or "fastest known time" to complete a long-distance route. It had never occurred to us that in saying no to those opportunities and choosing instead to have children, we would be opening ourselves up to set a whole new kind of record.

We were feeling a little nervous because we'd recently received the following email from Chief Ranger Carin Farley:

Dear Crawfords,

I have received several inquiries from concerned citizens after they have viewed your social media posts. As the chief ranger, I am responsible to help facilitate all of the law enforcement, search and rescue, and emergency response on the trail. Just an FYI, there has been considerable mention of your youngest and requests to my office for welfare checks. I believe the concern mainly rests with his position in the pack for hours at a time and the environmental concerns with cold weather.

As we were shaking hands and meeting everyone at the conservancy headquarters, a lady in a ranger uniform with a sidearm and handcuffs on her belt walked up and introduced herself. It was Chief Ranger Carin Farley.

She had dreadlocks and full-sleeve tattoos on her arms. She was nothing like we'd imagined. Kami and I smiled—she looked like us!

"It's a pleasure to meet you all," she said. "If there's anything I can do to help you out, just let me know."

As we were talking to her, Rainier ran around the gift shop playing with all of the stuffed animals in the miniature shelter they had set up. I asked her about the email she'd sent—did she need to question us, or was there anything we needed to watch out for?

"Oh, no." She waved my fears away with one hand. "That was just a formality. I think what you're doing is wonderful."

MILEAGE MATH

Because Harpers Ferry is home to the Conservancy, it's thought of as a halfway point on the trail, but it's seventy miles short of the actual halfway point. It's a dirty trick—that could be the difference of a whole week of hiking! We knew it was important not to celebrate too early. We'd walked 1,025 miles and had 1,164 to go. This meant in the second "half" of our trip, if we were going to make our deadline, we'd have do an additional 161 miles in nine fewer days than the first half.

We had arrived at Harpers Ferry on Day 85. For our entire trip, even with taking turns carrying Rainier, we had only averaged twelve miles a day. For the next seventy-six days, we'd have to hike more than fifteen miles per day—with no zero days. And we already felt pushed to our max. The prospect of no breaks was sobering. Doubt crept back in. Was sacrificing the ending worth a few days off for a marathon or walking around DC? Was a finish even possible?

It was more clear than ever that we could do it—we could hit our goal. We had walked more than fifteen miles a day numerous times now. But we had done it with the help of going home, being a tourist in DC for a day, relaxing in the hot tub with Silver at the vacation mansion...all things that felt like a giant release valve. Breaks like that had been a great lever to pull whenever we thought the kids needed it. The breaks were important for me too—supplying the motivation to keep everyone moving was a full-time job in addition to the hiking, and when I had to do both for days or weeks on end, the stress built up and exhausted me.

But going forward, even if we felt like we needed it, we would have to ignore that feeling. What would the cost of this be?

At this point, my worst fear—that the kids would hate us when we were done—was at its highest probability of coming true. No matter how much grit and determination they'd shown thus far, the kids still had a limit, and I was once again worried that in our deter-mination to make our goal, I wouldn't be able to recognize it until they were past it.

As we left Harpers Ferry, we walked along three miles of rail-road-grade trail called the Towpath. It's the flattest section of the entire 2,200 miles. We saw a passenger train running along the trail above us. It was headed to New York. We waved at the people on the train, and as it slowly passed us by, we could see some people waving back at us, their faces obscured by the grimy windows. Just then, a text message came in. It was from Silver. He was on the train headed to New York; he'd been offered a job doing legal work in New York City, and he didn't know when he'd be back. He was waving goodbye to us.

There was an ephemeral quality to relationships on the trail. Every A.T. book has statistics warning that something like 50 percent of people quit in the first one hundred miles, and 50 percent of the remaining hikers quit in the next one hundred miles, and so on, until only about 10 percent are left to finish the trail. But we never knew which people would fall away and who would stay. We weren't attached to many people, but we'd experienced so much with Silver—our first conversations about family over pancakes where he said, "The trail provides," sitting around a camp fire in the snow, the milkshakes and beer in the Shennies, the vacation-house mansion, the thunderstorms in Virginia, cigars and a piano concert at Bear's Den, and talks about expensive watches. We watched the end of the train disappear into the woods.

We didn't know then that that would be the last time we saw Silver. If we had known, we might have cried.

All we knew for sure was that we still had a hell of a long way left to go.

CHAPTER FIFTEEN

The Cult

"I don't want to be part of any club that will accept me as a member."

—Groucho Marx

One of the oddest offers we got while on the trail was from a man named Tobiah.

Hi Crawford Family,

I watched your videos and I want to help y'all out. We have a *free store* full of clothes for men, women, and children as well. I am the baker at an organic farm and market. We host hikers year round for free. We have three hikers' cabins and a big bath house as well as a bakery, cows, goats, fields of organic vegetables, and a nice farm store and cafe.

We all live together on this commune farm of thirty people, fifteen of them children that yours can play with. We are a spiritual group of believers and would be honored to lavish you with His love. You are welcome to come and stay for as long as you like. We can meet and shuttle you back to the farm for free.

It sounded too good to be true. When we stayed in a town or at a house, we estimated we got three times as many calories than on the trail. And calories were our most valuable commodity, our highest priority by far. Every member of our family had lost significant weight in the last few months. We had learned a lot about food since we started. Things like Little Debbie Cosmic Brownies contain the most calories per cent and ounce of any other snack, palm oil is a natural laxative, and tortillas are the best bread product to pack because they don't go bad, you can't squash them, and you can spread peanut butter and Nutella on them and call it a meal.

We also learned that Ramen Bombs are gross. These were a concoction of ramen mixed with dehydrated mashed potatoes flakes; they only weighed twelve ounces before adding water, but they filled you up instantly. However, they also left you feeling like you'd swallowed an anvil. The kids hated them.

We were all starting to get sick of *all* trail food, honestly, and it was sometimes a fight to get everyone to eat enough. I found myself pleading with Kami and the girls to eat more than they were comfortable with, but the only time they could stomach it was at a restaurant—at one hundred dollars a pop.

With this in mind, an email like Tobiah's, and the promise of plentiful free food, could not be ignored. However, we had some strict terms. Because of our new resolution after taking a zero day in DC, we actually had to walk past the road they were closest to to get sixteen full miles that day. They would need to pick us up at that location and drop us back off there the next day, which meant extra driving for them. Thankfully, they agreed.

When we arrived at the parking-lot meeting point that day, we were twenty minutes late, despite our attempt to hustle. There was a man waiting for us there; he had long hair held back with a headband, a beard, and loose, handwoven clothes.

We apologized for being late. He shook his head and said, "Don't worry about it, man, we're all about love here!"

At the farm, all the men had long hair, headbands, and beards. The women wore long skirts, and they all talked about love all the time. They had two little cabins set up for us, each with four bunk beds. It was pretty rustic, with electricity and a few fans but no air conditioning or plumbing. Each of the rooms had a gift basket with chocolate, kombucha, and fruit.

That night was Friday, so it was their celebration of Shabbat. Kami and I had rarely come across other Christians who had taken to celebrating this Jewish tradition as we had, and it felt cool to see it. They celebrated with a special meeting and dinner in a big tent. In the tent, everyone sat in a circle, and they handed us cold fruit-infused Yerba mate tea. Women danced in the center to Jewish-sounding music while children sat very calmly and quietly by their parents. Since our family had taken Hebrew lessons, we thought it was all pretty neat—it was certainly different, but we're the Crawfords. "Different" doesn't faze us.

After the circle, they served us an amazing meal of salad, fresh-baked bread, mashed potatoes, salmon, and key lime pie. They invited us to a service at 8:00 a.m. the next morning. They made it clear we didn't have to go, but that we were welcome. We asked them when breakfast was, and they just said it would be after the service. Then they invited us to the service again.

We were grateful for their hospitality, but we weren't interested in the service. What we wanted to do most was rest and eat, not worship. We told them we'd probably sleep in, and they mentioned the service a few more times before saying goodnight.

Back in our cabin, we saw that our gift baskets contained some newsprint literature that looked like it was from the '70s. There were all sorts of illustrations and black-and-white pictures that talked about various aspects of their beliefs. It mentioned "tribes" and "the 144,000 chosen." It talked about the "end times" and the last book of the Bible: Revelation. We learned more about this group that called themselves a "tribe."

According to the literature, they didn't have any individual money. When someone joined the tribe, they gave up all their possessions. They also changed their names. So it turned out that Tobiah was not originally called Tobiah. That was the "biblical" name they'd given him when he moved in. It all felt a little weird, and the kids didn't really like it. However, we had beds and pillows and nice meals, and we thought of all the money we were saving. The promise of sleeping in let us drift off soundly.

At 7:30 the next morning, there was a knock on our door. We were all still asleep and just ignored it, but thirty seconds later, it came again, louder. Kami and I looked at each other and groaned. We opened the door and it was Tobiah, asking if we were awake and wanted to go to the service at 8:00 a.m. Rainier was now awake and hungry, so we figured we might as well go and see if we could get breakfast.

The kids and I went to the service while Kami went hunting for coffee. The meeting was an open format where anyone could share at any time. One lady stood up and spoke about how she had sinned but wanted to make it right. She talked about how unworthy she was and how there was nothing she could do to make the badness go away. Trying to find a way to connect, I shared how we'd come to value a day of rest, and how stopping work helped us find value in who we were and not in what we did.

Meanwhile, Kami met a man outside who wasn't part of the community but stayed there each summer. He explained that he helped out on the farm and got to stay for free. When she asked about coffee, he said the community didn't drink it. They once did but had been told by the "higher ups" not to do so anymore. They were only allowed to drink the yerba mate that grew on their own farms and directly profited those higher up. Thankfully, he had some contraband coffee that he brewed in the shower house, and he kindly offered Kami some.

Alarm bells started to go off in Kami's head. Everyone at the farm was welcoming and kind, but something felt off. She joined back up with us over at the tent where the service was wrapping up and breakfast was beginning. Just as she arrived, one of the wives walked over to us and struck up a conversation.

"I loved what you shared this morning about your rest days," she told me. "Can you tell me more?"

I started talking about how we came to take rest days after our trip to Jerusalem, but before I could finish my sentence, she interrupted me, talking about the tribes in the book of Revelation and how they were part of the 144,000 chosen.

We could tell she hadn't actually been interested in what I shared. She was just using the conversation to start her pitch, which felt completely scripted. She and a couple of others brought out the Bible and started talking about the 144,000 of the remnant in Revelation. Because we grew up with the Bible, we knew what they were referencing, but their interpretations were things we'd never heard before—they were based off of obscure passages. We instantly felt claustrophobic and trapped; the kids went quiet.

We asked about getting a ride back to the trail. Originally, they'd offered to take us back anytime, but now they were saying it may work better if we stayed for lunch and maybe another night. Everything was free, they said, and we could stay as long as we wanted. We couldn't afford a zero day, but the thought of free food was so hard to turn down. We simply couldn't get these kinds of calories on the trail.

And then I looked over at Dove and Eden. The look in both their eyes said, *Get us the hell out of here!*

> The whole reason we had opted to stay here was for a morale boost, but it had backfired. The extra calories weren't worth the tingling of our Spidey senses telling us something was very wrong.

I looked at Kami and said quietly, "We need to go."

After some more haggling, a few of the tribe members finally agreed to take us back to the trail. "You're welcome back anytime!" they said as we waved goodbye to everyone on the farm.

It was a silent ride back to the trail, with our driver chattering obliviously while we all sat uneasily in our seats, wanting nothing more than to be back in the relative safety of the woods. When we arrived at the trailhead, he wouldn't let us go, describing another location farther up the trail in Vermont with great food and people who would host us. After about a million attempts to end the conversation, we finally got away and disappeared into the trees.

Back on the trail, we joked about the pamphlets and the coffee. Filia and Memory had found the whole experience funny, but the older kids were more freaked out.

"Everyone at that place talked in a really eerie way," Eden said. "It was almost like they were brainwashed."

I knew what she meant. None of the kids at the farm had their own opinions. When we'd asked them questions, they'd given short answers that seemed memorized, or looked to adults to speak for them. It was a stark contrast to the Crawford kids, who were outgoing and opinionated, perfectly happy to speak for themselves. It reminded Kami and I of where we'd come from as kids ourselves— being afraid to say the wrong thing, totally preoccupied with "behaving."

Later that day, at a water stop, we ran into a group of thru-hikers who were discussing a podcast they were listening to. It was called *Cults*, and there were two episodes on a cult in Virginia that was fixated on being in the chosen tribe of the 144,000.

Our whole family looked at each other wide-eyed. We had spent the night with a cult?

We learned that the cult goes back to the '70s and has around three thousand members. Their founder was incredibly wealthy and went through three or four wives. They were famous for hiding children from their parents, changing the children's names to biblical-sounding ones, then sending them around the world to their different locations. The podcast ended by saying that this cult is "alive and well, currently set up, and recruiting needy hikers along the Appalachian Trail."

We felt like we'd barely escaped. Kami and I were mortified. Here we were getting hate comments about our kids being cold—imagine what the internet people would say when they found out we'd exposed our kids to a cult! At least the food was good.

In a lot of ways, it also felt like the marathon; if it was a mistake, it was a mistake that none of us regretted. It gave us a great story to tell. Back home, we watched documentaries about cults on Netflix. On the A.T., we had lived for a night inside of one.

5·26·18
THE PLACE WE ARE
STAYING AT IS LIKE
A CLAN OF
"CHRISTIANS", THEY ALL
LIVE ON THIS FARM,
AND ON SHABBAT
THE GIRLS WEAR
DRESSES AND EVERYONE
DANCES AND SINGS.
BEING HERE MAKES
ME MISS HOME
EVEN MORE

Eden (15) and all the kids recognized traits in the ways the children behaved from our earlier, more religious parenting methods: quiet, well-behaved, and submissive.

That night, we got an email from Tobiah.

"What an amazing gift it was to host you and your family. God obviously brought us together. I will be praying for y'all and your epic journey. If you have any pictures or videos of us, please make them positive and we would love if any feedback you give would encourage people to come stay with us rather than discourage them. I love what you shared with us at the morning gathering and will keep you all near to my heart and in my daily prayers. My prayer for you is that you will remember what you learned here and know there is always a place for you to come when you need us. Hopefully you can stay with our friends in Vermont. If you do, tell them that Tobiah sent you."

CHAPTER SIXTEEN

The Grind

"[Rest] is not simply a pause. It is an occasion for reimagining
all of social life away from coercion and competition to com-
passionate solidarity."

—Walter Brueggemann

It had been weeks since we'd taken a zero day. The days blurred
together. We hiked sixteen miles, twenty-one miles, thirteen
miles, seventeen miles, eighteen miles, and seventeen miles.
Since our last zero day in Washington, DC, we'd increased our mileage to try and catch up with Hops and The Degenerates. We also
knew if we stood any chance of seeing the A-frame sign at the top of
Katahdin, we had to make miles. We started to call walking "grinding." Our legs were the factory, and each day was spent grinding as
many miles as we could.

We were getting stronger. Our legs felt like rocks. We got used to
the soreness. Our new shoes prevented our feet from hurting, and

we spent our time fine-tuning our efficiency. But our reinvigorated pace brought a new challenge: our lives were now consumed with walking. We'd wake up and start walking as soon as possible. We kept breaks short. We often arrived at camp in the dark after as much walking as was humanly possible for us.

I'd spent much of my work life as an entrepreneur, choosing what I wanted to do. Now, the trail sometimes felt like just another job. I had to clock in and clock out. It felt like the same thing every day. I started to wonder about diminishing returns; had we already experienced what we wanted on the trail? Did we need to go on when hiking felt so tedious and meaningless? It felt like a vacation that had run its course. We remembered the wisdom of not quitting on a bad day, but what about quitting after a bunch of monotonous and tedious days?

To keep on going, we had to think back on our original intention for starting the trip. It wasn't a vacation in the typical sense. We didn't go to the A.T. to escape our lives; we wanted to create an experience that would change our lives. So when we looked at our new normal, we didn't ask if we liked it, but rather, did we have a better alternative for bringing our family together back home?

We couldn't think of anything. Sure, we were miserable, but we knew the feeling we would get from going home. The comfort and rest would be nice, but after three or four days, we'd be right back to our old discontent. Plus, the walking gave us time to process some of the things we'd recently been through in our lives. Over the last three years, we had lost our entire community based upon spiritual decisions we had made. Most of Kami's family had stopped speaking to us, cutting us out of their lives entirely—just weeks before our hike, we'd endured a difficult, stressful split of the family business, for which we'd moved to Kentucky in the first place. There had been a lot of pain, therapy, and sleepless nights. We, and especially Kami, still had a lot of grieving to do, but that processing had been pushed to the side by the ever-present distractions of our lives back home.

In 1948, Earl Shaffer became the first person to thru-hike the Appalachian Trail after his service in World War II. He said he walked the A.T. to "walk off the war." Kami's family didn't even know about our hike. Much of her time on the trail was spent venting, processing, and working through the pain she still felt. She said she was using the trail to "walk off her family." So even though the sense of adventure had worn off, we decided hiking was better than returning to the numbing comfort of home. As long as we were still processing, and until we had something better to do, we wouldn't quit.

Our grueling and monotonous pace had a cost, and it wasn't just physical. One startling moment came in June. We woke up and started walking almost mindlessly. We didn't know what state we were in or what day it was. All we knew was we had to move, and we were never fast enough. We'd worked so hard to create freedom and teach our kids they were good enough as they were; now, our method of hiking was teaching them the exact opposite. No amount of miles was enough.

We had to make it to Katahdin. But what if we didn't? Would our already difficult journey feel like a waste?

Asking this question was making me push the kids harder than ever. Every break was counted down and timed; as soon as we arrived at camp at night, we would begin to mentally prepare to leave the next morning. I could barely remember who I was or why we were doing this.

At the thought of this, I broke down again and cried.

We had become thru-hikers first and humans second. Identities can creep in and take over at any time in life. When you think of yourself as an employee, a boss, or an A student, you prioritize elements that prop up those identities and push aside the things you really need in life, like relationships.

> There was a chance we could finish this hike, but it wouldn't be worth it if we lost ourselves in the process.

As we were walking, I shared my feelings with Kami and we both agreed that we needed to change something or find a solution. After two hours of walking we came up with an idea. We decided to implement regular rest days. We'd get more miles during the week, so that by Fridays, we could wake up extra early and hike a whole day's worth of miles by 3:00 p.m. Then, upon arriving in a town, we could have a meal, watch a movie, and do anything other than think about the trail. We'd sleep in, have a nice breakfast—which simply meant something warm that wasn't a Pop-Tart—and get back to the trail with enough time to get at least ten miles in. This plan would cost us five miles a week, which we'd have to make up in the other six days. But we'd gain almost twenty hours in which we weren't thru-hikers. We would just be human. We'd still have some jobs to do, like laundry and video editing, but we were okay with that because the most important thing was that we didn't have to take a zero—something we couldn't afford to do anymore.

Back home, Kami and I made life-changing decisions once or twice a year that shifted the course of our family. Out on the trail, it felt like we were needing to make them once a week just to survive.

Our first rest day created an instant boost. We lounged in a coffee shop and sipped kombucha and lattes while the kids played board games. We journaled and read and even sent out some postcards to friends. Then we went to an ice cream shop. Our twenty hours off trail actually changed the time we spent walking. It started to feel optional, and we even saw some joy return to the monotony of walking. The boredom and difficulty didn't disappear, but states started to fly by. West Virginia was only four miles long—a breeze compared to the 550 miles of Virginia. Maryland, a state we'd never been in before, was forty miles long and took us only three days. But the biggest benefit was not our increased speed; it was the fact that we were able to remember who we were and why we started walking to begin with.

SPACE TO HEAR THEIR DREAMS

On Day 96, more than three months after we started the A.T., we hit the trail late, at around 9:00 a.m. We'd crossed the Mason-Dixon line—the symbolic divide between the northern and southern states—and entered into Pennsylvania, the most notorious state on the A.T. In the garage eighteen years earlier, when we first heard about the A.T., Penguin and T-Time told us of the rocks in Pennsylvania. Hikers nicknamed the place Rocksylvania. There's a stretch about one hundred miles long where ankle-twisting rocks are known to shred shoes, and venomous copperhead snakes lurk in cracks underfoot.

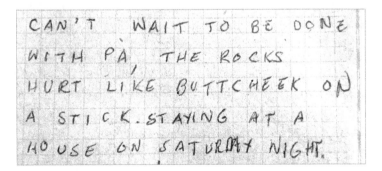

Eden (15) definitely has a way with words. The constantly changing weather and terrain brought us all new things to complain about.

We were all in a bad mood. We'd been driven more than an hour off trail to someone's house and had spent the night in a room covered in cat hair. The room below us, where the kids slept, had a radio blasting classic rock all night long. We could hear it through the cat-piss-stained carpet. Our hosts had fed us off-brand soda with white bread and margarine. We were trying to be grateful, but the "help" seemed to actually lower our morale instead of boost it, and we arrived on the trail two hours later than planned.

Then it started to rain.

We had a difficult decision to make. We were running low on food, but the next town, Hamburg, was 23.6 miles away. The classic advice was to lower the miles in Pennsylvania, even in good weather. With the rain, the already sketchy rocks were slippery, making them more dangerous. But Eden, who was in charge of lunch, told us that the lunch supplies were perilously low. We ate Nutella wraps—one jar of Nutella spread out on twelve tortillas, using a stick we found on the side of the trail as a butter knife. The wraps were so sweet and sticky they clung to our throats and were hard to chew. It didn't matter how hungry we were or if we enjoyed them—we needed the calories. We washed them down with stream water, but we were sick of drinking. Staying hydrated felt like a job. Eden said this was the last time she was doing Nutella wraps.

All together, we had a discussion about the pros and cons of pushing through to the town. At this point, we were still nineteen miles away, and it was lunchtime. I was struggling from the unsettled night and didn't have the motivation to push the kids, which had been my role so far.

Kami said, "We might make it by ten p.m. if we're lucky. That's without taking any breaks."

Dove thought it would be fun to have a challenge that pushed us. Filia was less confident: "Um, I want to get to the hotel, but I don't want to do it because it'll be really hard...but yeah, like, I want to stay in a hotel tonight and have good food..."

Then we found out two things. One: the only hotel in town was all booked up. So that was off the table.

Two: there was a Red Robin in town. Red Robin was a burger joint from Seattle that served unlimited fries. I'd even worked for them sixteen years ago as a server while I was trying to pay for Kami to get through nursing school.

We had zero ability to say no to unlimited fries. We saw it as a sign.

"What do you think, guys?" I asked the kids. Both Kami and I were keenly aware that we might be reaching their breaking point.

But they were enthusiastic. "Let's do it!" Memory said, and the other kids echoed her. The pull of Red Robin was strong.

We decided to go for it. We put our heads down and knew, for the next ten hours, we'd be doing nothing but walking. The only thing we had to take our minds off the pain in our legs was the rain and each other. The younger kids walked up ahead chatting with each other. Dove and Eden hung back near us. Usually, Kami and I would have our own conversation while our older kids talked.

The only trouble was, by that point, Kami and I had talked about everything there was to talk about. Seventeen years of marriage, and we'd never run out of conversation before—but the trail had done it!

We were bored of each other, and Kami, as an introvert, just didn't want to talk anymore.

We'd started walking about a quarter mile apart because Kami needed space from the socialization that I craved. Even though we spent so much time together, it was easy to feel lonely in the woods.

I edged up closer to Dove and Eden. For years, all Kami and I had heard was that teenage girls were a nightmare, and it's "impossible to connect with them." We'd hear friends say things like, "I've just become a human ATM machine" and "Oh, just wait till your kids are teenagers. Mine just mope around demanding to go to the mall."

On this afternoon, with the nearest mall seemingly worlds away, I had the chance to test those theories. I struck up a conversation with the girls. The topic was: the future.

And once again, my kids blew me away.

Out of nowhere, Dove began to share all about her dream life. She talked about where she would live, and how her brothers and sisters would all be on the same block. She described how when they all had kids, the siblings could take turns schooling each other's nieces and nephews in the subjects they were each passionate about. She talked about how she'd spend her time every week. She spent twenty-five minutes describing the kitchen in her dream house. She wanted a gas stove and high-end appliances; she wanted cast-iron pans and exposed cupboards like we had; she imagined a big coffee bar with a lot of counter space; she wanted good lighting and lots of containers to store baking supplies. (I related hard—in my opinion, the kitchen is the most important room in the house!)

The whole time Dove was talking, I never said a word, but inside, I was beaming. I didn't care if any of the dreams actually came true, and didn't spend time trying to critique them. I just took it as an opportunity to listen to our child share her heart. She was willing to be vulnerable, and she had my total uninterrupted attention. I got to know her better. It was one of the best gifts I received on the trail.

KIDS AS A GIFT, NOT A PROJECT

At 4:45 p.m., we crossed the 1,200-mile mark on our trip in the rain. We had less than one thousand miles left to go. We also got some good news when we called the hotel back: they had one room available. It was a smoking room with two queen beds, and although it would be the smallest accommodations we would have the entire trip, we didn't care. At least, it would be dry, and by now, the room was only ten miles away.

With three miles left, it was completely dark and pouring rain. We all stopped to pull out our headlamps. As soon as the lights flashed on, we could see that Filia was not doing very well. She was completely worn out. We gave her an energy gel pack with caffeine, the kind they give you during marathons. We'd been carrying it since Georgia just for emergencies. She was feeling better within a few minutes, so we started down the trail, following the little white circle of rocks lit by our headlamps.

We talked about the food we'd order. I wanted the Banzai burger, a teriyaki-grilled patty topped with a teriyaki-glazed grilled pineapple. It had "the big three," as Red Robin staff called it: mayonnaise, lettuce, and tomato. Of course, I would add extra pickles. Reciting memories of old training materials, I described how the Red Robin Smiling Burger was supposed to "wow" guests with "each ingredient fresh and visible 100 percent of the time, with the bun wrapped tightly but never torn." The kids were captivated. We talked about how we would dip the hot fries in the cold ranch, and I let the kids know about the honey mustard, which was sweet and complemented the saltiness of the fries.

As we walked through the most miserable situation down a steep section of trail, we laughed as our dreams of hot food became more and more detailed. Later, we learned that this section of trail was responsible for more ER visits than any other part of the A.T. We did it in the dark, while it was raining. But even though our bodies ached from the miles and we were soaking, even though we knew we'd soon be piled into one bedroom with two beds that stank with cigarette smoke, our main memory of that night was enjoying each other's company.

Growing up in the Western world, we had learned to treat our children as a project. We thought our primary job was to prepare our kids to be morally, academically, and financially prepared. These are great goals to have for our kids, but when life revolves around reaching those goals, it was hard to see kids as a true gift. To just enjoy them. Parenting becomes its own kind of grind—the same thing day in and day out, focused more on the destination than the journey. Most of parenting had been based on the premise that we were further along than our kids. That we had something to offer them based upon our age and wisdom as a parent. But on the A.T., we were figuring it out together. We were equals. And without the pressure to parent, we were free to simply enjoy our kids as fellow travelers. Our kids became companions, not projects. Our relationships with them were gifts, not jobs.

By simply being present with our kids, we could offer a simple gift back: ourselves. Most of our parenting years had been focused on the accomplishments of our kids. We thought about how quickly they could walk or read or learn their ABCs or Bible verses. As we grew as parents, we focused less on trying to change and form our kids into what we thought they should be, and spent more energy observing their uniquenesses and enjoying them for who they were in each moment. And if the trail took us one step closer in being able to see our kids as a gift, the rain and blizzards, the monotony and miles would be worth it.

At 10:16 p.m., we walked into the Red Robin in Hamburg, Pennsylvania, fourteen minutes before it closed. Less than ten minutes later, we had six baskets of fries in front of us with ramekins of ranch dressing and honey mustard. We toasted to our longest day on the A.T. at 23.6 miles. Less than three miles short of a full marathon, in the rain, with our packs, carrying a baby on the toughest terrain we had encountered. I was drinking a Blue Moon, Kami a Cherry Coke, and Rainier a plastic kids' cup of chocolate milk with a straw. Everyone had a smile on their face, and we were all laughing and talking about the day.

Seven said, "I never thought we'd get to this moment. I was dreaming of it, but I didn't think it would happen."

"Right now, it feels really worth it," Eden chimed in. "I'm eating fries. I feel like I'll know more tomorrow, but right now, I don't regret it."

Filia, who was feeling better, looked over as she was coloring on the kids' menu and had the last word. "It was worth it."

CHAPTER SEVENTEEN

"Real Hiking" or Not?

"It (trying to keep the law) grants you the power to judge oth-
ers and feel superior to them. You believe you are living to a
higher standard than those you judge. Enforcing rules...is a
vain attempt to create certainty out of uncertainty. ...Rules
cannot bring freedom; they only have the power to accuse."

—William P. Young

Pennsylvania was hard.

Wonderful moments like we had at Red Robin didn't change the fact that we'd been hiking nonstop for sixteen days. The warnings we'd heard about the terrain hadn't been wrong: it was nonstop rocks that chewed up our shoes and required careful, slow, tedious work. Shepherding six kids across dozens of miles of slippery rocks without a single twisted ankle was a testament to how carefully we put one foot in front of the other.

To pass the time in the steep, rocky, highly technical portions of Pennsylvania, we made up songs.

The kids wrote a song about one particularly dangerous section to the tune of "Dumb Ways to Die," which was a rip-off of an Australian Metro Trains song that had gone viral back in 2012. We all took turns adding lines of dumb ways we could die on the rocks as we climbed the steepest hill of our hike.

Eden: Vlogging while walking on a bunch of boulders...

Filia: ...while carrying a fat baby on your shoulders...

Seven: ...eating carrots that are out of date, hiking on the A.T. when it's way too late...

Memory: ...hiking on this trail for days, following that dumb white blaze...

Dove: ...duuuuuumb ways to di-ieee! So many dumb ways to die.

In the heat, Eden quietly carried Rainier for 90 percent of that section. She didn't complain for a single moment.

The trail allowed us time and space to know what was going on inside our kids' minds and hearts like never before, but it helped to be intentional in hearing about what they thought. Every night, we went around the circle sharing the highs and lows of the day. We called it "tent time."

I shared about getting a message offering us a place to stay. Kami shared about the lunch break by the stream. Dove shared how hard it was to miss our friends. Eden shared that it had been three days since she'd showered. Seven said he hated waking up at 6:30 a.m. Memory recounted swimming in the river and collecting berries. Filia said she didn't like it when she tripped and got her hands dirty. And Rainier said he liked gummy bears. There were no wrong answers.

Back when I was in recovery for addiction, I'd been a frequent participant in twelve-step groups. There, I'd heard a helpful phrase in twelve-step groups: "No crosstalk." This simply meant you were not allowed to respond to anyone's sharing with anything but the affirmative "Thanks for sharing." This was a helpful tool, and we implemented the rule at tent time. For us parents, this meant we were taking off our parenting hats that tended to try and provide solutions or critique. Instead, we focused on just being present and accepting each kid's perspective. It was hard at first, but we had observed this tactic made our kids want to come to us more and share things, knowing that we weren't going to try and fix them.

But the night of that difficult section of trail, some feedback was shared during tent time that made Kami and I feel terrible.

Eden spoke up quietly, obviously in the throes of an inner battle between her emotions and not wanting to complain. "I carried Rainier during that entire difficult section, and nobody even said, 'Good job,'" she said. "It was hard enough, but not being appreciated made it harder."

Honestly, this revelation stung. It was like she was saying that, though we were exhausted and felt like we were trying our best and doing everything we could, Kami and I weren't doing enough. It made me wonder again if I was pushing the kids too hard. Some of the meaner online comments crept back into my mind. I had to push all this pain down, though, and focus on our daughter and her needs.

If I was parenting in crosstalking mode, I would have said, "Buck up. You're not going to get compliments for everything in life. Stop feeling sorry for yourself." But the no-crosstalk rule forced me to pause, to set my ego aside. I was able to see Eden's expression as a gift and was grateful she'd shared her disappointment with us. It allowed us all to know her better. We could all identify with a time when we felt unappreciated or unrecognized for our hard work. Eden trusted us with her feelings and allowed us that opportunity.

> Accepting a child means accepting all of them, taking the
> good with the bad, the successes with the disappointments.
> We don't get to pick and choose. We can only decide if
> we'll accept the reality of our whole child or deny
> it, pushing them to share themselves elsewhere.

The next day, I apologized to Eden. "Sorry I never said anything before. It's easy for me to get self-absorbed, but I think what you accomplished is awesome and it has been an incredible help for you to carry Rainier. Thank you."

She looked back and smiled. "You're welcome."

Over the next day, I would find time to go to each of my kids and point out how much I appreciated their help and contribution to our trip. Eden vocalized what, deep down, everyone needed.

Tent time was a simple way to get a pulse on how everyone was. This helped us parents make decisions based on a constantly changing morale. But this wasn't the only benefit. We found our kids performed so much better throughout the day when they felt they had a place they could be heard (or even vent) every night. We were all going though incredibly strenuous experiences and pushing ourselves physically and emotionally every single day. Our kids had an incredible ability to put out the effort when they felt like they were valued and heard. The same is true for every person we've ever met, honestly. And the reverse is true: when someone doesn't feel valued or heard, their desire to participate in a job or relationship disappears.

Tent time was a constant opportunity to see the trail experience through the kids' eyes. We saw that kids could get the same benefits from the trail as any adult. In these conversations, we learned to treat our children like mini adults, valuing their stories, hearts, and opinions as much as those of our friends. While we sometimes used simpler words, the connection between us and our small humans was not at all diminished by their size or vocabulary.

Later, we found out the rocky section from that day Eden carried Rainier was called Lehigh Gap and is notorious for its difficulty. Ask any thru-hiker what their least favorite state is, and they'll say, "Pennsylvania!" For the rest of our time on the trail, people asked us, "How did you do on Lehigh Gap?"

Each time they asked, we pointed to Eden.

SLACKPACKING

On Day 100, we were met at the trail by a family named the Hesses. Their son, Tylor, had hiked the trail the year before and contacted us about helping out. His email said:

Hey Crawford Family!

My hometown (East Stroudsburg), where I grew up and my parents live is ~four miles from the Delaware Water Gap (mile 1294.7).

You're welcome to stay with us as long as you'd like.

We're happy to have you over for dinner.

We're happy to give you a ride, rescue you from the weather, or help you resupply.

I know what it's like to feel the need to "put in the miles," and I don't want to impede on your progress, so please let us know what works best for you.

Please email, call, or text. Hopefully, we can work something out! I look forward to meeting you IRL.

The Hesses had a suburban mansion they drove our family to. They made us cocktails and appetizers before dinner, gave us cigars, and then offered to slackpack us.

All along the trail, we'd seen people "slackpacking"—an activity frowned upon by many thru-hiking purists. Slackpacking was hiking without your pack. There were many ways this was accomplished, and they were all inefficient. The first time we heard of it was back in Virginia, when we were hiking north and saw a man up ahead coming toward us who looked familiar. It was Hops. He was going south, and he didn't have a pack on. He told us he was staying at a hostel that, for a small fee, would drop people fifteen miles up trail. Then they could hike back to the hostel and their packs. This meant you could still hike all the miles on the trail but with less weight, faster hiking, sometimes being able to avoid hiking up large hills (because you could take it in reverse) and shower two nights in a row. The next day, the hostel would drive them back up, and they'd resume the trail as normal.

This kind of trail-hacking seemed to violate the spirit of the A.T. Slackpacking seemed lazy, luxurious, and wasteful. As hikers who didn't slackpack, we felt we had a moral high ground over those who did. We were on a journey. Many hikers see their heavy packs as a badge of honor, not something to be avoided. The harder the trail was, the better. We were accomplishing something, not cobbling together a bunch of miles in the most efficient and comfortable way possible.

Then there was the cost. Slackpacking was usually provided by hostels to get an extra night off you, and they also charged for the multiple shuttle rides involved. For us, this crossed a line. It felt like cheating.

But now we were in a different situation. We woke up at the Hess's on Saturday, the day we were attempting to rest. We planned to hit the trail and head north, sleeping in the woods. It was pouring rain, and we were exhausted from the push through Pennsylvania. Tylor had been speaking in hushed tones with his parents. Then he came to us with an idea.

The family said they'd love to have us for another night of cocktails and cigars. Tylor had hatched a plan where his parents could drop us off, we could still hike 8.5 miles that day, and we'd end up back at the house for dinner and showers. And to accomplish this, we would just leave our packs at the house, taking nothing but our rain jackets, a few snacks, and the carrier for Rainier. We knew the excited look we'd get from the kids if we suggested another night in this mansion.

It forced us to ask ourselves how important our arbitrary rule of hiking purity actually was. We wondered how slackpacking would make us feel when we reached the A-frame sign at the top of Mount Katahdin. Many people hike the last three miles to the sign with their packs just for the picture, even though they will return to the parking lot without using anything in their packs that day. Would we feel like we cheated if we started hiking without our packs? What is cheating? Whose rules were important, and who made them, anyways? Would be able to live with ourselves if we broke them? We wouldn't know until we got there.

We thought back to our arbitrary rule from early on of avoiding hotels—it had been a huge game-changer to ditch that rule and stay in towns when we could.

And here was this family offering to help us. By saying no to protect our purity code, we would be denying them the ability to be a part of our journey. Once again, we thought back to Arnie-1-Mile's words: "Hike your own hike." We had changed so much. It made sense that the way we hiked would also change. Instead of asking if we were following the rules, we asked some new questions:

What was best for our group?

What do we want to do?

These questions sound simple, but we were never able to ask them as long as our focus was on the rules around us that everyone else had created. Now it was obvious. We knew it was time to say goodbye to our pride and the self-imposed ban on slackpacking. It was time to hike our own hike. So we said, "Screw it. Let's go."

Tylor joined us on the trail for that day, and without the packs weighing us down, we felt like we were flying. In the toughest state, we were going five miles per hour, in the rain, which for us was unheard of. We were used to doing about two miles an hour. We still had Rainier, but we were sharing that load, and for the first time, everyone experienced what it was like to hike without a pack. We hit the trail at 3:00 p.m. and did the whole 8.5 miles in less than two hours, laughing and running most of the way.

At 5:00 p.m., we crossed the border from Pennsylvania to New Jersey thirty minutes ahead of schedule. We were soaking wet, covered in mud, and smiling from ear to ear. It was the happiest we'd seen the kids in weeks. Tylor's parents arrived, and back to the mansion we went. There, we put our soaking clothes into the laundry, took hot showers, and celebrated with cocktails and cigars while the kids watched *The Incredibles*, one of their favorite movies, on the big-screen TV.

It was amazing to reflect on how far we had come. We thought back to our feelings when everyone was sick on Day 4 back at Blood Mountain Cabins: "We didn't start the A.T. because we were brave, but we did believe it would make us brave. We didn't start because we knew we had what it takes. We were just confident we'd pick up what it would take along the way."

Those first four days, we had struggled to get 8.5 miles a day. We were afraid of the rain. The result was pain, discouragement, and lack of confidence. Today, we had just killed 8.5 miles through pouring rain, in less than two hours, as an afternoon break. In a way, that day's miles felt like a party, and we were laughing about it with our new friends, who had offered us their fine cigars and booze.

The experience reminded us to be open to new perspectives on hiking, and not to get too attached to any particular rule set. We clearly had two options in front of us. We could try and remain purists, which meant satisfying an unwritten code of hiking that varied from person to person and was constantly changing—but was always, no matter what, strict and uncomfortable. Or we could challenge our self-constructed identities as thru-hikers and simply hike our own hike.

Slackpacking released any elitism, any sense of what the trail "should" be, prioritizing the experience we thought was best for our children and accepting help when it was offered.

For the rest of the trail, when we received an offer for slackpacking, we accepted it. It helped us feel incredibly light, and it allowed us to receive from others in yet another way. People wanted to help us. Several even took time off work to do so. It was obvious people truly believed in our journey and wanted to be part of it in some way. Some of our offers to slackpack came on weekends, which was a huge morale booster and helped us reinforce a rest day while still getting miles in. And so we adopted some new guidelines:

1. We would never pay for slackpacking as a service.
2. We would accept slackpacking whenever it was offered by a stranger.
3. When slackpacking, we would only move north.

It was humbling to "lower" our standards, but we could see that the trail offered the most to us when not used as a weapon to take the moral high ground over others. We realized others who had slackpacked earlier had perhaps been able to enjoy more aspects of the trail—while we were busy deriving our identity from an arbitrary and rigid standard. We realized if we were going to make the trail work for us and truly hike our own hike, we had to let go of any rigid ideas we formed before we even started.

It was the perfect time to make this decision too—because the trail was about to get even rockier. Literally.

6/1/18 92# PA FRIDAY
THIS MORNING WAS
KIND OF ROUGH BUT
AFTER LOSEING SAINTY
IN A SWARM OF MOSQIUTOS
A GETTING IT BACK
EATING ICECREAM,
WE ATE AN AWESOME
DINNER THAT SOME V
NICE PEOPLE BROUGHT
US. AND WALKED 2 MORE
MILES TO A SHELTER.
TOMOROW IS GOING TO
BE A LONG DAY, BUT
WE ARE STAYING AT A
HOTEL W/ A POOL THAT
SOME PEOPLE ARE PAYING
FOR. I'M FILTHEX
FILTHY RIGHT NOW.

For Eden (15) and the rest of us, the incredible difficulty of hiking,
bugs, and weather were always offset by the kindness we received
from people who invited us into their homes, bought us meals,
and in a few instances, even paid for a night at a hotel!

CHAPTER EIGHTEEN

"If You Make It to New York"

"It takes all of us to succeed, but only one of us to fail."

—Warren Doyle

What the Appalachian Trail guidebooks don't tell you is that the dreaded rocks don't stop at the Pennsylvania border. For several dozen miles after we crossed into New Jersey, the tough, picky, rocky terrain persisted.

But our family's morale was uplifted by crossing into a new state, and gradually, the rocks and venomous snakes disappeared. Our mileage picked up as we knocked out the seventy-two miles of New Jersey. We did 16.2 miles, 16.4 miles, 17.7 miles, and 17.7 miles, and before we knew it, we'd passed through yet another state. We were in New York.

Months earlier, before leaving for the trail, we'd done a livestream on YouTube, answering questions and saying goodbye. One guy, who called himself Stan the Man, commented, saying, "If you ever make it to New York, I'll buy you guys ice cream at Bellvale Farms Creamery, which has the best ice cream on the trail." At the time, New York seemed like a world away, and although we appreciated the offer, we didn't think much of it.

When we actually made it to New York, three and a half months had passed, so we didn't know if Stan the Man's offer was still good. After all, we'd only interacted with him once on the internet. But sure enough, he reached out to us as we got closer, and planned to drive two hours from New York City to meet us and take our packs so we could slackpack the last ten miles to the ice cream shop.

We arrived at Bellvale Farms Creamery by noon that day, full of energy. Stan said, "Get whatever you want! It's on me!" I ordered a banana milkshake made with six scoops of coconut ice cream and a whole banana. Kami got three scoops of coffee ice cream with a waffle cone and a cold bottle of birch beer. The kids couldn't believe they were allowed to order whatever they wanted; back home, we always shared dishes and never, ever got the waffle cone.

The ice cream really was the best we had on the trail, and the creamery had a log book where hikers signed their names. We opened it up and immediately zoomed in on a recent entry: Hops got his ice cream fix. He'd been there just the day before!

After more than a month and five hundred miles of trying, we were within a day of catching up to Hops. We wrote in the log book: "Crawfords, hot on his trail."

As a special surprise for the kids, we planned to attend the opening of *Incredibles 2* at the movie theater that night. We'd been looking forward to the movie ever since the first one, but none of the kids knew it was coming out because we had been away from the television for so long. After the creamery, we told them we'd go see the movie.

But there was a catch. We had to hike another twelve miles. At the beginning of the A.T., it took us a day and a half to hike twelve miles. Now, leaving our packs with Stan the Man and with more than one hundred days of walking under our belts, we were thankful for the opportunity. So, at 3:00 p.m., with bellies full of ice cream, we set off, feeling like we were on vacation. This was the power of being cared for by someone else and gaining the perspective to appreciate it.

As we went, we had a few amazing views. In one, we could see tiny gray sticks poking out over a distant green hill. It was the skyline of New York City. We could even make out the Empire State Building. Having spent some of our family's favorite moments in NYC—with Dove on her thirteenth birthday, and on a family field trip where we watched the eight-part, 17.5-hour New York documentary series and visited all the locations we learned about—it was like seeing an old friend in the distance. This was my favorite sight of the trip.

After ten miles, showers, and dinner, we walked in ten minutes late to the 9:45 p.m. showing of the movie. Even though *Incredibles 2* was a massive disappointment, that was one of our most memorable days on the trail.

It was Friday night and the start of our rest period. We wouldn't feel guilty sleeping in the next day because with Stan the Man slack-packing us the entire day, we had gotten twenty-two miles of hiking in, even with the stop at the creamery.

A TOUGH CHOICE

Even though moments like meeting Stan added relief to our trip, the facts didn't change: we had been hiking our biggest mile counts for nonstop days, sometimes from dawn to dusk. It was a grind, pure and simple. On the trail, we often grew frustrated and disappointed with each other. There were times we wanted to strangle our kids. This was high-pressure hiking that required all our physical faculties. We felt we could never mentally rest with our goal hanging over us, and the nature of sleeping in the woods meant we were always dependent on the weather, other people, and many things outside our control. As the team leader, I felt incredible pressure to keep the team moving forward, as though our progress was resting directly on my shoulders.

Before we arrived in New York, Seven started complaining about the trail and our pace. In addition to the hiking, Seven had been editing videos for one hour every night, often after the rest of us went to sleep. The videos had all started to feel the same. Trail life and the rigid pace felt unnatural and frustrating to him.

Complaining was a regular part of hiking. And while Kami and I had constantly reevaluated our reasons for being on the hike, working through numerous primary motivations to stay motivated over the course of three months, Seven's motivation was not clear. And without a clear motivation of his own, all that was left was complaining. We were always talking about our feet and our knees and our hunger and our shoulders. But his complaining was different. It was complaining about the whole trip. The complaining about our knees and shoulders went away the second we took our packs off every night and ate a bag of Doritos and mac and cheese. But this other, deeper complaining did not go away at night. It followed us to the next morning. "I don't like this." "I don't want to be here." "It would be so much better to be at home." "My friends don't have to hike." Seven's complaining crossed a fine line into blaming—mostly directed toward Kami, for the simple reason that she was willing to listen. "You guys made me do this." "You don't give us long enough breaks." "I don't want to edit."

We grew frustrated with Seven and the guilt he made us feel. Every time he complained, Kami would rethink the entire hike. She barely had the energy to take her pack off every night, let alone constantly reevaluate every decision we made. "Maybe the trip wasn't worth it," she'd often lament after a particularly brutal round of objections from Seven. We were fine with asking the question before, after, or every once in a while during the hike, but to be asking it ten times a day while hiking was not feasible. It was obvious Kami's desire to listen combined with her limited energy was unsustainable. We just wanted the complaints and blaming to end.

Even though Seven's behavior seemed normal for a thirteen-year-old boy, we weren't content with leaving it unaddressed. It would have been easy tell him to "shut up" or "be thankful" or remind him how good he had it compared to other hikers—or, hell, flick him in the mouth. It took everything Kami and I had not to resort to that kind of dismissive authority.

We thought of the newer posts that were still appearing online, criticizing us.

"Since their 'leader' is pushing for fifteen-plus miles per day and trying to act like it's a family decision, he has pushed me to dislike him more than I believed possible. Why CPS wasn't notified of their latest abhorrent behavior is beyond me. This family makes my blood boil. Selfish, dominating, creep of a man." —52er

"Does anyone have insight into why this family is getting so much positive attention on the trail AND on YouTube? How can people not see right away the abusive dynamics in this situation?" —Anonymous

"Every time they are taking a day off, Kami and Ben show them-selves kicking back, drinking coffee, smoking cigars, etc. Every time they happen to show Seven, there he is in a corner editing vid-eos. It's a lot of work, hours and hours. Doesn't he get to relax? Note how the kids set up the tents and prepare all the meals too?"
—DonnaPickles

Maybe the comments were correct. Maybe I had pushed too far. Wasn't Seven saying that he hated it proof that I had made this my trip?

Kami and I strongly believe in the adage "what you resist persists," and we knew that if we ignored the root of Seven's frustrations, those feelings would only resurface later, and the consequences to our relationship with him would be much worse. We needed a way to acknowledge Seven's feelings, yet still maintain our hike. We needed to get to the root of his complaining and have the patience to try and understand it, not just shut it up. Kami and I discussed the topic for hours as we strolled through New York State, which was more populated than the rest of the trail, far more hikers out for day and weekend trips at this point in the year.

Finally, we arrived at a conclusion we thought would work best for Seven and the family. It seemed risky, but we couldn't keep going as we were. It wasn't working for us or for Seven.

Even though we were deep into our hike, well past the middle, we decided to offer Seven the same option we'd given Dove and Eden back before we started the hike: we told him he could go home.

Stan the Man could take him to a train in New York City that went back to Cincinnati, where he could stay with my parents back home. He knew Halmonee and Papa would take care of him and there would air conditioning and video games. Given his complaints, it seemed like the obvious choice for a teenage boy.

Our YouTube channel had grown by tens of thousands of sub-scribers, with five thousand people watching our progress daily. They were consistently leaving comments about how inspiring and unique our family was and telling us that "we could do it" and that nothing could stop us. What would they think when they found out that we couldn't finish it together? That one of our kids didn't even like hik-ing anymore, and had gone home? It seemed like we'd given every-one hope through the picture of what was possible with a big family, and that if Seven left us now, we'd be letting everyone down. Forcing him to continue, though, would feel fake, or worse, destructive.

Losing a relationship with my child because he didn't
   fit in with our family goals was my biggest fear.

It was a fear born of personal experience. As I mentioned earlier, Kami was using the trail as an opportunity to "walk off her family," and the processing she needed to do went deeper than just being rejected by them. Kami and I had both been raised in communities where our voices were dismissed, or outright ignored, by parents and those with power. The message was that respect and honor were a one way street that kids gave to parents, who were wiser and deserved it. Even as adults, we were told that submission to authority was the only glue that could hold communities together. We had seen firsthand how that system worked for some, but not all—and that those who didn't fit in were marked as black sheep. There are only three options for black sheep: live authentically and get kicked out of the community, have the courage to move out on your own and rebuild from scratch, or hide your true self and desperately try to fit in (which you never will). The result of trying to fit in and spending a lifetime as someone you are not is that you will slowly lose your mind. Back in our spiritual communities, Kami and I had even seen kids commit suicide under the pressure of constant rejection.

Most of our lives we had both wanted to, and tried hard to, submit. We'd wanted to live up to the rules and fit in with our community. We'd given it everything we had, but inside, we just felt like we were going crazy. Suppressing what we really thought and how we really felt made us feel like we were dying on the inside. For a while, it was a feeling we just got used to. But eventually we broke, and we could no longer afford the price we would have to pay to fit in. Some of the leaders of the faith-based community we were a part of saw this as rebellion and refusal to submit to their authority.

For the two years before the hike, Kami and I had been in therapy for the deep confusion we felt in validating our own voices. We didn't know who we were or what we believed because we had never allowed ourselves the mental permission to explore, knowing it would mean losing all of our relationships. The stress and anxiety built in us until that first day we found ourselves in therapy. For the first time, we started to wonder if maybe we weren't crazy—maybe we weren't the problem. Maybe the problem was actually having to "buy" love and acceptance with submission and compliance.

We went back to therapy session after therapy session. It was the only place where we felt normal. Eventually, we learned that the relationships we'd thought were compulsory were actually optional; that demanding submission was just another form of violence and control, and that we had the power to choose who was in our lives. Slowly, we gained the courage to walk away from many of the relationships that didn't validate our voices, our feelings, or our humanity.

This meant we lost almost all of our friends, and Kami lost most of the relationships with her family.

Through our own journey, we'd learned an unshakeable truth: if we didn't find a way to validate our children's voices, then someday when they found their courage, they would choose to walk away from us too.

Just like Eden's sharing during tent time, Seven's complaining was a gift to us. The worst thing we could do was silence him. Instead of blaming him as being rebellious because his desires didn't fit into our family system, or appealing to some code of honor or respect that we, as parents, felt we deserved, if we wanted to have a long-term relationship with him, we would need to set our egos aside. We would need to simply listen, and take his feelings just as seriously as our goal. His complaining was showing us where our relationship was heading if we didn't pay attention to his thoughts and feelings. Giving Seven the option to leave was the only way we knew to validate his feelings and maintain the integrity of our goal. It wasn't easy—Kami and I desperately wanted to finish the trail as a family. It was hard even to consider giving up that dream.

But there was something else we wanted more: we wanted a relationship with our kids when the hike was over. This was the only way we knew how to save it.

For the hike to truly be a success for all of us, our kids had to buy in to the trail themselves. They had to make the choice themselves. Without allowing them that choice, we'd be invalidating their feelings—silencing their voices just because society had told us that ours, as the parents, was more important.

Once we gave Seven the option, all we could do was wait and see what he would choose. Would he choose to go home, where he could enjoy the rest of his summer with air conditioning and video games and without having to hike the remaining nine hundred miles? Or would he choose to stay with us and finish the trail together? The risk seemed amplified by the fact that Eden was also showing a bit of a mood downturn—it was obvious to Kami and me that, despite her best efforts to stay positive, she was seriously losing steam. If Seven left, would that make Eden or others wonder why they were still hiking? Him leaving would break the illusion of needing to stick with it; it would no longer be a whole family affair. Would the whole expedition unravel as each family member began asking the questions we had been trying so hard to avoid?

That morning, Stan the Man slackpacked us. As we hiked the 14.4 miles of our rest day, Kami and I were twitchy and nervous, waiting for Seven's decision. While we weren't bluffing on giving him the choice, we wondered if we'd really be okay with sending him home. After all, if he wasn't being forced to hike, why wouldn't he choose this easier path that had been so temptingly offered?

That day, we hiked through a state park. It was a holiday weekend, and the entire park was crowded; it felt like everyone in New York had come to swim in the lake. It would have been so nice to relax in the water, but because of our late start, it wasn't an option. We passed some vending machines. We'd never bought things from vending machines, viewing them as overpriced and preying on the impulsive. But now, hiking on a hot summer day, watching the locals splash around in the water, it felt hard to put a price tag on Popsicles and Gatorade. We spent twenty-six dollars at the two vending machines, and it felt like the best twenty-six dollars we'd ever spent.

After enjoying the Popsicles and Gatorade, Seven came to Kami and me. We braced ourselves.

"I've made my choice," he told us. "I want to stay."

I could feel Kami's huge internal sigh of relief next to me, and I knew she could feel mine. "Are you sure? We weren't bluffing. This is truly your decision," I said.

> MAMA JUST YELLED FROM THIER TENT THAT AUNT HANNA JUST HAD HER BABY AND IT'S CUTE AND HEALTHY. I WISH I COULD BE THERE NOW. WELL THIS BOOK IS FINISHED PLEASE EXCUSE MY HANDWRITING AND THE FACT THAT I OMITED LOTS OF THINGS BECAUSE MY HAND HURTS. JUST ASK ME IN PERSON (IF I'M STILL ALIVE) AND MAYBE YOU WILL REMEBER SOME OF WHAT I TOLD YOU AFTER I HIT YOUR HEAD WITH A FRYING PAN.

Eden (15) recounting the birth of a cousin back home. Being on the trail for five months over three seasons meant we missed many traditions and family events.

Seven nodded, and looked determined, not submissive. "I'm sure. I want to keep going with you guys. I don't want to miss out on the rest of the trail."

In that moment, Seven truly took ownership of his hike. He knew it would be hard, that it would continue to suck, but he was embracing it.

From that point forward, it was as if Seven's attitude changed overnight. The complaining stopped. Not because he was afraid to come to us, but because it wasn't our will keeping him out here anymore; it was his. It wasn't the hiking he had hated; it was feeling powerless, dragged along. But now he saw us, his parents, as allies instead of the source of his problems. We could now face the difficulty of hiking together.

He was all in on his hike for the first time.

FATHER'S DAY

June 17, our 108th day of hiking, was Father's Day. We crammed into Stan the Man's car and drove back to the trail. After saying our goodbyes, the kids announced their gift to me for Father's Day, of which Seven was a critical part: they would carry Rainier for the entire day.

As soon as I heard this, I started crying. It was the best gift I could have received. It would be the first day in three months I hadn't carried Rainier at all.

However, I did feel guilty. I knew how hard it was to carry Rainier, and I was worried the kids couldn't handle it. But I could see they really wanted to do this for me, so I decided to enjoy the rest of my day and accept the love and care from my kids.

New York is unique because the Appalachian Trail runs through the middle of a zoo there. That day, we walked right past the bear enclosure and saw three small black bears. For months, hikers had been telling us stories of all the bears they had seen; some had spotted more than fifteen bears in the Shenandoahs alone. Bears—and bear attacks—were a big concern on the trail. But those three bears that we walked past in the New York Zoo would be the only ones we would see on the entire trail.

That night, we sat in a deli parking lot eating Reuben sandwiches and blue raspberry Italian ice. I drank a twenty-four-ounce tallboy of Blue Moon beer out of a paper bag to celebrate Father's Day. Gift-buying has always been really important to me; I take great pride in selecting gifts for friends and family that are personal, meaningful, and often extravagant. This means that I'm not the easiest person to shop for or surprise. Over seventeen Father's Days, I had received my fair share of Hallmark trinkets and handmade items from the kids. This gift was different. It wasn't something that could be bought. This gift literally took a weight off my shoulders, made me feel cared for and loved, and skyrocketed my happiness levels. I've given many forced smiles upon receiving Father's Days gifts, but I've never received one that brought me to tears. This day I cried. It was the best Father's Day gift I've ever received.

A REUNION

It felt sad to be so close to New York City and not be able to stop there. At one point, we walked past a train station that could get us downtown in an hour and a half.

Having spent some of my favorite moments there, NYC was one of my top destinations on earth, and now, we could literally see it—so close, and yet so far. Silver had offered us his apartment across the river, and we even had a viewer watching our videos who offered us his apartment downtown. In any other situation, we would never have been able to refuse an offer like this; to take a day trip to a place this special, so conveniently, at such a low cost. Ultimately, though, even though it was so close, we were at a different place than we were when we took the day off to go to DC. We were in the northern states now. Katahdin felt closer, within our reach. We knew that every day could mean the difference between finishing or failing. We decided we couldn't afford the zero day it would take to go off-trail. In the blistering, humid heat, we trudged on, the NYC skyline shrinking behind us.

We couldn't have imagined the offer we were about to receive. A woman named Heather from Queens had seen our videos and reached out, offering to bring us New York City pizza. It felt like a dream. She planned to meet us at a state park that had a lake with a swimming area; we had to hike twelve miles to get there by lunch, but when we arrived, we walked across the sandy lakeside beach and saw a special surprise waiting for us.

There were two people on the lake shore. One was a man wearing a green shirt and, by now, very worn-out green cargo shorts. He was skinny and had a scraggly gray beard. Hops!

It had been almost two months since we'd said goodbye to him in the Wendy's parking lot after the forest fire and then been further separated by the marathon. He'd pitched his tent in the state park the night before, excited for a free meal and a reunion.

Hops had his arms spread out as wide as they could go as he walked toward us to give us a hug. "Hey, everybody! I missed you all so much!"

Rainier was increasing his vocabulary more and more as the months passed, and now he yelled, "*Bill!*"

"How have you guys been?" Hops asked. "You all look so different! Ben, your beard is amazing!" That felt good, after the jabs I'd taken online for my "gross" beard.

Filia ran up and gave Hops a hug. "I missed you!"

"There's my little Billy goat! Are you more excited to see me, or the pizza?"

Heather was a tall woman wearing a gray T-shirt and a bandana over her short hair. She was a union construction worker and spoke in a heavy New York accent. Heather had brought five huge pizzas with her—she said they were the best in NYC.

"It's Queens pizza. Our water is what makes it so good," she explained.

She also had a cooler full of Pepsi, nitro cold brew coffee, half-and-half, and chocolate milk for Rainier. She even brought a bunch of side dishes to complete the meal. As we ate, she talked excitedly about watching our videos.

"I was watching thru-hiking videos and came upon you guys when you first started. And I was just like, 'I can't believe they're doing that. That's nuts! They've got the whole family! That's crazy!' And, at first, I was like, 'They're never going to make it.' And then as I'm watching you guys get better and better, progressing, I'm like, 'Holy shit, they're doing pretty good!'"

We thought about Silver's mantra: "The trail provides." Heather had a tattoo of the NYC skyline running across both of her wrists. Even though we couldn't make it into the city, the city of New York had quite literally come to us.

At the state park we had a shower, outlets, and the whole lake to ourselves. It was like Disneyland for hikers. We spent the afternoon relaxing, smoking cigars, and catching up with Hops. We shared about the marathon and our trip to DC, and he told us about his family. It felt like we had been apart for years; there was so much to talk about. Moments like this were the richest on the entire trail. It was an experience we could never plan, re-create, or purchase back home.

That night, we walked with Hops to a place called RPH Shelter. It's the only shelter on the trail where you can order Chinese food. We ordered sesame chicken, Mongolian beef, broccoli with brown sauce, wonton soup, egg drop soup, chicken chow mein, General Tso's chicken, and special fried rice. Hops got two orders of spring rolls. We also asked for nine bubble tea smoothies—our favorite drink from back home, with fruit flavors and crazy colors and giant tapioca balls that you sip through an enormous straw. And it all came delivered to the shelter, a hollowed out shed with no electricity. Hops was so excited to see us that he asked me if he could pay for everything, with the condition that I wasn't allowed to tell Kami and the kids.

It was the perfect day, and as we went to our tents still thinking about the Chinese food, we thought about The Degenerates. The final group of friends we had said goodbye to before the marathon was the closest with our oldest kids, but they were also the fastest hikers we'd come across. It seemed impossible that we would catch up with them; we were starting to think we'd heard their conch shells for the last time.

CHAPTER NINETEEN

The Vow

"'You do not understand,' said Pippin. 'You must go—and therefore we must too. Merry and I are coming with you. Sam is an excellent fellow, and would jump down a dragon's throat to save you, if he did not trip over his own feet; but you will need more than one companion in your dangerous adventure.'"
—J. R. R. Tolkien, *The Lord of the Rings*

The next week was a blur as we celebrated our reunion with Hops. It was exhilarating to meet back up with someone who played such a huge role in the first part of our trip. We talked about the forest fire and discussed plans to go back and finish the miles; we shared about the support we'd received and our conversion to slackpacking. We talked of possibly finishing the trail together and discussed the upcoming obstacles—most notably the

White Mountain National Forest, known as the Whites, renowned for being the most difficult section of the trail.

Even though the statistics seemed to suggest that hiking with a group was a liability, Hops agreed to join up with us because he said there was some sort of magic with our group. "It doesn't make sense," he would say. "It's like one plus one equals three with you guys." He began calling this magic the "x-factor." By now, he had seen so many different single people and groups, he had a pretty good impression of what worked and what didn't. But we defied all his evidence.

"There's something about you guys. You seem to be getting more miles, less sick, and less injured." This validated what we'd felt before we started our hike, and what we'd started to feel: hiking with kids could actually be an asset, not just a liability.

Other hikers continually warned us that the Whites would be harder than anything we'd experienced so far on the trail. The Whites run through the final one hundred miles of New Hampshire; they're also home to Mount Washington, which holds the record as the windiest place on the planet.

On Day 112, June 21, just three days after reuniting with Hops, we crossed the state line into Connecticut. Earlier that day, we received a Facebook message from a woman named Lu who owned the Bearded Woods Hostel with her husband, Hudson. She invited us to stay with them, and they agreed to pick us and Hops up on the road and drive us to their place.

As we talked with Lu and Hudson on the drive back to their place, we could sense they lived and breathed the Appalachian Trail. Hudson, who had hiked the entire length of the trail twice, had been to the A-frame sign at the top of Katahdin five times. The entire hostel—downstairs, upstairs, and the outside eating area—reminded us of the trail. Everywhere we looked, there were custom wood carvings made by Hudson, and an educational display of pelts and bones he collected of animals that live along the Appalachian Trail (though not collected from the trail itself, which is illegal). The stairway had a display of snake skeletons and various animal skulls arranged in rows. The bunkbeds had been handmade from logs with white blazes on each one. There were license plates along the wall from every state the A.T. runs through. It felt like we were in a miniature Appalachian Trail museum and art exhibit.

Along the A.T., there are many nice hostels. This one, however, stood out above the rest. Not only was the place creatively designed, but we had it completely to ourselves. Hudson and Lu closed the hostel during our stay and made us feel completely at home. Hudson offered us adults a beer and Lu, a gourmet caterer, served us a delicious homemade meal, all made from scratch. They refused to accept any payment, saying only that they "wanted to support our journey."

The most memorable aspect of this stay was our late-night chat with Hudson. He was not your typical conversationalist. He was socially awkward and hard to read, but he could talk for hours about the trail. He treated the A.T. like a science and could explain it in detail like no one else we met. He knew the distance of every major town and hostel down to the nearest half-mile between Springer Mountain and Mount Katahdin. During this conversation, Hudson offered us an overwhelming amount of information about the rest of the trail. He told us the best places to stay and the best sections to slackpack. "Make sure you eat at Joe Dodge Lodge." "Make sure you take your zeroes at the right times."

And he had a completely different philosophy of hiking than we had ever heard. He called it smarthiking. "The slackpacking you guys are doing isn't cheating. Professional long-distance hikers are carrying less than ten pounds, and they're not cheating, they're just hiking smart! People say they're going to attack the trail, and get as many miles as possible, that's the wrong way to see it!"

Then he told us about a figure in the A.T. hiking community I'd heard of, but didn't know much about: Warren Doyle.

Warren was an out-of-the box thinker, to put it mildly. Warren had been committed to the trail for forty-five years. In that time, he'd had hiked the full length of it eighteen times—more than any human in history.

Warren was quirky. He famously hiked without a toothbrush, didn't filter his water, and had finished the trail twice without taking a shower. On his first time hiking it, he set the record for fastest hike, an accomplishment achieved in sixty-six days wearing blue jeans. Even though he had accomplished the solo speed record, he dedicated his life specifically to helping groups finish the trail from end to end—because in his words, "Doing the trail as a group, with everyone who started together finishing together, that is the greatest achievement."

He had dedicated his life to seeing groups of people finish this life-changing experience. To accomplish this, he started a donation-based five-day seminar called Appalachian Trail Institute. The seminar had more than five hundred graduates and boasted a 75 percent trail completion rate, which meant spending five days with Warren increased your odds of finishing by more than three times. His alumni included Jennifer Pharr Davis, who claimed the overall (male or female) fastest known time on the A.T. and became the first woman to set the mark; as well as Bill Irwin, the first blind person to hike the entire trail.

But a 75 percent success rate wasn't enough for Doyle. He believed that the 25 percent of people who quit could do better and was convinced that most of the hiking experience was "in your head." One of the most prominent lines in his one-page book reads, "Learn to be a smart hiker rather than a strong hiker. It is not your gear that will get you to Katahdin, it is your heart and your mind."

So, to increase his success rate, every five years Doyle leads a group of hikers on a thru-hike himself. There are strict requirements to join; each member of the group agrees to a start date and end date that are predetermined, promising to stick together the entire way—otherwise the hike is considered a failure for the entire group. Before joining, each member has to agree that "Anything short of finishing together, on top of Katahdin, will be considered a failure for all."

His most famous story is when Baxter State Park Authority prohibited his group from climbing Katahdin because it was raining. Warren thought this was ridiculous and that safety was a hiker's prerogative. He also noted how Baxter State Park was stricter and more random in its rules and enforcement than other government agencies.

When his attempts to get the policy changed failed, Warren protested by climbing to the top of Katahdin in the winter without a permit.

He was ordered to pay a fine, but chose instead to spend the night in jail in protest, in an effort to raise awareness about the unusual rules and regulations in Baxter State Park.

His protest was noticed; a few years later, the rule was changed. We could tell that Doyle had inspired Hudson, and it seemed like Doyle's experience and philosophy were just what we needed. I started taking notes, trying to remember everything Hudson was saying.

"Your mentality is everything," he said. "You need to hike smarter, not harder. This is going to be especially important coming up in the Whites. This is going to be your toughest mental and physical challenge of the whole trail." That's when he told us about the "Technical

200," a stretch that starts with the last one hundred miles of trail in New Hampshire in the Whites and ends with the first one hundred miles of "trail" in Maine. It's called "technical" because, while the rest of the trail can be walked, these sections of the trail require climbing steep grades, navigating slippery and difficult terrain. Injuries are common.

By the time Hudson was done describing the Whites, we felt completely demoralized. We'd been cautioned by so many well-intentioned people about snakes, ticks, bears, weather, and roads. We'd only made it this far by ignoring these warnings and taking one step at a time, one day at a time. Now, with someone we respected giving us so much information, we wondered how we'd ever make it through this section safely. Our immediate fear was the kids' safety; we knew the younger kids would be much more challenged by the technical difficulty of the section. One wrong move could mean one of the kids being seriously injured. It was a rehash of all the fears we'd had back in the blizzard in the Smokies, as though the neglect and recklessness we'd been accused of by the online crowd was now closer to coming true. But this time, instead of three days in the Smokies, we were looking at three weeks in the Whites.

To make matters worse, Hudson said that in the Technical 200, our speed would be cut in half. It was going to take us double the time. Which meant that, if we wanted to get the same number of miles per day, we'd have to hike twice as many hours per day.

We were in the process of hiking our most successful month yet in terms of miles. In June, we had averaged just over sixteen miles a day, partially because we took no zero days. Even with this improvement, according to Hudson's predictions we should only expect to get eight miles per day through the Technical 200. It would add almost two weeks to our timeline. That was time we didn't have.

But his main caution wasn't about speed; it was about safety. He shared horror stories of people slipping and falling down wet rocks because they were going at a pace that exceeded their abilities.

Seeing the toll our recent speeds had taken on the family combined with the unknown terrain ahead, Kami and I openly talked about the fact we might not finish the A.T. by August 9. At that point, it felt generous to estimate a fifty-fifty shot at success. The idea of taking the kids to Lakeside, then returning to finish the trail, was again mentioned, but quickly dismissed. It was just too expensive—it would cost $10,000 for roundtrip airfare and transportation back to Maine. There were no "outs" at this point—it was finish by August 9 or bust.

Seeing our downturned faces, Hudson said, "I know you guys are concerned, but it's amazing that you've made it this far. You're inspiring a lot of people. It doesn't really matter if you finish the trail."

When we heard his words, we breathed a little easier. He was right: we had accomplished so much. It didn't matter if we made it to the end. We waited for a moment in silence, feeling tension begin to ease from our bodies.

Then Hudson continued, "But if you don't finish, no one will remember you."

We were thrown right back off guard. From demoralized to encouraged to confused, we weren't sure what to feel. Hudson had been honest in his encouragement, but now we knew how he really felt deep down: we had to finish.

That night, we went to sleep feeling unsettled. Questions plagued us. How were we going to complete the trail with all of the obstacles in front of us? Would we kill our kids' morale forever and make them hate hiking if we attempted it? Or worse, would we put our kids, especially our youngest ones, in danger? Should we just give up, knowing that there was little possibility of making it to Katahdin? It seemed insane; we had all sacrificed so much. But was that sacrifice creating an illusion—a sunk-cost bias?

I talked earlier about the Mount Everest phenomenon where highly intelligent and disciplined mountaineers throw their common sense out the window when they see the summit. Most deaths on the mountain are related to this moment, called "summit fever." At that moment, we weren't immune to our own version of summit fever when we thought of Katahdin. We had invested so much money and so many years into our goal, and yes, there were no hard and fast rules—we didn't have to finish. But after the fourteen-hour days and relentless grind of hundreds of miles, now it felt impossible to quit. The more we had sacrificed, the more we felt like we had to lose. How would we resist summit fever when we were in sight of the A-frame sign at the top? Did we have the strength to prioritize our long-term safety and not push the kids or ourselves too much? By now, there were so many people cheering us on. Many people had brought us meals and offered places for us to stay and it felt like if we didn't make it, we would not only be letting ourselves down, we would be letting each of these people down as well. This would make things worse and not better. More pressure meant we were more likely to make a dangerous decision.

The next morning as we prepared to leave, Hudson once again threw us a curveball—only this time, he said the exact words we needed to hear.

"I swear a vow," he said, "that if it will help motivate you to finish the trail, I will meet you at the sign on top of Katahdin."

We were bowled over by such a tremendous, heartfelt offer. For a few moments, we were speechless.

"How far of a drive is that?" Kami asked.

"It's five hundred miles," he said. "I can be there in eight hours."

"We're not going to hold you to this," I said, as we loaded our packs into Hudson's car.

Hudson's response was short. "Hold me to it."

Just the night before, we weren't sure we could make it. We'd resigned ourselves to killing the dream, but now with Hudson's crazy promise, we were back in the race.

On the car ride back to the trail, a couple of the kids complained they felt sick. We were driving down small, windy roads in the middle of nowhere. We scrambled and found Eden a thin, plastic grocery bag. Five seconds later, she threw up in it. She was still hunched over, and we were trying to figure out what to do when Rainier threw up all over Dove. We pulled over on the side of the road and there was vomit everywhere.

I could read Kami's worried face like a book: *This is my worst nightmare.*

We felt terrible for the kids, and also for Lu. We'd only known her for about twelve hours and had made the most disgusting mess in her nice car. And we had nothing to clean it with.

But Lu thought nothing of it. She offered to wash our dirty clothes and bring them with her to the next place we'd be. It felt vulnerable to have her take some of our very few possessions, but we also knew she wanted to be a part of our mission and wouldn't accept a dime for anything. Back home, we'd architected our whole life to avoid situations like this. But now, we felt an indebtedness, gratitude, and connection we hadn't experienced before. In many ways, all our experiences with trail magic and people's kindness along the A.T. had trained us for this. With nothing at the trail besides our backpacks and no stores or car washes around, there was literally nothing we could do but say "thank you" and accept Lu's kindness.

When we arrived back on the trail with sick kids and walked away from the car and our only shot at running water, we felt like we were saying goodbye to our lifeline. We wondered what people would say about "what we were putting our kids through" by hiking when they were sick.

Since Hudson and Lu were slackpacking us, we'd planned on doing a twenty-mile day, but seeing as the kids were sick, the minimum we could do was 14.6 miles and still be able to get our packs. Popular opinion would say that the responsible decision would be to take the day off and wait and see if the kids felt better. But the days of doing what was responsible based upon what was popular were behind us. We offered the kids the choice, and they said they'd be fine. Once again, we made the decision for our kids' health that walking wasn't dangerous, and that we would have to assess as we went; we simply could not afford to stay at a road based on the chance that they might feel bad later. Thankfully, everyone felt better after we started moving, and it ended up being a relatively good day of hiking.

Hudson wasn't done with his generosity. When he dropped off the kids' clothes the next day, he offered to be our "trail mentor."

"I've only offered this one other time," he told us. "If you need help for any reason during the rest of your trip, call me anytime, and I'll answer. I'll help, no matter what it takes."

Our new trail mentor ended up being an important asset for us a number of times when we found ourselves in sticky situations and unsure how to move forward. He remembered every single mile, so we knew we could count on him for the answer. The trail isn't science—we knew there were no "right" answers, but we could depend on Hudson's experience.

It was fascinating to find allies who were so devoted to this strip of dirt that they were willing to drop everything to assist people they barely knew. Most importantly, it was a reminder that we weren't hiking alone.

In less than four days, we'd completed the fifty-one miles of Connecticut and reached the Massachusetts border. Hops was still with us, and he was blown away by the hospitality we received on a daily basis. It was like nothing he'd seen hiking alone. The YouTube videos combined with the family aspect meant people offered us trail magic almost daily in this densely-populated section that passed many large cities. We knew it wouldn't last forever, so we tried to take advantage of every opportunity for extra calories and companionship.

Eden and Rainier's sickness didn't last long, but Eden was struggling to stay motivated on the trail. It had been raining pretty regularly, and our shoes were always muddy, our clothes always wet, and the tent and sleeping bags started to smell like mildew. Eden craved order, tidiness, and showers. She started complaining more and more and regularly and blamed us for her discomfort. We listened and tried to offer her what little comfort we could. When that didn't seem to work, we reminded her that she chose to come. The complaining went on.

We decided to up the ante and give her the same choice to quit that we had offered Seven. We would be meeting up with Halmonee and Papa one last time in about a week, and it would be the perfect opportunity to get a ride home.

We could tell she wasn't happy with either option: stay and not complain, or leave.

"I'll think about it," she said with a frown, and looked troubled.

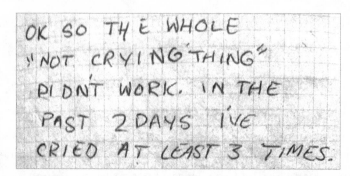

OK SO THE WHOLE
"NOT CRYING THING"
DIDN'T WORK. IN THE
PAST 2 DAYS I'VE
CRIED AT LEAST 3 TIMES.

Crying happened a lot on the trail, and Eden (15) was no exception. We often found ourselves at the end of our rope physically and emotionally. Crying could be triggered by conflict, physical difficulty, or even the sound of familiar music.

On Day 115, we hiked almost eighteen miles to get picked up by a family who had reached out and invited us to stay at their CrossFit gym for the night. Mike, the owner, was a tall man with spiky, gray hair. He wore a tight red shirt, and his arms were so big they stretched the sleeves. He looked like a G.I. Joe action figure and talked like a high school coach. His family met us at the trail with Capri Suns and Cherry Coke and transported us and Hops in a private school bus back to the gym. We joked we had to go on the A.T. for our kids to experience what it was like to ride in a school bus. The gym didn't have a shower, but they made a makeshift one for us outside—two sheets of plywood and a hose connected to the hot water inside. While each of us used the hose outside, someone else had to correct the temperature inside, receiving directions shouted through the window. "Hotter! Hotter!...*Ouch, too hot!*"

We gave Rainier a bath in a big metal feed tub in the janitor's closet. He even had a rubber duck that we'd been given by another couple who'd housed us. The whole scene made us laugh.

A blog post published on REI's website estimates that the average person on the A.T. needs $5,000 to cover food, lodging, and gear.

Since we had eight people, we'd need $40,000. In factoring our costs, we added a 20 percent bump for "just in case," which meant that we budgeted $50,000. But with all the connections we made and offers we received, we were spending much less than that.

In addition to tangible benefits like lodging, food, and slackpacking we were receiving, we were bolstered spiritually by people's stories. People shared how seeing our videos had changed them, how they reinvigorated their hope for family, how they helped them realize there was another way to live and that "the grind" was optional. One lady named Jennifer drove two hours to deliver lunch to us. She shared that she'd planned to leave her family to hike the trail solo next year. It was her dream, and that was the only way she knew to make it happen. Now, she was reconsidering and making plans to do it with her whole family. Not only were we receiving, but we were giving back; we were sharing a story that resonated, showing people another picture of their possible future and life. When they met us, they said it made a different story feel more real, more attainable.

The next morning in the gym, at 6:00 a.m., the music started blasting as the first round of CrossFit classes started. Hops was asleep in the middle of the gym floor. Our family was spread out in the dressing room and locker area, and people working out could see our kids still asleep. It probably looked like the owners converted the gym into a homeless shelter for the night. We awkwardly ate bagels, salmon, and berries as the gym members jumped on boxes, swung ropes, and smashed tires with sledgehammers all around us.

OLD FACES, OLD FRIENDS

As we continued through Massachusetts and Vermont, we started to pass hikers we'd seen earlier on the trail. Now that we were no longer taking zero days, and people were helping us out by slack-packing us more regularly, we were catching up to some of the people who had quickly passed us, and passing them in turn. Many people were surprised and seemed to take an ego hit that they were being outpaced by a seven-year-old. At one point, we considered going slower to stay with people we knew, but we couldn't. We had to keep moving. We'd been hiking with Hops for more than a week now, and it looked like we could be traveling companions for the rest of the trip. Hops introduced us to his friends he had met, Eddie and Kat from Brooklyn. Eddie had spent the summer playing saxophone in the New York subways and had landed a gig playing on the nationally syndicated *Colbert Report*. Now he carried a tin whistle that he played while walking, taking requests. He played all of Rainier's favorites: "Twinkle Twinkle Little Star," "Old MacDonald." It felt like our own personal concert-turned-parade.

On the night of June 29, we walked into Melville Shelter after a long twenty-mile day—thirteen straight hours of walking. It was dark and hard to see, but it looked like the shelter was completely full.

Then we heard a familiar sound: a conch shell.

A dark shadow ran up behind me and grabbed me in a big bear hug. Culligan!

The farm boy from Iowa who sang Disney songs at the top of his lungs laughed excitedly as we hugged.

With the help of those who slackpacked us, it had taken us two months of nonstop hiking while the faster Degenerates had lived up to their name and spent three days partying in the previous town, as was their pattern. We'd done it! We'd caught up with The Degenerates!

All thoughts of exhaustion went out the window. We gathered around the picnic bench outside the shelter and everyone embraced happily. There was Nubs, the Australian veteran; Not Dead, the ambulance driver; Mama Kish, Not Dead's slave driver; and Fun Facts, who, true to form, had a pack of Haribo Frogs in her hand.

They all looked skinnier and more scraggly than we remembered. Not Dead and Fun Facts had new haircuts; they'd both buzzed the sides of their heads. Besides that, they were the same old irreverent, playful friends we'd fallen in love with more than eight hundred miles ago.

Dove made rice and beans for dinner while everyone gathered around. On the trail, we were careful about making noise at shelters; ever since hearing that people on the forums had criticized us for the noise they assumed our kids made, we'd gone above and beyond to be courteous of other hikers at bedtime. This night, though, it didn't matter. The Degenerates loudly told stories and jokes, and the kids couldn't contain themselves. Dove was thrilled to finally be with her friends. She'd been pining for the last two weeks, hoping we were close and suggesting we hike longer and longer days to catch up.

Every once in a while, it would get really loud, and we'd look over to the shelter in concern. Culligan would say, "It's okay. We know everyone over there, they're cool." So we stayed up talking until almost midnight.

The kids' moods instantly changed. Catching up to The Degenerates was the single biggest milestone we'd achieved on our trip. Over the next few days, we'd see The Degenerates and loosely keep in touch, trying to camp in the same places. At one point, they announced they were going to slow down to our pace for an hour because Filia had asked if they'd hike with us, and the five of them promised they would. Online, our seven-year-old was being critiqued for being an assumed nuisance on the trail, but these hardened thru-hikers were willing to change their entire itinerary because they enjoyed her company. They joked with Filia and walked in a straight line with all the kids, singing Disney songs and laughing the whole way.

Culligan and I shared stories. I told him about the matching tattoos Kami and I had: "Everything was beautiful and nothing hurt." It was a quote from the Kurt Vonnegut novel *Slaughterhouse-Five*, but Culligan was surprised by the ironic fact that neither Kami nor I had never read it. This somehow evolved into a heated debate about whether people would still be reading Harry Potter books in one hundred years.

Eventually, The Degenerates went on ahead at their normal pace, leaving us all with significantly uplifted moods.

The summer days on the trail days flew by. It was hot outside, but after the cold and rain we had been through, we were thankful. We didn't think much of the record we might break as the largest family to hike the A.T., but on two other occasions, we met people on the trail going for their own records. There was Harvey Lewis, a school teacher from our home town of Cincinnati. He was running the entire trail in an attempt to get the fastest known time. In preparation to meet, Harvey wore a Flying Pig Marathon shirt—the marathon we'd gone home to run. Like us, he had started on Springer Mountain. Unlike us, he'd started on May 30—more than three weeks after the marathon. He was averaging forty-five miles every single day. He hugged our family, and it felt like we were hugging a skeleton. We talked and had the chance to jog a mile with him. He said he recognized us from our weekly runs back in Cincinnati.

Another unique hiker we met went by the trail name Pappy. Pappy was eighty-seven years old. He'd hiked the A.T. before, but if he finished it this year, he would be the oldest person to do so in history. We took pictures with him. It was fun to see Pappy standing next to Filia, an eighty-year gap between the oldest and the youngest hikers on the trail at the time.

It was amazing and humbling to see what a footpath could do to the human spirit and how it had brought many people to challenge themselves and redefine what their best life could look like. Maybe Hops was right. Maybe the Appalachian Trail really was sacred ground.

Around 5:00 p.m. one day, when we were worn out, we crossed a small gravel road and saw a paper plate hanging from a tree with a black arrow pointing to the left. When you're in the woods and you see an arrow on a plate, you follow it. We crawled through some branches and up a small embankment until we heard voices. Up ahead, there was a Toyota Camry with a bunch of bumper stickers on it, just parked in the middle of the woods; we couldn't see how the sedan had gotten there. It was surrounded by branches, and behind it was a bespectacled man in his fifties cooking hot dogs on a stove next to a giant orange beverage cooler.

"Ya hungry?" he asked in a Southern accent as he handed each of us a slice of watermelon. "Wash your hands first. That's the bleach, there's the towel. Don't want no germs in my setup."

He gestured to the makeshift hand-washing station. "I'm Fresh Ground. I feed everyone, and everything's all you can eat." We'd been hearing stories about Fresh Ground for months—all the way back to that first trail magic breakfast cooked by MacGyver. Legend had it he quit his job to feed hikers, starting in Georgia each year and driving his Camry, named Stinkbug, north until he ran out of money. He was famous on the trail.

Fresh Ground cooked us homemade potato fries, which the kids dumped in ketchup. Rainier kept chanting, "Fwesh Gwound, Fwesh Gwound, Fwesh Gwound!"

Kami and I were a little more wary at first. We'd run into quite a few people who called themselves "trail angels." Some of them made brownies or gave you pop—but with some of them, it felt like they just wanted to talk to you about religion, or they treated you like you were just a notch in their belt.

But things felt different with Fresh Ground. We couldn't figure out why or how he was there; we asked if he had a donation jar, and he said not to worry about the money. He ran his "kitchen" super efficiently, and we were surprised at the quality of food he prepared with so few ingredients and supplies. Also, unusual for trail angels, he was dressed like a hiker, using the same gear and brands we'd seen all over the trail.

We couldn't figure him out, but we appreciated our time with him immensely. It was some of the best food we'd eaten on the trail.

With four miles still to go that night, we finished our meals quickly. We had plans to meet The Degenerates; we didn't know how long we'd be able to stay hiking with them, and we wanted to take advantage of it. In a hurry, we cleaned up our plates and said a heartfelt goodbye to Fresh Ground, hoping we'd run into him again on the trail.

We would.

CHAPTER TWENTY

Naked and Drunk

"Go to heaven for the climate, hell for the company."

—Mark Twain

I t was on Day 120 that we'd caught up with The Degenerates, and for the rest of Vermont, they were our trail companions.

Hiking with The Degenerates was incredibly fun. It put a fresh charge of energy into our hike. Dove, who's always been social, smiled for days, saying, "I can't believe we finally caught up!"

But Eden was different; the excitement of being with our friends could only pick up her spirits so much. Eden has always been the most structure-oriented of our kids. She missed the order and cleanliness of being back home, our days planned out, our house kept tidy, her special areas that she could keep orderly. Eden had always kept her bedroom neat as a pin. From Day 1 on the trail, surrounded by dirt, uncertainty, fatigue, and very little structure, she was way out of her comfort zone. By Vermont, her nerves were beyond frayed.

On Day 123, Eden began the day crying. She wasn't sick or injured; she was just done with the trail. As we hiked up mountain after mountain in Vermont, mountains so steep that in the winter they were ski slopes, she sniffled miserably.

Our offer to her, like we'd made to Seven, still stood—it was up to her if she wanted to leave the trail. She told us she was still deciding.

We were all worn out. The terrain was tough, which made relationships tougher than they already were. It felt like we all needed space, but there was nowhere to go. It was incredibly hot and humid, and we were hiking up to a very exposed area. I was at the end of my rope, but for different reasons. All I could hear was Eden sniffling, and it seemed like she was just feeling sorry for herself. I'd slow down so I wouldn't have to listen to her, and she would slow down to match me. I'd speed up to try and get ahead, and Eden would speed up too.

Finally, I'd had enough.

"Can you hike somewhere else?" I snapped at her.

"I don't want to be here!" she snapped back at me.

The opportunity we had given to her to leave was becoming more and more appealing to both of us.

We'd had a late start that day, so after hiking for ten miles, it was already 5:00 p.m. We stopped for break at a crystal blue lake where The Degenerates, Hops, and a few other hikers we recognized had pitched their tents and spent the late afternoon swimming and relaxing. The kids begged us to stay. We'd planned on hiking another five miles, but this was too perfect an opportunity to pass up. After a swim, we sat around the fire drying off and reminiscing about our time on the trail.

On the A.T., time is measured by states. It had been four months and twelve states since we started. We'd been through an eighty-degree temperature change as the seasons shifted.

I pulled out a raspberry dark chocolate bar that Eden had given me for Father's Day that I had been carrying for four hundred miles. It was smashed to pieces, but now seemed like the perfect time to share it. Dove pulled out a bag of marshmallows, which helped the shifting mood. Eden finally started to laugh and joke as we roasted them.

One of the things we loved about The Degenerates was that they treated our family just like any other hikers. They were crude, they swore, and they didn't treat the kids differently. Earlier that week, on the summer solstice, it was Hike Naked Day. There had been discussion online about how we could stay off the trail to "protect our kids from nudity." The word "protecting" seemed like overkill to Kami and me, but the prospect of a horde of nude hikers streaming past our relatively sheltered kids and robbing them of their innocence was definitely awkward. However, we were committed to fully embracing the trail, the people on it, and the opportunity to expose our kids to real-world situations we didn't want them to be afraid of. In the end, we didn't see any nude hikers—but The Degenerates had participated, and now we had the opportunity to hear about it.

"And then we were all walking in a line, and we came across this whole row of school kids...there were, like, twenty of them!"

"You should have seen the girl's face in the front."

"You should have seen the adults' faces in the back!"

"We just walked past, said 'hi,' and pretended nothing was up."

Smoking pot was also a big thing on the trail. People called it "having a safety meeting." Often, we'd walk past hikers smoking, and when they saw the kids, they'd try to hide their bowl, looking sheepish.

We didn't care if our kids saw people using drugs. Kami and I were both raised pretty conservatively and didn't have a party background, but we wanted our kids to see the reality of the trail. This was real life. Why hide it from them?

We would always rather our kids be exposed to lifestyles outside our own, and be able to ask questions and process it with us. The alternative is that they leave home and learn about the world for the first time with a bunch of strangers. A huge benefit of the trail was our kids seeing real life, all of it, unvarnished and true. So, while new people we met apologized after swearing in front of our kids, The Degenerates knew better.

That evening, Eden came up to Kami and me.

"I made my decision," she said. "I want to be here, and I'm thankful to be on this trip. It's just hard. Thanks for listening, and sorry I was complaining."

"Eden, we're glad you're here." I said.

Kami hugged her and said, "You're doing great. You'll be okay. I know this is really hard for you, but we think you'll be glad that you stuck with it."

Just like it had been with Seven, this was a huge relief, despite how annoyed I'd been with her earlier. I hadn't been actually worried that Eden would choose to leave. We'd seen what giving Seven ownership over his hike had done for his attitude and motivation, and up until then, Kami and I had had to externally motivate Eden to keep going. Now Eden owned her hike.

This also took a burden off my shoulders—it took me out of the role of coach, and meant I could hike alongside her as a fellow journeyer. We could share our struggles and feel companionship instead of me feeling like I had to constantly push her, and her feeling like she was being pulled along.

The kids, together, had made another decision that day. They opted to stay the night at the lake with our friends even though they knew that meant getting up at 5:00 a.m. the next day to make up the miles.

Out here, friendship made a much more immediate impact than back home. It meant more miles, more calories, more laughing, and more enjoyment, and it helped keep our family going. And, as Eden had shown us, it meant immediate motivation not to quit, the kind of motivation that the abstract, faraway promise of Katahdin just couldn't offer.

Four days later, we left Vermont and crossed into New Hampshire. We looked forward to a visit with Halmonee and Papa for a fourth and final time on the trail. But this time would be different; we couldn't stop and spend a day with them. We still had to average fourteen miles a day, every day, for the next thirty-three days straight. This sounded easy, but the next 450 miles were through the Whites and the Technical 200 that Hudson had warned us about. We expected our mileage to be cut in half there.

As we approached, the Whites were constantly on our minds. Would it be dangerous? How much harder would it be than anything else we'd done? Would we be able to finish it? We imagined steep cliffs, slippery granite rock faces at high altitudes—trips to the emergency room. We had no way of knowing what was in store for us. All we could do was keep walking, one step and one day at a time.

I THINK ITS DAY 86 .... IDK ANYWAYS,
I'VE MISSED A TON OF DAYS SO, FACT TIME.

1. WE TOO GOT PICKED UP BY THIS LADY NAMED KATE WHOSE BEEN WATCHING FROM The beginning

2. SHE is an awesome person.

3. We took a zero day in Washington DC becuase it was only 20 min from her house.

4. That was cray cray being there back after 4 years and really fun.

5. She is super funny.

6. The next night we stayed at a cult that was worse than WOODS HOLE

7. I HATED THAT PLACE

8. 4 days later met STAN The man and

9. stayed with his sister, Sue.

9. We stayed with Mennonites last night.

10. TODAY, WAS NOT That bad. WE hiked, 16 miles to a road where a lady, Heidi and her husband Jeffery and their kids. They had this awesome setup and brought a ton of drinks, pizza and

Dove (17) had a lifetime's worth of experiences in a few months. Also, it's such a contrast to note how, at this point, sixteen miles is seen as "not that bad" compared to how difficult eight miles was in the beginning.

Halmonee and Papa drove for more than fourteen hours to meet up with us and slackpack us. They also delivered our second round of free shoes that Altra had offered. Our last shoes had holes and were starting to wear through after nine hundred miles of walking. This would be the third and final pair of shoes each of us wore on the trail.

For three days, the grandparents dropped us off at the trail in the morning, picked us up at night, and joined us for dinner. My mom even hiked eleven miles with us one day.

During this time, Kami and I celebrated our eighteenth wedding anniversary. Halmonee and Papa watched the kids, and we went off alone for only the second time since starting the A.T. We took the van into town and bought Kami a dress at a discount store. Then we shared a sushi dinner. We'd planned to meet up with The Degenerates in town, but they'd had too much to drink back at their hotel and didn't want to leave, so we picked up a six pack and joined them.

Upon arriving at the fancy hotel room one of their parents had paid for, we found the five of them drunk and near-naked on the beds, watching television and waiting for their laundry.

For the first time in months, we had the clothes, transportation, and childcare to go wherever we wanted, and yet we could think of nowhere we wanted to be more than crammed into a smelly hotel room with a group of friends fifteen years younger than us, sharing cheap beers. We'd celebrated previous anniversaries in places like Maui, British Columbia, and Lake Michigan—but this was an anniversary to remember.

The next day, after three days hiking, slackpacking, and spending time together, it was hard to say goodbye to my parents. If everything went according to plan, we'd be seeing them in exactly one month at Lakeside. It had been 130 days since we'd said goodbye to them in Georgia. That first time walking away had been hard because we didn't know what we were walking into. This time it was hard because we knew exactly what we were walking into: the Whites.

About a month earlier, we'd received a mysterious email from a trail angel who called himself The Omelet Guy. We didn't know anything about him except that he'd be waiting for us when we reached the Whites. We'd told him the date we thought we'd be there, and we were on track. He'd said he normally only stayed on the trail until 5:00 p.m. but would make an exception to wait for our estimated arrival of 8:00 p.m.

We reached his tent right at 8:05 p.m. and saw a big sign:

"Welcome to the Whites."

CHAPTER TWENTY-ONE

Into the Whites

"And those who were seen dancing, were thought to be crazy,
by those who could not hear the music."

—Friedrich Nietzsche

The Omelet Guy's real name was Carl. When we arrived at Carl's spot, we saw a bunch of equipment running off a generator. There were Christmas lights strung around the trees, music was blasting, and he had a bunch of collapsible tent chairs set up to welcome visitors to a carport-style tent that looked like it was from Walmart. His set up was five feet off the Appalachian Trail, within walking distance of a gravel road. There was a large fake plastic tree adorned with bananas, which he encouraged us to take and eat. It felt like we'd arrived at an oasis.

Carl the Omelet Guy was retired, and he used his free time and Social Security checks to feed hikers. He had started off by feeding hikers the standard Snickers bars, sodas, beer, and other mass-packaged goods, and then calculated he could feed more people better food by making gourmet omelets. After a long day of hiking, we were all ready to eat, and our orders were serious business. He gave us a choice between one, two, or three eggs. He chopped up onions and peppers, grated lots of cheddar cheese, and cut chunks from a ham hock, which he diced and added to each omelet. He did all this on a counter assembled from miscellaneous pieces of lumber and commercial kitchen surplus that had been cobbled together in the woods, and a propane grill. It felt like Swiss Family Robinson meets Master Chef.

As he cooked, he smoked his cigar and told us all about how he had to go to bat with the National Park Service because they said leaving bananas out for the hikers was bad for the local animals. He said, "They can come after me and sue me. I'll go to court." We believed him.

Before our hike, we knew we'd meet all kinds of interesting people on the trail, and boy, had we. But this took the cake: a man who could think of no better way to spend his retirement than battling the Park Service over feeding bananas to strangers. He was a man on a mission, and like no one we'd ever met. Over the months, it had become clear to us that the A.T. was a magnet for people who thought outside the box. It served as a place where people unsatisfied by a comfort-driven society flocked to feel something real. It was a place where people wanted more—more depth, more relationships, more challenge.

Eventually, Carl handed each person what appeared to be a seven-egg omelet regardless of what we'd ordered. He handed them over and said with a grin, "Your Social Security dollars at work."

After the main meal, he made us a dessert using angel food cake, frozen fruit, and whipped cream. By the time we were finished, we were stuffed. He made a point of saying, "It's all you can eat, all you can carry out." He handed out Ziploc bags so we could take leftovers. It was incredible food, especially in the woods.

Carl had heard Rainier liked chocolate milk, and he'd made a special trip to the store to get chocolate milk for him and Cherry Coke for Kami. He had made individual care packages for the kids with candy, lightweight toys, and hand sanitizer. He also brought us four packages of cigars. He apologized, saying they weren't the fancy kind, but they were the best they had at the closest Walmart, which was forty-five minutes away.

Trail magic was always nice to receive, but this was on a whole other level. Some people treat hikers like a novelty or a mission project. Carl treated us like we were his family at a holiday dinner. We didn't want to leave.

"It is like Christmas for me," he said. "Every day I get to see new people from all over the country and the world." Carl treated us like royalty. And he treated every hiker this way—he was out there from 9:00 a.m. to 5:00 p.m. every day. He approached it like a job, except that he refused to get paid. Anyone that offered a donation was refused. He said, "Anyone that wants to donate, save it. Just buy yourself a steak when you summit."

We later heard a rumor that someone once tried to leave twenty dollars and Carl had threatened to break both their trekking poles.

We compared Carl's life to our typical vision of retirement, relaxing by a beach or playing golf. Carl was making a huge difference in many people's lives; he shared about the range of people he'd met, the conversations he'd had, and the purpose he found in his work. We were amazed at how far he could stretch his Social Security dollars. He taught us you don't need to be rich to care for people. You only need to be creative and willing to meet them where they're at.

We left Carl's tent humbled, impressed, and puffing on the best cigars Walmart had to offer.

Seven (13) comments on smoking one of the cigars from Carl. Some people have a problem with us allowing our kids to occasionally smoke, but we would rather our kids try new things with us.

On July 11, we walked into the Whites. It was Day 131 of our hike, which was also my thirty-ninth birthday. We prepared ourselves for the trek up Mount Moosilauke and down the other side. This was the beginning of the section our trail mentor, Hudson, warned us about: the Technical 200.

We joked about celebrating my birthday by waking up at 5:00 a.m. and climbing a 4,800-foot mountain in eighty-degree heat. It was not my idea of a party.

ADOPTED

We had a two-hour head start on The Degenerates, but they easily caught up to us near the top of Mount Moosilauke. It was great to be back with them again. After briefly seeing them in Hanover for our anniversary, we hoped we could hike together moving forward. It took our minds off of the upcoming nine hours of uphill hiking. We were also boosted by our "trail grandparent," Hops, because as we were all complaining about the dust, heat, and elevation, he kept using words like "sacred experience" and reminding us this was a beautiful, once-in-a-lifetime opportunity.

We all took a break together at the top of the mountain. The view was breathtaking. At 4,800 feet, we were above the tree line and exposed to the wind and the sun. The peak was crowded with tourists, day hikers, and kid camps that had come up for an adventure. We sat on some stacked rocks, taking a break. Fun Facts ate Haribo Frogs, Hops ate chips, and we shared gummy bears to celebrate our first major climb into the Whites.

That's when The Degenerates pulled out their conch shell necklaces. We'd been hearing these necklaces for the last four months every time we said "hello" or "goodbye."

"We have a surprise for you," Culligan said. "Will Memory step up here, please?"

Memory stepped forward and gasped in delight as Culligan pulled out a new, matching conch shell necklace and put it around her neck.

"I now proclaim The Family...honorary Degenerates!" Everyone clapped, whistled, and cheered. The honor and joy we felt in that moment is impossible to express—suffice it to say, we were moved.

Ever since we started the trail, we knew people thought we were crazy to bring six kids along. This made us shy around hikers early on, assuming the worst, that they'd find our kids annoying and disruptive.

But seeing The Degenerates award Memory with a conch shell, their vote was clear. To them, our parenting style wasn't an issue to be debated. Our kids were not annoying add-ons ruining their hike. Our kids were their friends. And now we were part of their tramily.

On the top of our first White mountain, The Degenerates' ceremony ended, and we all blew our ridiculous-sounding conch shells together. I blinked the tears from my eyes to take in one last look at the spectacular view.

PLANNING A PARTY IN THE TECHNICAL 200

We didn't have much time to celebrate; the downhill section of Moosilauke to the parking lot would be our steepest and most technical terrain to date. There was a two-mile section where we'd descend one thousand vertical feet per mile. We walked alongside multiple waterfalls, descending at the same steepness as the water. It was more like down-climbing than hiking. It was scary to imagine how far someone would fall if their foot slipped or they grabbed a loose rock. This is the first time we could see what Hudson had warned us about. Thankfully, we had a birthday party to distract us from the scary climb.

In the days leading to my birthday, Kami was stressing about what to do for it to make it feel really special. It would be our third and final family birthday on the trail, and she felt the pressure of living up to the amazing red velvet cake from her birthday, and the eggs Benedict from Dove's.

In Hanover, a couple named Caitlin and Jodeob had met us on the trail with a backpack full of drinks. "Just so you know, we know the Whites. If you need anything, just ask." Kami had their contact information, so she reached out to ask if they could bring some beers and steaks to the bottom of Mount Moosilauke to surprise me. They were both vegetarians, but said they were glad to help, and drove hours to do so.

Coming down the mountain, we were so excited to get to the finish line that we didn't even realize how difficult the terrain was. Walking alongside the waterfalls, we balanced on wooden boards while holding little metal rungs. We'd been stressing about this section for months, but in this moment of excitement, we didn't pay much attention to it. Later, we realized the experience down the mountain was downright scary, with the sheer heights and slippery metal, especially for Filia, with her small legs, and me, carrying Rainier.

When we were finally off the mountain, we saw a bunch of people we knew up ahead. Hops had arranged a trip to the store and was sitting in a trunk filled with cheese, chips, and pretzels. The Degenerates were all there with pizza and my favorite—fresh blueberries. Caitlin and Jodeob had brought the steaks and beer along with a tiny grill to cook on. And everyone was sitting on the ground in the middle of this small, eight-car parking lot on the side of a two-lane highway.

I sat in awe, looking around the parking lot at this funny type of party that we'd never, in our normal lives, be guests at. Everyone was laughing. We didn't have balloons or cards or presents, we didn't even have chairs, but we had everything. It was the happiest we'd seen the kids in a long time—which was wonderfully ironic, given that we had just climbed the most difficult mountain on the most difficult section of the trail.

The Degenerates taught me how to shotgun a beer; thirty-eight years, and I'd never done it. It turns out it's the kind of thing you should learn young. Kami and the kids laughed uncontrollably while I sputtered and coughed up bubbles. I only made it three-quarters of the way through the can, and came in last place to The Degenerates, who, unsurprisingly, were pros.

It was my favorite birthday ever.

A few local hikers saw the party and joined in. They sat around, ate some food, and enjoyed the companionship. Toward the end of the night, as the sun started to set, we overheard one say to the other, "If this is what the Appalachian Trail is like, I want to do it."

During the birthday party, Caitlin and Jodeob introduced us to Serena, the owner of the Notch Hostel. We had planned to illegally pitch our tents near the parking lot, but knowing it was my birthday, Serena offered us room in the Notch Hostel for free. At first, we politely declined, but instantly regretted that decision. In the Whites, and in the whole of the Technical 200, the opportunities to rest, recharge our phones and the laptop, and consume more calories were far more scarce. We realized we'd be crazy to turn down this opportunity. The fighting in the tents at night had gotten worse. Eden was getting fewer showers than ever, giving her more to complain about than ever, and everyone was sick of each other. We'd mostly declined out of politeness and not wanting to impose; but on the trail, necessity and survival have a way of putting manners in the backseat. We went back to Serena and gratefully accepted her offer. On our first day into the most difficult section yet, we were thrilled to go somewhere where everyone had their own space and bed.

Serena put us up for two nights for free. Caitlyn hiked with us, and Jodeob slackpacked us—which didn't just help with comfort and speed, but in the Technical 200, made a significant positive impact on safety.

The second night at the hostel, we all went out for pizza. At the restaurant, Kami talked with Serena and her husband, Justin, about our doubts, the Whites, and our timeline. Justin was concerned that we only had twenty-eight days to make it to the top of Katahdin. He and Serena made a living helping climbers in this area and spent their off-hours summiting the Whites, so they knew this terrain better than anyone. They also knew the area's statistics for injury and speed. With 372 miles to go through the toughest terrain, and virtually no opportunities to slackpack through the remote Technical 200, he didn't think we'd finish by August 9. Over pizza, he broke down his logic. If our speed in the Technical 200 was cut in half, as everyone said it would be, we could expect a maximum of ten miles a day. It would take us eighteen more days to finish the Whites. Then we'd enter into the final 192 miles of Maine with only ten days remaining. We'd have to do more than nineteen miles a day for ten days straight. We'd never done that before. The entire plan left no room for zero days, errors, injuries, weather, or sickness.

I could tell Kami was deeply shaken. That night while lying in bed, Kami admitted, "I've never been scared of the trail before. I don't think we're going to make it."

I reassured her, but inside, I had the same fear. What were we about to get ourselves into?

CHAPTER TWENTY-TWO

Weather Reports

"The mountain decides whether you climb or not. The art of mountaineering is knowing when to go, when to stay, and when to retreat."

—Ed Viesturs, American mountaineer

Hiking in the Whites was slow and tough. We did thirteen miles, ten miles, and fourteen miles. In order to get more than the ten miles a day we'd projected, we started waking up at 5:00 a.m. to get in more hours of hiking. There was no room for error at this point if we wanted to make our deadline. It's telling that, over the course of our entire hike, we took fourteen total zero days—and only one of those days was in the last three calendar months of the hike.

The weight loss we had experienced for the last four months was starting to become serious. Kami's spine protruded out and poked me while we slept. Although we hadn't adopted personal trail names, we started calling Kami by a new trail name: Gandhi. It was all we could do to make light of a very serious situation.

Of the kids, Dove was having the most trouble eating, and we were worried her weight loss could be dangerous. Rainier, as usual, was actually gaining weight, which made him heavier and slowed us down even more.

So far, the one positive thing was the weather. And that was about to change.

As we approached Mount Washington, the forecast called for thunderstorms. Mount Washington is known as the most dangerous point on the A.T. for weather, and it's the highest point of the north section of the A.T. Everyone is hyper-aware of the conditions. The mountain is also a tourist spot, with a train line and a road ascending the mountain to a gift shop and restaurant at the top. In the visitor center, there's a list called "Casualties of Mount Washington." It lists the 161 known deaths since the state park started recording them in 1849. The cause of most of these deaths is summarized by the six words tacked to the wall in huge type: "The Worst Weather in the World."

Most of the hikers saw the forecast for thunderstorms and planned a zero day, but we had our deadline in mind. It didn't feel like we could take a day off unless it was an absolute necessity. If we stopped just for a weather report, it could set a precedent for the final northern leg of our trip. Now that we'd shown the world we might succeed, the criticisms online had grown quieter. But we wondered what would happen if they heard about our decision to keep going in the face of bad weather on dangerous terrain. Worse still, what if something terrible happened?

Weather reports, just like a lot of other information, can be paralyzing. For months, people had warned us about snakes, ticks, bears, the Pennsylvania rocks, the Whites, the Smokies, and Maine. They'd say, "watch out for..." or "get ready for..." We found that although well-meaning, this type of forward thinking was never helpful because there was no practical application. There was no way to take the information and actually prepare. All we could do was worry.

The weather report looked daunting, but we concluded, just as we had back in the blizzard of the Smokies, that our comfort was more at risk than our safety. The two main dangers were the cold, and slipping and falling. We were prepared for the cold. We'd been through much worse, and as long as we kept moving and kept our tent and sleeping gear dry, nothing would be fatal. For safety with falling, we would just have to assess the risk as we went and trust the kids knew their footing and leg strength. So, even though many hikers were waiting out the weather, including The Degenerates, we decided to push through.

The night before we got to the mountain, we stayed with Hops in a hut. The huts are maintained by a trail organization and provide food and a roof in exchange for work. We slept on the floor of a dining hall with other hikers who stayed up late, whispering under the lights of their headlamps in anticipation of the next day's weather.

On Day 136, we woke up and saw the sun rising behind the mountains. There wasn't a cloud in the sky. It ended up being a sunny day, and we summited with no problems. The view at the top was disappointing, though. The summit was covered in giant antennas, a parking lot, and gift shops. We'd heard there were chili dogs at the gift shop, but we had arrived at 7:30 a.m., and everything was closed. Rainier was especially disappointed about that. For weeks after, every time we mentioned Washington, he'd say, "Washington closed."

As we hiked down the mountain, we saw the train heading up. It felt like the people on board were taking the easy way out. As thru-hikers this far north, we felt the trail was our home, and others passing through were just tourists.

Hops was struggling to go downhill. He'd had problems with his foot since the CrossFit gym, and now he was starting to lag behind. We asked if he needed help. "No," he said. "I'm fine."

We knew he wasn't telling us everything, but we had to keep moving, so we told him we'd meet him at Joe Dodge Lodge, our destination for the night at the bottom of the mountain.

JOE DODGE LODGE

Joe Dodge Lodge was three miles away at 6:30 p.m. It was one of the few facilities in the Whites with food and lodging, and it was on Trail Mentor Hudson's "Must Stop" list. The restaurant was open until 7:30 p.m. At our normal rate of one mile per hour for the Technical 200, we'd get to the buffet two hours late. We held a quick family meeting and told them that if we wanted to go for it, we'd have to torture ourselves for the next hour and run—and we still shouldn't get our hopes up. We maybe had a 10 percent chance of getting there in time.

"We can do it," said Eden. Dove and Memory offered to run ahead and stall them from closing the restaurant. Seven said he'd carry Rainier. And then everyone started running. The kids called it "orcs in daylight mode," a reference to *The Lord of the Rings*. We ran the last three miles with full packs on.

They say the Appalachian Trail is a marathon, not a sprint. That day it was both. We walked into Joe Dodge Lodge at 7:25 p.m. covered in dust and sweat. The staff was kind enough to keep things open an extra fifteen minutes for us. It was a top-notch buffet with organic ingredients and everything made from scratch. After our run, we were famished; we filled up our plates and finished them before we got back to our seats, turning right back around for more. We ate spring mix salad with blue cheese and berries, mac and cheese, caramelized buttered carrots, key lime pie, penne shrimp pasta, and coffee with real half-and-half.

As we ate, we had time to think back on the rush to get there. Dove said, "That was pretty fun running through the forest with a common goal. I can't believe we made it."

Memory reflected, "I was praying we would make it, and I ran the fastest I've ever run in my whole entire life with a pack on."

Eden said, "I'm in a lot of pain, I'm really gross, and I'm really tired. But I am so glad we made it here. It feels like we just won a race!"

By the time the buffet closed, we each had up to five full plates of food in front of us, including dessert. There were times on the trail when our eyes were bigger than our stomachs; this was not one of those times. Our stomachs were way bigger than our eyes. When we left, all the plates were scraped clean.

As we walked out of the restaurant, Kami yawned. "I feel a food coma coming on."

A few weeks prior, a European man named Harm had reached out to us and said he'd been inspired by our videos and wanted to sponsor a night for us in the Whites. He was a member of the mountain club that owned the lodge, and he made all the arrangements. All we had to do was give the lady at the front desk our name. Harm even took care of the buffet check.

Even though Joe Dodge Lodge was on Hudson's recommended list, at $500 a night for our family, we couldn't have done it unless it was a gift. Harm's generosity got us two basic rooms with bunk beds, shared bathrooms, a buffet dinner, and breakfast. The lodge had a piano in the common area, which was a wonderful sight. Back home, the kids played the piano voluntarily for up to an hour a day; on the trail, music had been absent since Bear's Den, the last place we saw Silver. Now, we sat in the cozy living room as it rained outside, listening to the kids' fingers come alive on the keys while eating Ben & Jerry's that Hops had bought from the gift shop. It felt more special than any concert we'd ever been to.

> The music reminded us of home, and how much
> we had changed. Tears streamed down our
> faces as we sat and watched and listened,
> soaking it all in. We felt alive. The music
> itself sounded different having hiked
> eight hundred miles to get to a piano.

Dove and Memory played and sang a duet, "Good Old Days" by Macklemore. The song is about cherishing the present moment, knowing that someday you'll look back on it as magical days long gone. Hearing their two beautiful voices together was mesmerizing.

We had one final twenty-mile stretch before leaving the Whites. It was a notoriously dangerous range of mountain peaks called the Wildcats; the rocks were steep and slippery, and some of the climbs felt technical compared to the rest of the trail. And now, the weather report was calling for nonstop thundershowers.

Staying another day at the lodge would put our timeline in jeopardy and cost us $500; but as much as we wanted to get to Katahdin, we were yet again forced to ask if it was worth risking this type of danger. The thought of spending $500 on one extra night in plain bunkhouses was sickening, but then again, if we had the money, what better use for it could there be than staying dry and together next to a piano, pounding buffets with our friend Hops?

Maybe these were the moments we would remember in ten, twenty, or fifty years. These were the good ol' days. We booked another night.

PLANE TICKETS

We went to the front desk, paid $500 for a second night, and instantly felt relief. It felt nice to give Hops our extra bunk, since Rainier and Filia could sleep in one. It was like we were contributing to the trail magic we'd benefitted from since that first roadside breakfast.

That night, we fell asleep to the sound of Eden and Hops arguing over the ethics of taking advantage of Darn Tough Socks' lifetime guarantee. We'd heard that you could poke holes in your socks and get new ones, no questions asked.

"It's unethical," Eden said. "The warranty is for when they actually wear out, not for when you just want new socks."

"I'm just saying, when the cashier looks at your socks, gives you a wink, and tells you they need a little more 'help' before the warranty kicks in...who's getting hurt?" Hops replied.

After thirty minutes, they quit arguing—not because they had agreed to disagree, but because everyone else in the bunk room was telling them to shut up.

As soon as they fell silent, we all heard it: the rain was pouring down outside. It lulled us all to a deep, satisfied sleep.

The next morning, we slept in and walked through the still-pouring rain to the buffet. It was only at breakfast that we realized how long it had actually been since we took a full day off with no walking. Washington, DC, where we took our last zero day, had been fifty-three days ago! We'd walked through all of West Virginia, Maryland, Pennsylvania, New Jersey, New York, Connecticut, Massachusetts, and Vermont without a single day off. We'd forgotten what it felt like to wake up and not walk.

Caitlin, who'd helped us celebrate my birthday, had introduced us to her friend Whitney, a thru-hiker alumna. After Whitney hiked the A.T., she slept outside in a tent for three months because the transition back to the real world was so hard for her. Whitney was happy to help hikers and do anything to reconnect with the trail people and life. She took our kids into town to get supplies and do laundry. She even bought us beer to drink back at the lodge.

Celebrating our first zero day in fifty-three days was a mixed experience. On one hand, it felt wonderful not to walk, but on the other hand, we had more tasks than ever to catch up on. Our hiking schedule and the terrain had meant no energy at the end of the day and no internet. We were behind on email, social media, and editing and uploading our videos to YouTube for the first time in our entire trip. Even our gear had suffered. Instead of being able to see ahead where we were going to stay and order new equipment for when we arrived, we'd opted to make do with what we had and just hope it lasted. My rain jacket was no longer even waterproof and stuck to my arm like wet Saran Wrap.

While the kids were off enjoying their time to themselves, Kami and I looked into a task that seemed foolishly optimistic. We had to buy plane tickets to Lakeside for when we finished the trail.

We'd told the kids that as long as they gave it their all, we'd go, whether we finished the hike or not.

The kids had given it their all. We were going to Lakeside.

Eight one-way tickets to Seattle, Washington—the nearest airport to Lakeside—was a total of $1,900, which seemed like a great deal for last-minute flights. The only little problem was the flight was from Portland, Maine, so we'd have to arrange transportation

Tuesday July 17th 2018 Day # 136

ZERO DAY!! WOKE UP AT LIKE, 7:30 WENT
TO BREAKFAST WHICH WAS PRETTY FANCY
AND WATCHED THE RAIN COME DOWN AND WATCHED
HIKERS SHOW UP ARMOUR, ALASKA, ROCKET MAN, HOPS,
& FLASH ALL CAME AND ATE BREAKFAST WITH US.
THAT WAS FUN. AT 11:30 WHITNEY CAME AND
PICKED EDEN, FLASH, AND I UP TO GO DO
LAUNDRY AND RESUPPLY. I HAD TO RESUPPLY
FOR EVERYONE 8 MEALS, BREAKFAST, LUNCH & DINNER AND
A BUNCH OF OTHER RANDOM THINGS. IT WAS STRESSFULL
AND I FORGOT THE CREAM CHEESE. BUT IT WAS FUN
CHATTING WITH WHITNEY, WHO THRU HIKED IN 2014.
HAD A REALLY RELAXING 9 AM TIME IN THE LOBBY
AREA WITH THE PIANO AT NIGHT. BILL BOUGHT PHISH
FOOD. ITS NICE THAT WE'VE DONE ENOUGH MILES TO
BE ABLE TO TAKE A ZERO. HOPEFULLY WON'T HAVE
TO TAKE ANOTHER TILL WE'RE DONE. BILL & EDEN ARGUED
ABOUT DARN TUFF SOCKS LOL.

Dove (17) recaps our first zero day in 53 days which was a welcome surprise
but also a much-needed opportunity to catch up on a bunch of tasks.

from Mount Katahdin to Portland. A shuttle ride would take more than six hours, but the tickets were bought, and there was no turning back. We were totally committed to finishing.

We bought the plane tickets on Day 138. We were twenty-three days from the finish line, with 318 miles to go. This meant fourteen miles a day, which would have been okay on easy terrain. We still had more than one hundred miles left of the Technical 200, though, and we were being held back by a thunderstorm.

The next morning, we left an envelope with the receptionist containing buffet coupons that we'd squirreled away for The Degenerates. We'd heard they'd taken a few days to celebrate in town—the excuse, not that they needed one, was that Not Dead had been awarded an educational grant. After writing "Degenerates" on the envelope and handing it to the receptionist, we hit the trail.

The Wildcats were tough. Kami fell once and banged her knee, but she was able to keep walking. We didn't reach the campsite until 9:20 p.m., which meant an hour of hiking in the dark. There we found Hops nestled up in a pile of pine needles. Besides that, we had hiked the Whites with no serious incident, and two days after leaving Joe Dodge Lodge, we walked out of the White Mountain National Forest. We were finished with the first half of the Technical 200.

Rainier was super excited to hear that Fresh Ground (or Fwesh Gwound, as he called him) was up ahead, and ran the last half-mile himself. And the rumor was true: Fresh Ground was at a road crossing cooking lunch. Fresh Ground planned his food stops by choosing a hiker or a group of hikers that he referred to as his "engine." He would follow this person and time his cooking setups at road stops based upon their arrival. At the road stop, the person was guaranteed to be fed along with the dozens of other hikers traveling in either direction who just happened to be there. In this way, he would proceed up the trail at the pace of his chosen engine.

In this case, his engine was a woman named PeeWee, who, like us, had been filming her hike and posting the videos to YouTube. He had been following her hike across multiple states.

"I knew you guys were comin'!" Fresh Ground said as he held out a piece of watermelon.

He was serving sloppy joes with homemade french fries, and had even picked up some macaroni and cheese for the kids. Hops showed up, and we sat around enjoying the food and celebrating our completion of the Whites.

Hops said he didn't want to leave.

"You've been Fresh Grounded!" I said. This became the term for the universal hiker experience of not wanting to leave Fresh Ground's tent.

Eventually, we got our packs on and said goodbye to Hops. He said he'd meet us at the campsite up the trail. On the road, we passed a hostel. It would have been nice to stay there, but we had eight more miles to do that day, so we kept on walking.

We later found out that Hops had stayed at the hostel we'd passed. He'd broken a bone in his foot and not told us about it. That was why he'd been dragging behind for the last few weeks.

We felt terrible for him. Hops had helped us since the Smokies, where he saved us spots in the shelter. He'd offered our kids pizza at the hostel, helped us get our feet sized for Altras, arranged transportation and lodging with Jordan and Kristen during our sickness and the forest fire, and paid for our Chinese food. And now, it looked like his lifelong dream was at an end.

That was the last time we would ever see Hops, and we hadn't even said goodbye. Once again, we were reminded that no matter how close Katahdin felt, we could not let our guard down. One slip up and our trip would be over.

CHAPTER TWENTY-THREE

Bad News

"Man is born to die, his work short lived; buildings crumble, monuments decay, wealth vanishes, but Katahdin, in all its glory, shall forever remain the mountain of the people of Maine. Throughout the ages it will stand as an inspiration to the men and women of the state."

—Percival Baxter, former governor of Maine

On Day 141, we walked into Maine, our final state. Now that we had made it halfway through the Technical 200, we still had one hundred miles of difficult terrain left.

Maine seemed like a cross between Alaska and Texas. The people there call themselves Mainers. They're proud, independent, and enjoy their isolation; they think of themselves as wild and rugged. The A.T. in Maine is known for moose and dangerous river fords. There's a story that says the trail in Maine was built through the state in a month, not a year, the timeline it would typically take to find the most walkable path and clear the trail of massive obstacles. Instead of creating a trail, they just took a bucket of paint and splashed white blazes across existing boulder fields.

THE HARDEST MILE

We started the morning with PeeWee, Fresh Ground's "engine" who had arrived in camp with us the night before. We set out for the most famous mile of the trail, the Mahoosuc Notch. It's essentially a mile-long boulder field obstacle course. We strapped our trekking poles to our packs because we had to use our hands, paying close attention to every step. Our packs were still heavy and there were times we had to squeeze through tunnels and cracks so small, we had to remove our packs.

PeeWee, who had never hiked with our family and was used to hiking alone, filmed our family and provided commentary for the whole experience.

"This is a nice camera, I hope I don't drop it...We are now standing in a single-fiiiiiiiiile line with Rainier in the front, and it is verrrry slooooow."

Right in front of PeeWee, Dove squeezed through an especially narrow section and popped her head out into the sunlight.

"Look! The mountain is giving birth to a Crawford!"

There were ten-foot drops. We had to pass Rainier back and forth and coach him to crawl through tiny cracks. We often sent the kids ahead to find the easiest path. There were large, cavernous gaps in the rock that sometimes went down for twenty feet into the dark. It was so remote and deep, there was still snow and ice on the ground in August. At one point, PeeWee dropped our camera.

"It fell into a hole that's in a hole that's in a hole," she said. With some hard work and help reaching from the smaller hands in the family, we eventually got it back. The whole thing would have been a great weekend excursion back home, but it was hard not to focus on the danger and our slow pace.

Finally, after a lot of climbing, crawling, some laughing, and one cracked camera screen, we reached the end of Mahoosuc Notch. It had taken an hour and a half to cover what we thought was one mile. We walked around the corner and saw much bigger boulders and another sign announcing we were only halfway through. Normally, navigating a boulder field that felt like an obstacle course combined with a natural playground with kids would be fun. But when you need to be averaging more than fourteen miles a day, spending three hours to do a single mile takes the wind out of your sails.

We came up with a tedious but effective process where we would go up twenty feet, set Rainier down, and go back and help everyone else. At one point, we lost track of Rainier. He popped out of a different hole than the one we expected—a hole no one else could fit through.

Once in the Notch, there was no place to stop for food or bathroom breaks. This was something Kami and I took notice of; the weight loss of our group was starting to reach red-alert levels, and force-feeding everyone snacks at regular intervals had become a normal discipline just as important as walking itself. We had started off with Memory carrying all the snacks, but now each person carried two mandatory snacks that needed to be eaten every hour.

Three hours later, we finished the mile-long Mahoosuc Notch together and sat down to have a snack together. What a relief.

As I walked, a thought crossed my mind: what if I offered Fresh Ground $1,000 to join our family for the rest of the trip and cook food for us?

It seemed like a practical arrangement; he'd get money, and I'd be ensuring our success. There was virtually no amount of money I wasn't willing to pay to make sure we made our goal. The single biggest thing I could do toward that end was invest in nutrition, because Dove and Kami were teetering on the edge of bonking out and not being able to hike at all. They'd lost the most weight of any of us, and couldn't seem to eat enough food.

As we sat there debriefing with PeeWee what it was like to hike with a family, something about my idea didn't feel quite right. I thought back to how I first offered Fresh Ground a donation and he turned it down. He didn't seem like a man that was motivated by money. The hardest challenges of the A.T. can't be solved with money. And even if this one challenge could, I felt like an offer like this might offend Fresh Ground and compromise why he was out here. We could tell that he was out here to find fulfillment of his own, and the way he did that was by going to the hikers who he perceived had the greatest need. Offering him money would, ironically, cheapen what he was out there to do. Even though we were heading into the most remote section of the trail, away from towns and the amenities of the southern sections, we would have to put the trail's provision to the test. Would the trail continue to provide?

THE CABIN

That night, we stayed at The Cabin, a hostel run by an older couple who called themselves Honey and Bear. We'd heard it was the longest-running hostel on the A.T. All the guidebook said was, "Alumni hikers welcome by reservation only."

That was not very welcoming, as we were not alumni. But we bumped into a veteran hiker named Odie who gave us the owners' contact information and said The Cabin would be a great fit.

Odie had a mohawk and a big beard, drove a short school bus, and was known for putting together *The Hiker Yearbook*, a scrapbook of images from the hiking year that looked like a high school yearbook. He spent six months creating the yearbook and posting things on Facebook like, "I'm considering buying more clothes so I don't have to do laundry naked, or at least start going to a less popular laundromat." The other half of the year, he walked the trail with copies of his yearbook in his backpack, giving out bracelets advertising *The Hiker Yearbook* and trying to inform people about trail culture and history. Every year, he gave a famous speech at the Trail Days Festival in Damascus, Virginia. He stood on top of his van with a megaphone, delivered his speech, and passed out $1,000 worth of candy bars to hikers.

Odie knew we were close and offered to take us to The Cabin in his school bus. We told him we weren't alumni. "Don't worry about it," he said. "You guys will really like each other."

Honey and Bear were both in their eighties. They had a home that had been literally made for hikers, and every night, they served a family-style dinner around a huge dining room table. They finished by bringing out a three-gallon tub of the locally famous Gifford's Moose Tracks ice cream. They served a fresh-cooked breakfast every morning.

We still had about ninety miles left of the Technical 200. Maine was slow, with steep climbs up smooth, granite rock faces and treacherous river crossings. Where Pennsylvania was known for its rocks, Maine was known for its roots. Very slippery tree roots covered most of the trail. We had more falls on those roots than all the rest of the trail combined. They were the same color as the dirt, but when you stepped on them, your foot would slide in an unpredictable direction. We started logging days that were barely ten miles, sometimes less.

Most hikers, including PeeWee, were taking zero days at The Cabin because of the weather, which was consistently cloudy and rainy. They said it was too wet, too dangerous, and too miserable. You could do damage do your feet if they were wet all day tromping through puddles.

We desperately wanted to take a zero, but we had less than eighteen days until our deadline, so we left the hostel in the morning while other people sat inside watching movies, waiting out the weather, and soaking their feet in Epsom-salt baths. It was downright depressing to walk out into the rain, knowing that others with more relaxed timelines were enjoying themselves and could hike at their leisure once it became sunny. It was especially demoralizing because we weren't even sure we could finish. There was every chance we were torturing ourselves for no reason.

Right on cue, the trail provided.

Odie, who was preparing to fly to the West Coast to try and start a hiker yearbook for the Pacific Crest Trail, dropped everything and offered to slackpack us for the next four days. The farther north we got, the more rare these offers were because the trail became more and more remote. The towns were fewer, the stores were more difficult to get to, and cellphone reception became nonexistent. Gratefully, we accepted his offer.

Slackpacking through the Technical 200 helped our bodies burn less calories, increased our speed—which at this point meant we could get a full eight hours of sleep—and meant we were safer walking on the slippery roots and rocks. Every day, we ended at a road, and Odie picked us up in our own private school bus and drove us back to The Cabin. We never could have dreamt up this scenario. We had never even asked him for help. Although the trail was almost always wet and slippery, being pack-free and knowing we were returning to The Cabin for warm meals made the tough terrain feel so much more doable.

Numerous mornings, we headed up a hill into the rain and saw thru-hikers and day hikers turning around, saying it was "too dangerous" or it "wasn't worth it." Every time, we were prepared to turn around if it got too sketchy, but we moved forward knowing Odie would be waiting for us in his school bus. Usually, he'd hike up to meet us in the rain. On these days, the difficult terrain meant our miles were short. We walked ten miles, ten miles, and thirteen miles—well below the average we needed. It looked like Justin from the Notch Hostel was right. Ten miles was the max average.

No matter what, every day, we went out and hiked. We moved forward.

Honey and Bear hosted us for four nights. Because of Odie being willing to shuttle us around, it was the longest we'd stayed in one place on the trail. For that, they charged us the standard rate of twenty-five dollars per adult. This included the all-you-can-eat, home-cooked breakfast, and dinner and ice cream every day. They even sent our family out with all of the leftovers and packed us lunches, which are not usually included.

I tried to pay for some of the kids, saying they ate as much as adults, and all I heard back was that kids and veterans were free. I argued about the size of our family and how they'd be losing money if they fed our six kids two meals a day, but Bear, who didn't say much, simply said, "The price is the price. We want to see more kids on the trail."

THE PHONE CALL

Our third night at The Cabin, we made a phone call that we were not looking forward to.

We'd heard rumors that children six and under weren't allowed to go above the tree line to the summit of Mount Katahdin for safety

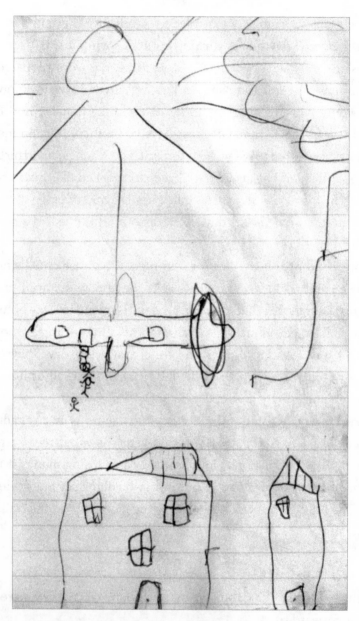

Another drawing from Filia (7), who had planes on the brain. Now that we'd bought tickets for eight people, we would be flying out on August 10 (Day 162) whether we made it to the top of Katahdin or not.

reasons. Mount Katahdin is 5,267 feet above sea level.[1] On its peak is the famous A-frame sign that marks the official northern terminus of the A.T. It's the end. The tree line, the farthest point Rainier would be allowed to go, is the point of elevation at which the trees stop growing. On Mount Katahdin, this is at about three thousand feet above sea level, two miles short of the sign at the top.

We'd heard about this rule for a while, but we'd also heard numerous stories of exceptions that had been made, and we were fairly confident that we qualified to be one of them. In 2013, a five-year-old hiker named Christian Thomas, who was known as Buddy Backpacker, was given permission by the rangers and summited Katahdin with his parents after hiking half of the A.T. In 2015, Lisa Murray took a picture at the sign with her two five-year-old twins, who'd completed the trail over two years. In 2014, Roger Poulin completed an A.T. hike that took him four years. Although he was an adult, he was deaf and blind and had to be accompanied to the top. So, we knew there was some flexibility in the regulations.

We weren't the first thru-hikers to bump up against Baxter State Park regulations—not by a long shot. In fact, the relationship between Baxter State Park and the Appalachian Trail hikers has been strained for quite some time.

Here's some of the context we'd heard about Baxter State Park vs. thru-hikers. Percival Baxter, the governor of Maine from 1921–1925, was a *very* interesting character who bought up all the land

---

1   There are differing opinions on how high it is. Hudson and several pamphlets put out by Baxter State Park insist it's 5,267. Wikipedia says 5,269. This is an important two-foot discrepancy that must be noted; after all, as Hudson says, you can't trust everything you read online.

that makes up Baxter State Park. When he died at the age of eighty-seven, he bequeathed the park to the people of Maine, along with a trust of $7 million to maintain it—money they could only access as long as they followed an incredibly specific list of requirements he set forth. To this day, according to the park's own staff, it functions "like a cult" because the park and money are dedicated to carrying out the vision of Percival Baxter.

The goal of Baxter was to keep the land "forever wild." This means that unlike the US National Parks system, which is set up to encourage as many visitors as possible, Baxter's list of rules is bent toward making access to the park *difficult.*

Some of Baxter's strange rules: all employees must be from Maine. No paved roads allowed. And, of course, no one under the age of six is allowed above the tree line.

A recent example of "rule breaking": on July 12, 2015, ultrarunner Scott Jurek set the record for the fastest supported time on the A.T., beating Jennifer Pharr Davis's record set in 2011 by three hours, finishing in forty-six days. When he reached the sign at the top of Katahdin, he popped a bottle of champagne to celebrate his incredible achievement. Baxter State Park promptly issued him three citations for consuming alcohol, littering (presumably from the champagne spray—because as a staunch environmentalist, he carefully packed out the bottle and cork), and traveling in a group larger than twelve (since his summit was attended by his support crew, some family and friends, and news media).

While Jurek was happy to admit that he did indeed consume the alcohol, he said he'd checked with park rangers first. "I had a couple of sips of champagne," he explained. "A friend brought the bottle without my knowledge to surprise me, and two rangers at the bottom gave him a verbal okay."

The last two charges were eventually dismissed, but Jurek had to pay a $500 fine for consuming the champagne.

Baxter State Park also took issue with the fact that Scott wore a headband with the name of his sponsor, something that they claim violates their rules prohibiting commercial activity in the park.

Immediately after Jurek's accomplishment, BSP posted on their Facebook page: "With all due respect to Mr. Jurek's ability, Baxter State Park was not the appropriate place for such an event."

After the incident, it was pretty universally agreed upon that Scott Jurek was being made an example of for an outstanding issue and ongoing contradiction of values. According to its mission statement, the Appalachian Trail's goal is to provide first "for maximum outdoor recreation potential as an extended trail," which essentially means that the goal of the ATC is to get as many hikers out on the trail as possible. Baxter "State" Park's goal is uniquely opposite.

Because Baxter State Park contains the A.T.'s northern terminus at Mount Katahdin, thru-hikers have been butting up against the park's rigid rule system for decades. Increased tensions have caused BSP to publicly threaten pulling permission from thru-hikers to summit Katahdin—which would obviously necessitate moving the terminus. While many have said this is unlikely and was a political move, the impact upon keyboard warriors has been dramatic, with a rise of people blaming thru-hikers who try to skirt the rules. Online, you'll see a lot of rhetoric like "it only takes one" and "you could jeopardize it for everyone." They essentially (unfairly, in my opinion) put the pressure of the entire future hiking community into the hands of one hiker. So, for us, asking for an exception to Baxter's rules wasn't just about us, unfortunately. We'd started the hike by just walking along the trail, but now our finish had the potential to be turned into a hinge in a political debate between factions. Even just *asking* for an exception to the rules was political.

We'd waited until now to ask for an exception for Rainier because we wanted to be taken seriously, not as some rookies in Georgia with big plans and a high chance of quitting. By now, we were confident we had a chance to make it to Baxter State Park, and thought we could prove to the officials we were at least as qualified as those who had been allowed to summit previously. We'd hiked more than 1,900 miles and been above the tree line more times than we could count in rain, heat, and snow.

Taking a picture with that A-frame sign was synonymous with finishing the trail. By now, it had been burned into our minds by all the postcards and pictures hanging in homes, museums, hostels, and even restaurants that standing on the sign meant success. If it persuaded the Baxter officials, we were even prepared to hire a guide or let them know Kami had a nursing degree. We would make any accommodations necessary to be able to give the kids and ourselves the finish we'd dreamed of for the last five months.

That evening we sat outside The Cabin after hiking through the rain all day. Out on the lawn, Memory giggled as Fresh Ground applied bright purple dye to her brown hair, a treat he'd picked up on a trip to the grocery store. Kami and I watched as I held the phone to my ear; I was waiting for Eben, the superintendent of Baxter State Park, to pick up. Apprehension gnawed at my belly.

When Eben finally did pick up, the conversation was brutally short.

"It's not possible for you to go to the top with your two-year-old. We don't allow it."

We asked if there was anything we could do to give Baxter peace of mind and said we knew other people had done it. Could we hire guides or sign waivers?

Eben repeated himself. "It's not possible. We don't allow it." And then he denied the stories that we knew were true. "We can't make exceptions, and we never have," he said. Eben was friendly, but he wasn't telling the truth, and there was nothing we could do about it.

"Thank you for your time," we said, and hung up the phone.

It was a huge letdown. It felt discriminatory. It was bureaucratic bullshit. We were crushed. For five months and fourteen states, we had kept moving by telling ourselves we were A.T. thru-hikers. And thru-hikers hike until they get to the sign.

But due to a technicality, we weren't going to finish together. At least, not legally.

The thought of telling the kids made us sick to our stomachs. While we'd been on the phone, they'd been keeping an eye on Rainier. Seven was watching movies, Dove was making Oreo balls because she had access to a kitchen, and Memory was dyeing her hair with Fresh Ground and PeeWee. We decided to let them have their fun that night.

The next day, during our lunch break in the rain, we gathered the courage to tell the kids. "We have some bad news, guys," I said. I explained what was happening.

The kids were flabbergasted. "That's so stupid!" Dove said.

"But we've carried Rainier this whole way. Up so many summits. It doesn't make any sense," said Eden.

"It's unfair," said Seven. "I feel like it's right in the middle between not being a big deal, and destroying our entire trip. I hope we can figure something out."

As the parents and leaders, Kami and I knew we had a tough decision to make. But we would have to figure it out later; it was still raining, and we had sixty miles left of the Technical 200.

CHAPTER TWENTY-FOUR

A Friend Returns

"...it is very important simply to accept wherever one finds oneself and to trust each unique process of discovery and resolution. There are heavens and hell in all of us, and much to learn in each realm."

—William A. Richards, psychologist,
author of *Flight Instructions: Insights from
Four Decades of Navigation Within Consciousness*

We soon found out why Maine was known for being wild. Other states had bridges over the bigger creeks; Maine doesn't bother with bridges. On a few nights, it rained like crazy, and we wondered if the rivers would be impassable. One flooded river could prevent us from finishing the trail or even making our flight to Lakeside. It was a constant reminder of how outside of our control finishing actually was.

Getting started on rainy days was hard. We'd spent months trying to keep our shoes dry, and now we had to deliberately submerge them in rushing water, which felt more "wild" than even we were used to. Most of the time, we'd just look at each other, stare at the water, and then take a step. The cold water would instantly fill our shoes and soak our socks—even reaching our shorts in deeper rivers. At one point, we were up to our midsections in water, thanks to the heavy rain. Three or four of these river crossings were difficult for the smaller kids. At times, I had to carry the younger ones on my back, returning to help another person and making multiple trips across. Thankfully, we passed through the rivers without any serious mishaps.

We weren't the only ones struggling with the rain. PeeWee had dropped behind, taking several zero days; we were now forty miles ahead of her. It was unlikely that she'd ever be able to catch up. The trail was getting to her; her YouTube videos showed her constantly breaking down and crying on camera. Everyone was going through difficult times as established tramilies broke up—people, even this close to the end, were quitting left and right, simply reaching the end of their ropes. It was something I'm sure would have happened to us if we didn't have a group and a deadline. We had no idea where The Degenerates were, but it was looking like we might never see them again either.

Leaving PeeWee behind meant saying goodbye to Fresh Ground. I had mixed feelings about remaining silent about my idea to try and buy his help. Making the offer didn't feel right, but to have his help would have been so nice. In some ways, not making him an offer to join us felt irresponsible. If there was something I could do to increase our odds of finishing, especially since it involved the kids' nutrition, logic said to do it. But even though his support had been so important to us, and we were sad to lose it, something felt wrong about the offer, and I didn't make it.

I decided to trust in Silver's mantra. The trail provides.

Fewer and fewer hikers were out because of the dangerous terrain and storms that we were walking right into the middle of. After six days straight of rain and river crossings, we finally came across another hiker, a man coming down from Crocker Mountain as we were going up.

His head was bandaged; we could tell it had been pieced together out in the field. "I'm not going any farther. The storm is too dangerous. I fell back there and smacked my head," he told us.

There was nothing we could do but hope we were stronger, more careful, and luckier than him. Our time in the Technical 200 had worn us down. We were only doing twelve or thirteen miles a day; before entering this section, we had no problem hiking twenty-mile days. It felt like we'd gone backward, like we'd lost whatever magic or strength we'd built up.

GROWTH IN OUR DARKEST MOMENTS

During the tail end of the Technical 200, it was raining. We were wet and had been walking through rivers all day. Literally, the trail was a makeshift river, and often times, we couldn't even see our ankles underwater.

I had been pushing our family nonstop. The deadline we had set for ourselves was a constant pressure I had felt for five months. Every day since we had started the trail back in March was work. Even the days not spent walking, we thought about and prepared for walking. Every day was forward. Every day, we were not finished. Every day, there was more pressure.

If we finished, we would be famous. We could tell the internet haters, "We told you so." We could show Kami's family, who had written her off, that we were valuable after all. We could finally check off the bucket-list goal we had set for ourselves sixteen years earlier. And yet no matter how far we hiked, we were always one step away from failing. One literal step. Failure meant we spend the rest of our lives remembering how we had almost finished the A.T. Our pictures would be a constant reminder of a section of trail that was incomplete. And if we couldn't finish it this year, the chances of us ever trying it again were nonexistent. This meant that every moment now could have an impact on the rest of our lives. If one child twisted an ankle, our entire group was finished. With the kids running around and playing, jumping off rocks, every optional activity that wasn't moving us forward was a threat to our mission. It wasn't worth it. At moments, I'd become a tyrant, wanting to stop everything that wasn't walking. Halt all play; there would be time to play later. For now, we had to hike.

I had been pushing nonstop for 150 days. "Let's go." "Almost there." "C'mon!" "You can do it." Different words, all saying the same thing. I'd repeated these phrases thousands of times for the last five months, and I didn't even know if I believed them. I felt like the youth pastor talking to kids about abstinence when he already knows most of them are sleeping around.

I'd been in a battle with myself that harkened all the way back to the moment in Georgia when I'd flicked Rainier's lip in frustration. I wanted to be able to let go, to let everyone react to the trail naturally instead of rushing for the deadline. I wanted to be able to let each kid hike their own hike. But the pressure I felt to keep our family moving wouldn't go away.

A breaking point came in Maine. Seven was carrying Rainier, and I had been in a constant war with Seven to keep moving. On this particular day, he seemed particularly mopey and was lagging behind constantly. Because of our rule to never have a kid be the last person in the group (especially when carrying Rainier), our group was getting more and more spread out, and I was having to hang farther and farther back. I was getting increasingly frustrated. Everything I said passive-aggressively, or even aggressive-aggressively, wasn't working. There was nothing I could do to speed Seven up, and I felt helpless.

We were walking single file, and I was pushing Seven by Rainier's backpack kid-carrier. There was a bar on the back that I could apply a little pressure to. I kept pushing harder and harder because I knew Seven was capable of more. It was obvious Seven was getting flustered, because I'd raised my voice, and it looked like there may have been tears in Seven's eyes.

But instead of stopping to listen, I pushed harder.

We had gone fifty or sixty feet like this, and then, it happened. Seven tripped and fell into the water.

Rainier started crying because even though his head didn't go under, he was scared from falling. Seven's face landed in the water, and his arms and jacket were soaked. He fought to control the tears welling up in his eyes.

Instantly, I tried to yank my two boys back up. My first instinct was to blame Seven for not watching his feet (something we had remind the kids to do constantly) and scold him to be more careful.

Then Kami looked at me with wide, angry eyes, confronting me. "Did you push Seven down?"

I hadn't; Seven had tripped. I stammered and hawed and defended myself, but now everyone was looking. Everyone knew what had happened. If I hadn't been pushing Seven, he wouldn't have fallen.

Whether I had pushed him down or pushed him so he tripped was irrelevant. What mattered was that

> I was out of control and saw my son as something
> that was preventing me from achieving my goal.

It was a sobering moment. While my pride had taken too much of a hit to apologize right then, I was plagued with thoughts about what could have happened. Seven could have been permanently hurt. He could have broken a bone. Rainier could have hit his head. Either one being injured would have ended the hike for the whole family.

But instead of just thinking about what could have happened, I also thought about what did happen.

I had humiliated my son. I had bullied and physically manhandled him. I had ignored his feelings, his voice, his pace, and his struggles.

People often choose to see stories like this as anomalies to be swept under the rug, explained away. They say, "That's not really who I am, that's an exception."

But, just like back in the cold in Georgia, what if these moments— when I was at the end of my rope, when I lost my temper, when I was failing—were actually the truest look at who I was, and how I needed to grow?

We had paid a therapist thousands of dollars over the course of three years to help us heal because he could give us frank and objective observations about who we really were. To offer us a glimpse into ourselves that wasn't always pleasant but was objectively true.

In contrast, this lesson was free. It was a glimpse into who I really was, and I didn't like it.

Being raised by an Asian mom and a perfectionist dad, I wasn't raised seeing failure as an option. My mom would sacrifice sleep and comfort to avoid failure; my dad would simply keep his hidden. So I never saw it. Failure was not allowed. I didn't allow it in myself. And when I saw it in my kids, I couldn't allow it in them either. While

I had grown away from this mindset through therapy, there were deep parts of me that were still afraid of failure and made themselves known on rare occasions. They only appeared when all of my camouflage and coping skills had run out.

And now, the arbitrary goal of touching a sign at the top of a mountain had taken precedence over the acceptance and free will of my son. Instead of listening and trying to understand his perspective, I had used force to further my own agenda and satisfy my own fears.

For Kami, this was the lowest emotional point of the whole trip (so much so that we made it through the first eight drafts of this book before realizing we needed to include it in the story). She would later say that she was embarrassed to have been a part of that incident. She couldn't help but wonder if there were warning signs she'd missed, or if she should have stepped in and stopped me earlier.

My biggest moment of not living up to my own standards as a father didn't come from a mundane incident. It didn't come from dragging the kids through a grocery store, or a mall, or a parking lot. In those instances, it's easy to blame the kid: they're tired, they're not behaving. My moment came in the middle of a high-stakes adventure, when my kids were pushed to their limits. On the trail, no one claim the kids were lazy; no one could claim they were just complaining, like kids do. And so I was forced to look at the other side of the equation: me.

I would have to dig deeper, and look deeper. I knew I would need to make amends with my son in the form of an apology and being willing to make it right. But more than a singular apology, I would need to lean on my humility, and the commitment I'd made to constantly be willing to self-reflect, to examine the drive that makes me parent the way I do.

> The trail gave us the full spectrum of
> experiences: beautiful ones, and horrible ones.
> We couldn't pick and choose what we took away.
> We'd gone out there to experience it all.

My task now was to accept what the trail was showing me. Had I changed at all? Was the trip a waste? If I had hiked two thousand miles and was still a controlling dad prioritizing my goals over the kids' well-being, could anyone really hope for growth? And what message was I sending to the kids? I was supposed to be a role model, but through my behavior, I was telling them that the end goal is more important than individual choice.

How would this affect them as they started to make decisions on their own?

BEYOND MISTAKES

On Day 149, five days after leaving The Cabin, we went into the final difficult section of the Technical 200: the Bigelow mountain range. Just as we entered this part of the trail, a couple named Brad and Beth contacted us. They'd attempted a thru-hike that same year but had quit due to the cold and difficulty early on. Having seen our videos, they wanted to host and offer to slackpack us one last time. Maybe we wouldn't have to finish the trail on our own.

Beth told us that watching me lead the kids reminded her of her father. "Back when I was knee high to a grasshopper, he started running around the neighborhood, and he got us into running," she explained, tearing up at the memory. "We'd run around the block and see how fast we were, and then he'd have us running this cross-country course under the power lines. We were little kids running five miles out in the woods. Our neighbors thought he was off the wall."

There was obviously more to the story that she wasn't sharing; no parent is perfect, and I'm sure her dad hadn't been. But I was blown away that, in a whole childhood, these were the moments she remembered, the scenes that really stood out.

She looked me up and down, as though she was remembering her dad. "Doing what you're doing with your kids at this age is just remarkable, and the communication that you have with them is beyond belief. I can't even express what feeling it gives me to see that. You know, you don't have that anymore in families. I think it's phenomenal what you guys have accomplished. And no one getting hurt, and you guys have come two thousand miles and you're way stronger than you were six months ago...I don't know what else to say." She was crying.

I hugged her, tears in my own eyes. I'd never had anyone tell me I reminded them of their dad in a positive way. Usually it was with a tone of voice that revealed resentment and bitterness. It felt really good to be used to reignite Beth's beautiful memories of her favorite person.

In general, I believed that I was doing what was best for my kids, but the barrage of comments online combined with my failures on trail had made me constantly wonder if I really was. What we were risking with the lifelong relationship with our kids was far worse than anything we risked climbing mountains in the rain. To hear stories for the first time of someone from the other side made me feel like maybe the risk was worthwhile.

It was just the boost I needed, and that we all needed at that moment. It's hard to really convey what the Technical 200 meant to us. We'd been warned about it all along, and the warnings hadn't even prepared us fully for the difficulty and exhaustion of the section. We were totally drained at this point, mentally and physically.

Somehow, with the help of Odie and his school bus, Honey and Bear and their Cabin, Serena at the Notch Hostel and Harm at Joe Dodge Lodge, and Brad and Beth in the last two days, we finished the section. We finished in the rain while other hikers were stopping. We kept moving forward. In the nineteen days it took us to travel the 226 miles, we ended up averaging just under twelve miles a day. That was two more miles a day than Justin had forecasted back on the night he'd scared Kami. This may not seem like much, but when you multiply that by the nineteen days it took us, we had done more than an extra thirty-five miles as a team.

On top of Mount Bigelow, at the end of that difficult section, we took some pictures of the sprawling views. It was the most beautiful scenery we'd seen on the trail.

We usually had our cellphone turned off, as we rarely got a signal on the trail and wanted to conserve its battery, but in the few minutes we had it on to take pictures, we got a call from Fresh Ground. He wanted to know our plans for the next few days so we could meet up. This was unexpected—Fresh Ground had never contacted us before, and it sounded like he thought it was better to give PeeWee her space in finishing the trail without him—so the possibility was very exciting.

"Never plan on me being there, but if I can, I'd like to help you guys," was how he signed off.

As we headed down Mount Bigelow, relieved at finally finishing the Technical 200, the kids reminisced about Fresh Ground's great food and how much they'd enjoyed watching movies with him at The Cabin. It felt like the hardest part of the trail was over.

Then I got sick.

I started to feel like I had the flu. Kami had to lead everyone in the dark for the last two miles to our campsite. Some of the kids were crying by the time we arrived, and by that point my body ached everywhere.

We quickly put up the tents, and everyone went to bed right away—everyone except Kami, who lay awake, worrying.

"Ben still doesn't feel good. If he's really sick—if he has the flu—I don't know. This might be the end. All this work, all this time…and it might be over," she said into our camera that night.

We were ten days from finishing and still had 135 miles to go. What if I couldn't walk the next day? If I actually had the flu, we were done. We couldn't take a day off, let alone a few days.

The next morning, Kami and the kids woke up at 6:00 a.m., preparing for the worst. They let me sleep in while they ate packaged doughnuts for breakfast.

I woke up feeling fine. Better than fine—great. Whatever sickness I'd had was mysteriously gone.

That day, we hiked 19.7 miles. The last time we'd managed that many miles was exactly one month before, back in Vermont. But with me feeling better, the easier terrain, and the motivation to meet Fresh Ground for dinner, we finished the miles and three river crossings with no problem.

After dinner, the owners of Shaw's Hiker Hostel picked us up. This hostel is featured in Bill Bryson's book *A Walk in the Woods: Rediscovering America on the Appalachian Trail*. In the book, Bryson refers to Shaw's as the most famous accommodation on the entire trail. It sits on the south side of the Hundred-Mile Wilderness, the longest A.T. stretch without any resupply areas. This section isn't technically difficult, but it's called a "wilderness" for a reason: there are no public roads, no resupply stores, no hotels or hostels, and no phone service for emergencies for one hundred straight miles. This means hikers must carry nine days' worth of food, which significantly increases pack weight, especially the first few days.

While we had been through a lot, nine days of wilderness presented some new challenges. Everyone had lost so much weight, and we were sick of the sight of tortillas, Nutella, and granola bars. We had to force ourselves to eat on the trail. This was especially true for Kami and Dove. They'd continued to lose the most weight, and I did all I could to get them to eat. I bought all their favorite foods; I pushed more food in front of them at every opportunity. I cheered them on, and when that didn't get them to eat, I tried cajoling them. I tried sarcasm. I tried guilt. Nothing worked. All Kami could say was, "I'm trying my best, but I should've eaten more earlier."

I felt helpless and frustrated because it put the entire group at jeopardy. At any point, either Kami or Dove could completely bonk out. We'd seen other hikers experience it already—they said your sweat starts to smell like cat piss, or ammonia, because all your fat reserves are gone and your body is burning protein to stay alive. When this happens, you go from hiking twenty-mile days to literally being unable to get out of bed the next morning. If that happened to Kami or Dove, we would be done. Our desire to stick together meant we would only be as strong as our weakest link, and those weak links were starting to show. This was why people in Vegas had been willing to bet against The Family. This was why most tramilies had split apart. This was why Hops was so amazed at the "x-factor" that had gotten us to this point. But where was our x-factor now?

I worried quietly about Dove or Kami bonking out; I genuinely didn't know what I'd do if this happened. If one of them bonked, would I have the strength to pull the plug on the trip this close to the end? At this point, it felt more realistic that I would strap one of them to the top of my pack and haul them up Katahdin, even if it meant permanent damage to my knees—or the relationship.

Honestly, I didn't want to think about it. I kept holding on to hope that they'd be fine, and we'd make it. But it felt like playing roulette, a game I'd always hated because the results are random and completely outside of your control.

For those last miles, good food through trail magic and towns, combined with the slackpacking offers, were the only things that kept us going. We couldn't make good food on the trail, but in towns, we could consume twice as many calories as usual. We were willing to pay almost any restaurant bill to keep the family eating; on the trail, we were literally starving to death. It felt like we had lit a fuse on a bomb that was burning every day and we didn't know how much time we had left. Going into our longest section without access to good food, carrying our heaviest packs, the fuse would burn even faster.

All these thoughts ran around our heads, and we didn't tell anyone. We couldn't afford the criticism.

Other hikers knew, though. The same thing was happening to them.

THE TRAIL PROVIDES

Fresh Ground met us at Shaw's. The hostel owners were a married couple who went by the names Poet and Hippy Chick. Fresh Ground and Poet got talking in a corner of the hostel, hunched over maps and gesturing toward the nearby woods. After a couple hours of this, Fresh Ground came to us.

"I have a plan," he said. "I've never done anything like this, but I have a way to make your last one hundred miles great."

Fresh Ground told us that Poet knew all about the back roads in the region. There was a whole system of private roads with gates, fees, and select open-hours keeping them from public access. Traveling the dirt roads required experienced navigation, as there was no GPS or cell signal. With Poet's back-country knowledge, Fresh Ground could slackpack us for the entire Hundred-Mile Wilderness, something we'd never heard of being done before.

But he wasn't finished. That was only the first part of the plan. He also offered to cook thirteen meals for us—and The Degenerates, if they caught up. We would only have to carry food for five meals. That was less than a normal two-day resupply.

It was an incredible, game-changing offer. It might make all the difference in getting us to Katahdin. I had a sudden vision of certainty—we would make it. We would make it to the end.

We couldn't wait to share this news with the kids. "You guys, circle up. We have amazing news. Fresh Ground…"

I suddenly found myself choking up, overcome with emotion. I swallowed hard so I didn't lose it.

"Fresh Ground has offered to slackpack us through the entire Hundred-Mile Wilderness. And he's going to make meals for us the entire way. I've never heard of anything like this happening; I can't believe it." I couldn't hang on to the lump in my throat anymore; I put my head in my hands and started sobbing.

The kids had tears in their eyes, too, especially Eden and Dove, who were responsible for lunches and dinners. They had just been getting ready to resupply for the entire six days—which meant meal selection, shopping, and packing food for eight people. It was a total of ninety-six meals, a huge responsibility. Now that burden had been lifted from their shoulders.

If you'd asked us what an ideal Hundred-Mile Wilderness would look like, we'd have said, "Nobody getting injured" or "Making it through with no major fights." We didn't think anything better was possible. Fresh Ground's offer was beyond anything we could have ever dreamed.

The trail was providing. Until this moment, we hadn't fully understood everything that phrase encompassed. We had thought that "the trail provides" referred more to a mystical randomness, kind of like the concept of "everything happens for a reason." But now we could see that it went beyond randomness. We had created space for the trail providing. It wasn't just that we were getting offers of help from strangers; we were in a place where we were willing to accept them. If someone had told me back at home that when we did our hike, our family would be accepting offers of food, shelter, and care at forty different strangers' homes, I would have rejected the idea completely. At home, I was still living into the story that self-sufficiency is better than interdependency; that the ultimate sign of success is never asking for help and never showing vulnerability. But on the trail we learned that by making ourselves vulnerable, we became a target for people's resources. When we left the comfort of our home, we created a void, an opportunity to be cared for in ways we never would have accepted before. We started to trust in humanity in a way we had never considered—to a point where, now, we were willing to put our family's health and well-being wholly into the hands of one man.

The plan was a little scary. We would be giving Fresh Ground our packs and just trusting he'd meet us at the agreed locations and times. It meant literally putting our lives in his hands; without him, we'd have no access to food, no tents for shelter, and no phone service to call for help. We'd only known this man for a matter of weeks. If he changed his mind, we'd be stuck. If he even got a flat tire, there was no way to get help in the wilderness. He'd have to find a way to get seven packs and food to us by foot, horse, or helicopter.

But on the other hand, we had seen this man operate. He'd been feeding hikers for four years and was more comfortable with a tarp and duct tape than anyone we'd ever seen. Even though he had never been in a newspaper or magazine, and you like wouldn't be able to find much about him online, word on the trail spreads quickly, and hikers talk. Among the people we met, Fresh Ground was among the most trusted and respected people to be found. Fresh Ground could prepare meals in a blizzard with rain blowing sideways. When all the other trail angels sat waiting out the weather, Fresh Ground would head into the storm because he knew hikers still needed to eat. He had a heart for hikers, and more importantly, he cared for our kids. We had complete faith that if his beat up Camry broke down, he would walk each backpack twenty miles on his own, one at a time, if that's what it took. Considering the combination of Fresh Ground's attitude and ability and Poet's knowledge, it felt like the least risky decision of our entire trip.

The plan had to be coordinated by the meal, the minute, and the mile. Everything was exact. We detailed the mile markers we'd meet at and the unmarked dirt tracks we'd take. We'd have to average 15.7 miles a day through the entire Hundred-Mile Wilderness to make our meet points, but we were in the best shape of our lives, and we wouldn't be carrying packs. Our new itinerary had an added surprise: with only 113 miles to the top of Mount Katahdin, we'd have an extra day. This meant we could take tomorrow off and relax in the hostel while preparing to make this final push. As long as nothing went wrong, this would be the easiest hiking of the entire trail.

The Degenerates were four days behind, but we sent them details of the plan. They'd need to meet us at the beginning of the Hundred-Mile Wilderness by Thursday morning—thirty-six hours away—if they wanted to join us. It seemed like a long shot, but we were hopeful.

ZEROOOOO. ~~The break~~ Woke up early to journal and ended up talking with Fresh Ground which was better. I ~~went~~ had an amazing breakfast and ate so much. Got dropped off and walked 3 miles to the beginning of the 100 mile Wilderness. So I guess not a zero but basically. FG walked with us. Rainier walked some of the way. It was relaxing. Got a

Dove (17) showing that when you've walked nearly 2,000
miles, walking three miles feels like taking a zero.

With all these momentous plans under our belts, we still had to make the most important decision of our trip.

CHAPTER TWENTY-FIVE

Hiking Our Own Hike

"The way kids learn to make good decisions is by making decisions, not by following directions."
—Alfie Kohn, *Unconditional Parenting: Moving from Rewards and Punishments to Love and Reason*

On our final evening at Shaw's, we gathered the kids around a picnic bench outside the hostel for a family meeting.

"Okay, so, we're not allowed to go to the top of Mount Katahdin with Rainier. He's only allowed as far as the tree line," I started, laying the problem out on the table.

"Allowed?" piped up Rainier. "Why?"

"Because they say it's not safe."

"Why?" asked Rainier again. For a two-year-old, he seemed to understand the absurdity of the situation remarkably well.

I looked at him and sighed. "I don't know."

The kids were still confused about the Baxter rules. "Did you explain that he's hiked the whole trail with us? Did you ask if they could make an exception?"

Kami shook her head, her expression grim. "I was on the phone for a long time with the park rangers at Baxter, and they won't budge. They won't let him summit."

"So, we have to decide what to do as a family," I said.

We all talked about the only options we could think of.

1. *We could ignore the rules and just go to the top.* The park rangers weren't playing fair. They'd lied to us. We knew they'd made exceptions in the past, proving it wasn't just about safety; something else was behind this seemingly arbitrary rule. We heard that the maximum fine would be $1,000 if we took Rainier to the top. Having already invested five months and tens of thousands of dollars into this trip, we thought a few more bucks to give our kids the storybook ending we all had earned was well worth it. On the other hand, stirring up an already tense contention between A.T. thru-hikers and the Baxter State Park officials didn't seem like an action that would serve the hiker community in the future. We were already getting YouTube comments to the tune of, "Don't piss off Baxter and wreck the summit for everyone else." We didn't agree with that ethos, but ignoring the rules would put the focus of our final day on outside forces, instead of on us—on being together. Just the heightened intensity of the online debate would be so loud it would be impossible to ignore. As a result, this was our least favorite option.

2. *We could leave Rainier at the tree line, and the rest of the family could go to the top.* This would allow those of us who'd actually hiked—and those old enough to actually remember it—to feel the sense of accomplishment at the top and have a picture with the famous A-frame sign. Numerous people had offered to babysit Rainier while we finished the last two miles.

As news of Baxter State Park's stance had been shared online, the comments had flooded in.

"Rainier deserves to summit just as much as the rest of you. Break the rules! You deserve to finish! You earned it and will regret it forever if you don't go all the way!"

"Wait!! You carried Rainer through the Whites and Mahoosuc Notch; that should already qualify to let Rainer go to Katahdin. I say go for it. I usually don't like breaking rules, but there are times you have to do it based on principles."

"Do it...folks will love it all when they see that bad ass SUMMIT shot. I'm for you guys to set the record and enjoy yourselves."

"The fine is just one more obstacle that will be overcome—and it makes your story even better!"

"Carry a small tree up. Keep Rainier a few feet back below the tree line."

"A rule that is designed to protect you from yourself is a rule designed to be broken."

Many commenters were outraged with the park officials. We heard from almost one hundred people who wanted to see us at the top so bad that they offered to pay the fine for us.

"Fight for Rainier too. One for all, all for one. I'll pitch in for the fine."

"I will definitely support a gofundme to help pay for that fine!"

"I would help pay the fine. Just do it."

It was obvious there was no easy decision. We couldn't have it all. It was a lose-lose situation. We wondered what we should give up. Should we sacrifice the happiness of the Baxter State Park rangers? We didn't know or care about them, and we'd probably never return to the park. Should we give up on being together every step of the way? Would preventing those of us who were able to finish just because of our principle make us just like the thru-hiking purists we'd tried to avoid becoming? Were we just sticking to a principle of togetherness for no good reason to prove a point? What would our decision look like to the tens of thousands of people who were following our journey on YouTube? We'd hiked for five months together, but we didn't need to do everything together. Would not summiting together cancel out all we'd accomplished on the rest of the journey? Would we feel any less close to each other, or any less triumphant?

We'd come out here to fight for together. Now there was no clear answer what the end of the fight looked like, and what it would take to win.

Filia (7) draws a picture of our family. For some reason, only seven of us are pictured. Was this what our group would look like if we finished without Rainier?

CHOOSING TOGETHER

Kami and I knew what direction we were leaning in. We'd been thinking about it for the last one hundred miles. We didn't want to break the rule and take Rainier to the top of Katahdin without permission. It wasn't that we had a problem with fudging the law—for us, it was on par with driving over the speed limit, which we did all the time. And our time in religious communities had taught us that blind submission to absolute authority is dangerous.

But if we took Rainier to the top, our last day would turn from a celebration of achievement, and a culmination of a months-long goal, to a silly game of cops and robbers. We didn't want our moment of triumph finishing the trail to be tainted by the memory of running from park rangers.

The second option, leaving Rainier with someone else while we went to the top, made the most practical sense to us. When the forest fire closed those nineteen miles of trail, we'd established a definition of thru-hiking that felt really good to us: a thru-hiker is one who hikes every mile of trail that is available. For seven of us, the last two miles were hikeable. We could finish the trail, touch the sign, and get a picture. Rainier had been carried 95 percent of the trail, anyway; and at the age of two, he wouldn't remember being left with a babysitter. As heart-wrenching as it would be to summit without him, we had to think of our other kids. At the same time, in the back of my mind, I pictured Rainier's confused little face watching us walk away from him—maybe wondering what was going on, and why, for the first time, he was being left behind. We had sacrificed so much to be together up to this point. The thought of walking away from him just to touch a sign didn't make sense to me.

It seemed like the choice before Kami and I was between two options: breaking the law, or breaking up our family. It was the definition of a no-win scenario.

We hadn't shared our thoughts with the kids. We didn't want to influence their thinking. For the first time on the entire trip, we fell completely silent and sat back, waiting to hear how the kids felt before we made the decision.

Seven was the most supportive of the option to leave Rainier with a babysitter, and the rest of us summit.

"It sucks, but also, Rainier won't even know," he said. "If Rainier doesn't care, why torture ourselves for no reason?"

He was just mirroring the most common sentiment that had been expressed online (besides flat-out breaking the rule, which was the runaway winner among the internet crowd).

"Take a group pic with the mountain in the background...then the rest of you hike up for the finish. I doubt that Rainier would sweat that too much."

*"I think it would mean so much to your other children to touch the
sign after hiking the entire the trail. They should summit!"*

*"Rainier will be back to summit on another journey when he is old
enough to appreciate it. You will remember that he needed to stay
behind, but Rainier will not remember in any kind of traumatic
way as long he is having fun while the seven of you are summiting."*

As we all considered the options, we thought of the hundreds of people who'd invested in our journey. We felt the weight of their help and expectations. In choosing to turn around two miles from the finish, would we be letting them down? What would Hudson, our trail mentor, say? What would someone like Warren Doyle, who had gone to jail for his right to summit, think?

If we didn't summit, would any of this matter? Would anyone remember us?

Then Memory, who had been sitting quietly with a thoughtful look on her face, spoke up.

"Those two miles matter. They're symbolic. They tell a story."

And suddenly, with a clarity as sharp as the night air, I understood my role as a parent in that moment. I understood it in a way I hadn't understood it yet for the entire hike. I understood it in a way that had escaped me when I flicked Rainier in the Georgia cold, when I snapped at Eden to stop complaining, and when I pushed Seven along until he tripped into the stream. I understood it in a way that no amount of self-reflection could have shown me.

This wasn't my and Kami's decision at all. This decision belonged to our kids.

My role as a father now was to step back, to hand over control. After all, I'd already done what I'd set out to do: I'd presented an agenda and an epic goal, and I had pushed and pushed our family until reaching that goal was actually within our grasp. I'd painted in my mind a picture of a perfect trip: us standing at the A-frame sign, with a caption that read, "The largest family to hike the A.T." And I had led the kids to the very edge of that picture.

Now it was up to them to decide how to live into the picture on their own terms.

> It was suddenly so clear to me: leadership
> wasn't about getting my way. It was about
> enabling people to have their own.

I looked at Kami, and I could tell she'd read my mind yet again. It was time to let go.

No matter what the kids decided, whether or not to finish the Appalachian Trail would be their decision. Kami and I would not push them. We would let go.

It wasn't easy to let go of control of the decision, and I wrestled with the instinct to grab it back even as I watched the kids talk through it. Were they qualified to make such a complex and high-stakes decision? After all, they were children. Finishing the A.T. was the ending to a bucket-list item I'd had from before five of them were alive. As much as I believed that our hike was about our family experiencing something epic together, I also knew it would be all too easy for Kami and me to take our perspective as older and wiser parents and just make the call. The kids wouldn't even have to know it had been a choice; they probably wouldn't contest the decision. We could get our way and have our ending.

But then I thought back to what the kids had been through. I thought back to every step they had taken, and every choice they'd made to stick with it, to stick with their family through something hard. I thought about how they all pitched in on adult responsibilities like cooking and setting up the tents and carrying Rainier. Again and again, they had proven that they were willing and able. I thought back about their performance in the Smokies, and how that day they had hiked to safety while other adults waited it out in the shelters— how they had been our heroes. I thought about the conversations they'd had with The Degenerates and how we had all been adopted by that tramily, signified by the honorary conch Memory still wore around her neck. I thought about how Eden had shared her frustration about the CPS callers back at Lehigh Gap; how Dove had shared her dreams of the future with me. Even though Filia was seven, she had woken up when we did, hiked up to twenty-three miles through the rain and into the dark, just like us, and even taken time to run a marathon. I thought about how both Seven and Eden had independently made the decision to stay on the trail when given the option to quit, how they truly owned their hikes.

If anyone was qualified to make this decision, it was these five kids.

I'm not sure when it happened, but I started the Appalachian Trail in Georgia hiking with my kids. By the time I made it to Maine, I was hiking with my friends.

This had become their trip. I was no more a hiker than they were, and this was no more my ending than it was theirs. The most important decision of the trip was theirs to make.

For thirty minutes, Kami and I sat and listened to the kids' opinions, offering no input of our own. It was fascinating. They were processing the issue with more depth than we had expected. They discussed the ending they wanted for themselves. They spoke about their disappointment, the possible ramifications, and the message we'd send to others. They considered what we were most likely to remember and regret. They agreed that it was a no-win scenario, and that something would have to be sacrificed.

Then something happened that stunned us.

"There's actually a third option," Eden said.

I was about to ask, "There is?" when Memory chimed in. "Yeah, totally. We can just decide that our trail ends at the tree line."

Kami and I looked at each other. Her face was inscrutable, as I'm sure mine was, as well. We were in disbelief.

Our kids were doing something we had never considered: they were owning not only the hike, but the trail as well. They weren't just living up to the title of thru-hiker; they were reinventing it.

They'd come to a conclusion I hadn't seen—the two options, breaking the law or breaking up the family, actually represented a false dichotomy. There was a third option. We could hike as much of the trail as was "hikeable" for our group, just like skipping the impassable nineteen miles scorched by fire. We could hike to the tree line together, and call that our summit.

Dove agreed with Memory. "We'd still be on Mount Katahdin. And we'd still be at a summit. We can't leave Rainier behind; I'd miss him."

"It wouldn't feel right to be at the sign without him," said Eden. "He's added so much to our trip."

One by one, we listened as everyone talked about how they'd received much more from Rainier than they had given. These kids had carried Rainier, fed him, and packed out his dirty diapers. They'd helped him learn his ABCs and sang countless songs about the wheels on the bus. But even with how much they'd done for him, they didn't feel like he was the primary benefactor. They were. They didn't feel they'd done it for him solely; they had also done it for themselves. He benefitted us. Just like Kami and I had learned our kids were actually an asset to our journey, not the liability our culture had warned us about. Our kids had come to the same conclusion about their youngest brother. The child that others had seen as a liability was now the driving force behind our decision on how to finish.

No one was blaming him or dismissing him. They were choosing him. He had been more than a burden. He had been a companion.

Kami and I teared up as we listened to all the kids agreeing, even as we felt disappointment wash over us.

It was official. We would never touch the famous A-frame sign.

But the disappointment faded quickly, and in its place was a singular feeling: pride. Left to their own thoughts, their own feelings, their own beliefs, our kids had chosen each other. They'd chosen to be together, no matter what it cost them.

There were so many reasons to hike that we had to say no to, all so we could maintain the reason we were here. We did this hike to be together. We wanted our final moments to make a statement to the world that together was most important. And the kids wanted to make that statement to themselves. We could tell from hearing their discussion: hiking to the top of a mountain was symbolic, but so was stopping at the tree line. They just symbolized different priorities. And we had chosen ours.

Our most valuable accomplishment would not be in a picture or a sense of completion. It would be in what we prioritized and sacrificed for our completion. It would be the perspective we gained on our relationships over the last two thousand miles. If we sacrificed our five-month journey to stay with our two-year-old, it would make the statement there was nothing we wouldn't do for each other or to sustain the relationships we had built together. And unlike the sign, which was controlled by Baxter State Park, no one could take that statement of our kids' importance and the value of our togetherness away from us. We would reinvent what the word "summit" even meant. We would reinvent the top of our mountain, and we would reach it together.

Maybe our belief in togetherness was real. Or maybe through the course of walking two thousand miles together, it had become real.

We wouldn't make it to the A-frame sign, but we would get to the tree line of Mount Katahdin. That would be our finish line. And now, with our new clear ending goal in mind, there was one obstacle left between us and Mount Katahdin: the Hundred-Mile Wilderness.

CHAPTER TWENTY-SIX

The Hundred-Mile Party

*"A beautifully told story is a symphonic unity in which struc-
ture, setting, character, genre, and idea meld seamlessly."*
—Robert McKee

O n Day 154, eight days before our flight was set to leave, we
were ready to leave Shaw's Hiker Hostel with or without The
Degenerates. We now had a timeline of concrete minutes and
miles. The kids had enjoyed the rest day watching movies with Fresh
Ground, and we'd smoked cigars and shared stories with some southbound hikers who were only one hundred miles into their journey.
Before heading out, we enjoyed the hostel's famous all-you-can-eat
blueberry pancake breakfast.

We wanted to show Fresh Ground how much we appreciated him,
so we decided to pick up his meal tab for the two days he was there,

which felt like the absolute least we could do. But when we went to pay, Poet wouldn't accept our money.

We tried again, but Poet wouldn't budge.

He explained when he sees people who support hikers, he wants to support them. Poet wasn't rich. He had kids and was running a seasonal business. He wanted to pay for Fresh Ground out of principle.

Just then, Fresh Ground walked in to pay. He took one look at us and knew what was going on.

Poet said, "It's been taken care of," and Fresh Ground walked out sobbing.

There was so much goodness in that moment, it's difficult to express the emotion that we felt. It was purely genuine. No one was trying to be kind for appearances. In that moment, we only wanted to support and enrich each other.

While driving us to the trail, Poet recited a poem he'd written about the view from Whitecap, the first place on the trail where you can see Mount Katahdin ahead.

> The view of Katahdin is the axe that breaks up the frozen seas
>   within us
> and the steely parts of our soul that have been hardened,
> by the long and arduous miles, will shatter
> and you'll feel the tears rolling
> down your dirt-streaked face.

We arrived at the trail and saw a hiker lying on the ground. It was Culligan!

It had been more than three weeks since we'd seen The Degenerates at my birthday party in the parking lot. Thanks to our relentless hiking without breaks, we'd kept ahead of their faster hiking pace.

But The Degenerates, receiving our message about Fresh Ground's support, had picked up the pace, hiking forty-two miles in thirty-six hours without sleeping to meet us on the edge of the Hundred-Mile Wilderness.

Culligan walked up to me, and to my shock, handed me a book.

It was a copy of *Slaughterhouse-Five* that he had bought for fifty cents. He had carried it for 150 miles to give me as a gift.

Carrying optional weight that is not yours feels like one of the most soul-killing activities you can do as a hiker. You feel every single step of what you carry; every single ounce contributes to your overall speed, comfort, and efficiency. We thought about our packs for hours a day and curated what was in them ruthlessly, constantly weighing the value-to-weight ratio. Hikers were always throwing things away, cutting tags off of jackets, removing labels, and throwing away boxes to save a few ounces here and there. Carrying extra weight was not something you'd do for any other hiker; it was something you'd only do for tramily. And in the hiker's code, as the kids had shown me on Father's Day, the kindest, most extravagant thing you can do for someone is carry something for them.

This book meant more to me than just a book. It was the only object I had been gifted in five months. And it was given in a way that told me I was worth it. I was worth carrying extra weight for.

"I thought you should read about where your tattoo came from," was all Culligan said.

THE HUNDRED-MILE SIGN

There was a sign on the trail marking the beginning of the Hundred-Mile Wilderness.

CAUTION

THERE ARE NO PLACES TO OBTAIN SUPPLIES OR GET
HELP UNTIL ABOL BRIDGE 100 MILES NORTH. DO NOT
ATTEMPT THIS SECTION UNLESS YOU HAVE A MINIMUM
OF 10 DAYS SUPPLIES AND ARE FULLY EQUIPPED. THIS IS
THE LONGEST WILDERNESS SECTION OF THE ENTIRE A.T.
AND ITS DIFFICULTY SHOULD NOT BE UNDERESTIMATED.

We were carrying one day's worth of food. Not long ago, this would have felt daunting. Now, it felt like an invitation to a party.

The Hundred-Mile Wilderness is a beautiful area. It's known for its trees, water, moose, and blueberries. There are beachheads on lakes along the way, and we often swam in the lakes at lunchtime. But what made this section of trail truly special was we were carrying less weight than ever. We were slackpacked for six consecutive days and ate the best food we had on trail. We were provided for in every way possible. With Fresh Ground's home-cooked meals, we didn't worry about the kids' and Kami's weight. We weren't gaining any pounds, but we weren't losing any either. Our quality of life went through the roof.

Each day, Fresh Ground met us at a predetermined point. He would make us dinner. We'd camp there overnight, and he would make us breakfast. Then we'd hike to the next spot. Sometimes, Fresh Ground even met us for lunch. We kept a rigid schedule, but it was worth it. Our pace had increased considerably. Over the next five days, we hiked 14.3 miles, 15.4 miles, 14.9 miles, 13.8 miles, and 17.5 miles. Every night was another party around a campfire with Fresh Ground and The Degenerates. We hung out, smoked cigars, and laughed the nights away.

As we hiked, we talked. Culligan wanted to know how to play blackjack. I'd played professionally in casinos for almost ten years, and I answered all of Culligan's questions. "How do you deal with six-decks?" "How much did you win in the Bahamas?" "What do you do when the casinos catch you?" "Was it dangerous?"

After laughing for five months with Not Dead, we joked and told her she should start a comedy YouTube channel. She had a crass way of talking that made us parents and kids laugh at everything she said. Fun Facts told us about college life. She described her friend-lover and explained their preference of they/them pronouns, a concept that was totally foreign to us and opened our eyes to a whole new way of defining identity. We made a miniseries on our YouTube channel called Meet That Degenerate in which we interviewed each of them and tried to help our audience understand why different people would quit their life to walk for five months—though really, it was just to capture some of the memories of our favorite people during a time that felt like a dream.

There was some awkwardness in talking to The Degenerates about our situation with the summit of Mount Katahdin. "That sucks," was all they could really say. A few other hikers said they'd boycott the summit to show their solidarity in opposing the park rangers' decision. But we urged them to hike their own hike and go to the top. It felt good to be supported, but it didn't make sense for them to suffer in a way that wouldn't change the result for us. We all had our own hike to finish, and we couldn't let our baggage weigh anyone else down.

They say hikers talk about three things: food, gear, and trail gossip. But it always comes back to food. With Fresh Ground's cooking, we had all day to talk about the meals we'd just had and fantasize about dinner that night. We swam in lakes and streams and took long lunches in the shade. It felt like we were on vacation.

On our longest distance day in the Wilderness, we woke up at 6:00 a.m., had blueberry pancakes and coffee, and were still able to leave camp by 6:45 a.m. We fit all of our packs into Fresh Ground's beat-up Camry like a smelly Tetris game. Until you've smelled what clothes and packs that are worn seven days a week for five straight months, constantly being soaked with rain and sweat and never fully allowed to dry, smells like, you can't fully understand why his car was appropriately nicknamed Stinkbug.

We met Fresh Ground for lunch at a river crossing and spent two and a half hours swimming and lounging. Kami and I even had time to do a nude photoshoot in the middle of the day for The Degenerates' Tastefully Nude Hiker Calendar 2019. Us parents took a photo with the conch shell necklace that we have been gifted in the foreground; we were eventually featured as Mr. and Mrs. July.

We got back on the trail and finished at 7:30 p.m. with burgers, hot dogs, and fries for dinner. It had been a memorably relaxing day, and yet we'd hiked 23.4 miles. This was just 0.2 miles less than our longest previous day of the entire trail, the night we had walked into Red Robin at 10:16 p.m. It was almost three times longer than our first day, when we had been desperate to quit.

Throughout the Hundred-Mile Wilderness, we ran into dozens of southbound hikers, or SOBOs, who were just starting the trail from Mount Katahdin and heading to Springer Mountain, Georgia. They weren't even a week in.

It was a little like staring at our former selves. They walked past us energetically, naively, with brand-new shiny gear and clothes, clean hair, and no trace of windburn or sunburn. I suddenly flashed back to all the kids packing up their own new shiny gear in the hotel the night before we woke up early for Cracker Barrel. Could that really only have been five months ago? Had it even been in this lifetime?

We felt like utterly different people. How had we become so transformed all within the boundaries of a single portion of one year?

Without fail, all the SOBOs had a stupid grin on their faces as they passed. Us NOBOs joked that we'd like to see how they looked in five months.

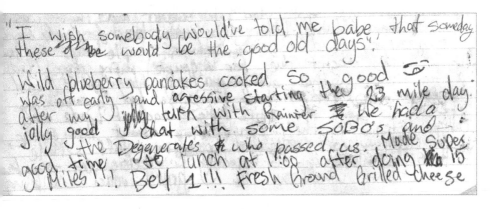

You can tell from Dove's (17) tone that our attitude had dramatically
changed even though at this point we were clocking some of
the highest and most remote miles of our entire trip.

A LESSON IN LOVE

One night, we were all sitting under Fresh Ground's tarp joking and smoking cigars. A woman came through our camp site and stopped to talk. She was a SOBO. Her stuff was disorganized, and judging by her inadequate gear, like many fresh starts, she wasn't going to make it far. She'd only hiked five miles that day. Fresh Ground had just had his usual three chairs, and she sat in the best one under the tent, eating all the best food for an hour. She went through Fresh Ground's bins under the table and was squirreling his bananas and Kool-Aid away into her pack. We wanted to speak up for Fresh Ground. She hadn't earned any of this, like we had.

But then we remembered Fresh Ground's policy, which we had heard him recite many times: "I feed everyone, and it's always all-you-can-eat." Then, the realization hit: this was who Fresh Ground was here to feed. This was us. Fresh Ground wasn't ours. He wasn't for sale, couldn't be bought, and just like all of most lavish gifts on the trail, he hadn't been earned. The trail had provided, and the only thing we had done was shown up. This was why I never felt it would be appropriate to offer him money to follow us.

I thought back to the things people had said about us in the beginning: The Family will never make it. The Family sucks up all the resources. I realized that, when it came down to it, we didn't deserve this food any more than she did. It was humbling how easy it can be to feel entitled to a gift and forget where we had come from. This lady, just like us, had shown up, and now the trail was providing for her.

"The trail provides" applies to everyone who leaves home. You don't have to successfully walk across thirteen states; you don't have to vlog, or share your story at all. "The trail provides" is a promise: that if you leave home and make yourself vulnerable, you will be cared for. At first, trail magic felt like a scarce and evasive miracle that could be missed if our timing was off or if we didn't make the right offer at the right time. I thought back to my fleeting idea to pay Fresh Ground for trail magic, and understood even more deeply why that hadn't felt right at the time. It would have been me trying to exert control over trail magic, bend it to my will. I couldn't control trail magic any more than I could control my kids. "The trail provides" wasn't something that could be bought. It was something that you earned. But you didn't earn it with money or even hard work. You earned it by letting go of whatever comfort you held the most dear.

As we hiked, the consistency of the trail providing also showed us that it wasn't random, and it wasn't just for us. It was for anyone willing to leave the comfort and safety of home. Fresh Ground knew that.

We reflected on our own hike. It started with two invitations: one from Nicole and John at the farm where we spent Easter, and one from Mike and Claudia in Damascus, where we spent Kami's birthday. Since then, we'd had thirty-four nights of accommodations donated by people wanting to support us. Some were in strangers' homes, and others were at hostels or hotels. We'd been slackpacked for twenty-three days. And we'd had eighty-six meals delivered to us on the trail or cooked at someone's home for no charge. We never asked for any of it, these were people that sought us out and drove for hours sometimes taking days off of work to be a part of our journey. We had not done the trail alone.

What we didn't know was that the home stretch with Fresh Ground and our friends was going to show us a picture of togetherness that we still were unable to imagine.

CHAPTER TWENTY-SEVEN

To the Tree Line

"Because in the end, you won't remember the time you spent working in the office or mowing your lawn. Climb that goddamn mountain."

—Unknown (commonly misattributed
to Jack Kerouac)

When we finally made it out of the Hundred-Mile Wilderness, we celebrated with a case of beer and some ice cream from a small convenience store.

Fun Facts and I borrowed Fresh Ground's car and drove toward town to find cell service. Before heading into the Wilderness, we'd texted Hudson, our trail mentor, to tell him our estimated time of arrival at this point, just as he'd requested. We said he didn't have to meet us, especially as we didn't think we were going to summit Katahdin. We hadn't spoken to him in more than a month, and didn't expect a reply, but wanted to check.

When I finally found cell service, I called Hudson, and he answered right away.

"Can I come see you?" he asked. I asked where he was. "I've been waiting here for you. I'm in Millinocket, fifteen miles away." We wondered what he thought of our decision to abandon the A.T. two miles before the end.

Before retiring to his hammock, Fresh Ground announced, "I'll be gone before you get up. I don't do goodbyes, but it really has been a pleasure hiking with y'all."

Well, the Crawfords *do* do goodbyes!

We thanked him as best we could for everything. There was no real way to repay him. We'd tried numerous times to slip one-hundred-dollar bills into his jar, and it was always a bit finicky. He made it clear he wasn't for sale, and we were worried we'd offend him. And even when we did manage to get money in there, it felt so inadequate for what we had received. We were here in part because of him. The kids had spent some of their hardest and happiest moments with this man, and it felt like something special. We knew we'd be meeting again.

Soon enough, Hudson arrived and found us sitting around our camp fire in the woods. He carried over beer from his truck and smiled as he gave us all hugs. He had driven for more than eight hours and been waiting for us to come out of the Hundred-Mile Wilderness.

Hudson then made a speech. We could tell he'd been thinking about it on his eight-hour drive.

"Being a thru-hiker is hiking the entire length of the Appalachian Trail in one hiking season." He paused. "That's the entire hikeable trail. You guys missed nineteen miles back in Virginia. That legitimately wasn't hikeable trail. When you guys get to the tree line, those last two miles, and the park rangers tell you to divide your family, well...you're fighting for together. Those two miles are legitimately not hikeable trail for your family to hike together! So that's where you finish. And if I'm there, I'm going to make it special."

He reached into his bag and pulled out a handful of custom-carved deer-antler necklaces. Just like every detail back at his hostel, they had been hand-crafted with painstaking detail. He'd engraved the A.T. symbol into the antlers by hand and presented each of us with a necklace, hanging them around our necks like medals. It felt like we were being knighted.

Everyone was tearful and grateful. Coming from our trail mentor, someone with such expertise, this felt like more validation than we could get from all the books and hiker forums combined.

Before he left that night, he took Kami and I aside and, in hushed tones so the kids wouldn't hear, said, "I'll see you guys up there."

He pointed to a garbage bag in the back of the truck, winked, and said, "I'm proud of you guys." We didn't know why he pointed at a garbage bag, but we didn't think much of it.

When we awoke on Day 160, Fresh Ground was gone. We hiked ten miles to get to the foot of Mount Katahdin and stopped to pick up the required permits for Baxter State Park. Of the 3,862 people who had registered at Springer Mountain to thru-hike north that year, only three hundred people had made it to the mountain so far. We would be numbers 306 to 313.

Back in Monson, where we spent the night, I opened a box that had been shipped to the hostel. It was a banner. After we decided not to summit, I'd ordered it from a twenty-four-hour printing place online and had it shipped while we hiked in the Hundred-Mile Wilderness.

On thin black vinyl, simple white lettering read:

Springer Mountain, Georgia

to

Mount Katahdin, Maine

2,190 Miles

161 Days

March 1 to August 9, 2018

I'd ordered it because I felt bad there would be nothing for the kids to touch after hiking more than two thousand miles in five months. I wanted to take this piece of vinyl up and let each kid touch it to signify the end of our journey. It was kind of pathetic, but it was something.

OUR FINAL DAY

On Day 161, we were more than ready to finish.

It was August 9, and our plane tickets for Lakeside were stamped for a departure the next day.

When we arrived at the parking lot, it was raining, and there was no sign of Hudson or his truck. The trip up to tree line was only three miles from there. We left our heavy packs at the hostel and started hiking straight up the mountain.

As we walked, I thought about all that we'd been through. Our kids had grown up. We'd celebrated three birthdays. Rainier knew the alphabet now. We'd walked through three seasons; the snow in Georgia felt like a distant memory. We remembered the Smokies and our run-in with CPS, and we thought of all the friends we'd made. We wondered how Hops felt with an injured foot and his lifelong dream in jeopardy.

I thought about everyone who helped us. We remembered Halmonee and Papa dropping us off at the trailhead and visiting us three times, riding in the van with Arnie-1-Mile and G, getting sick at Jordan and Kristen's, and staying at the vacation home mansion in Virginia with Silver.

And then there were all of our moments with The Degenerates. They were ahead of us, already on their way to the summit. We were sad we wouldn't finish with them. We'd been through so many highs and lows together.

We hiked our final three miles as a family, The Family. Hiking that morning felt like an out-of-body experience. We'd dreamed of finishing, and now that it was here, we felt a little sad—it was impossible not to, after becoming so immersed in an epic adventure that was at an end. But also, we were overjoyed and excited for everything that day represented, and those feelings outweighed everything else.

Katahdin is a popular day hike. It was incredibly strange and surreal being passed by groups of Boy Scouts laughing and making fun of each other as they raced to the top of the mountain. I wanted to shout, "Don't you know what we've just done? Don't you know what this day means?" It felt like everyone that passed us should have said congratulations. If they only knew what we'd been through, and that the seven-year-old they'd just passed had been walking in the woods past venomous snakes, up mountains, and through rivers for five months, they'd be in awe. But to them, we were nobody—just another tourist group in their way.

The trees started to thin. We could see an area up ahead with boulders the size of cars. At this point, the hike required some scrambling, but nothing that felt dangerous—certainly nothing compared to the Whites.

And then the last tree was behind us. We could see a little clearing about fifty feet ahead, so we decided to keep walking and end our hike there.

On the A.T., I'd cried close to twenty times just from thinking about finishing. I'd played the scene in my head so many times. Every night when we'd arrived at a road or to camp, I'd said, "Rainier, we made it." I'd imagined I would cry again, knowing this would be the last time I'd say that to Rainier.

But now that we were at the end, it didn't seem very emotional. There were too many distractions and mixed feelings about the summit situation.

Just above the trees, it became windy. There was one last boulder to pass before our clearing, which had been obscured from sight since we'd first spotted it. It was a tight squeeze through the boulders, and we lined up in single file. I went first, since I was carrying Rainier.

As soon as I got through, I stopped. Behind me, I could hear the kids bumping into each other and protesting loudly.

A few seconds later, they all found out why.

Instead of being empty, the clearing was full of people. There was Culligan, Fun Facts, and Not Dead—The Degenerates. They had put off their summit bid to wait for our family. Next to them was Hudson. Because parking at the Katahdin trailhead had been fully reserved, he had to park two miles away and walk in the rain to get to the trailhead before starting the three-mile hike to the tree line. There were other hikers there, all waiting for us with huge smiles on their faces.

And behind them was something we never could have imagined. The Degenerates and Hudson stood aside and revealed a miniature, hand-built A-frame Katahdin sign. Just like the original, it said:

Katahdin
Northern Terminus
Appalachian Trail

We couldn't believe it.

We'd reinvented our summit. And now we had our own sign!

"When I found out a while back that you couldn't go to the top, I went to work," Hudson said. The sign he'd made was a replica of the official one that stood two miles above us, and he had hand-carved each letter into the wood. It was scaled small enough to incorporate a special step on the back, so that Rainier could stand on it, like every postcard we had ever seen, and have his picture taken.

This is what had been in the garbage bag in the back of his truck the night before. In this moment, even though he never said it, we had our answer to what we'd wondered—if Hudson approved of our decision to finish the trail at the tree line. His kindness to our family told us everything.

Surrounding the sign was our own cheering section made up of our favorite people—those who'd hiked with us and supported us for the last five months. I looked around at all their thrilled faces cheering for us and almost broke down. When I started off the trail, I was worried that I would never find companions because of the size and limitations of our group. I had swung from believing that finding a good fit in a friend or hiking partner was impossible and unrealistic, to wanting to commit to people prematurely and force companionship that wouldn't have worked for either them or us.

But here we were, five months and nine days since we started, having walked 2,189 miles over the span of fourteen states, having made it through blizzards, sickness, zero days, side trips, and a marathon, and we were still surrounded by six friends at the summit. Five of them had started on the same week as us back at Springer Mountain, and one of them had driven eight hours just to share the moment with us. We never could have found these relationships had we sought them out or tried to force them. By focusing on our own hike and staying dedicated to our own journey, the trail had revealed our truest companions, the ones that were perfect for us. Hiking our own hike had formed the relationships we were meant to form.

I looked around at the faces of all six kids; they were in shock. Dove was grinning ear to ear and clapping her hands. Eden cracked a smile and headed for Hudson's sign to take a look. Seven stood in stunned silence. Every kid who had started the trail had finished.

I met Kami's eyes. Over five months of sweat, tears, and hard decisions, we had grown together as allies, depended upon each other more than ever, and tested the limits of our relationship. As partners, we were closer than ever, more capable than ever, and more thankful for each other than ever.

We looked at each other and nodded. "Okay," I said. "Let's do this."

Our friends whistled and cheered as we approached the sign, and Hudson led the crowd in, singing, "Hip hip hooray!"

We walked up and, one by one, we touched the sign.

And then I looked at Rainier and said one last time, "Rainier, we made it."

VICTORY BEYOND EXPECTATION

When we got to the sign, it felt wonderful.

But also, in a way, it felt like nothing.

For five months and nine days, we had dreamed of this moment. We had fantasized about being here, about being done. And now that we were here, we didn't have the feelings that we thought we should.

After we took pictures, there was nothing left to do. The kids' line of thinking was clear on their faces: So...can we go now? Rainier didn't know what we were talking about, didn't care about any sign, and seemed more excited about the granola bar in his hand. As far as

THURSDAY AUGUST 9TH 2018
DAY #161
LAST DAY!!!

LASTDAYLASTDAY LASTDAY LASTDAAAAY!!!

Woke up at 4:50, and it was raining. The weather report of thunderstorms all day was seeming to be accurate. Walked down to the Appalachian Trail Cafe, which opens at 5am, for some breakfast. Met Not Dead's mom, Amy, and some other family of hers, that was fun. Ate food, but not as much at I wanted. Not much appetite for some reason. Left at 6:30 very much on time, with Ole Man. Still raining steadily. But we were like, this is our last day, like who cares? And we started this mother fucker in bad weather, why not finish it that way too? So we charged off into the rain. The 1st mile was incredibly gradual. Within a half hour we came to a sign and checked the map, and we had 1.7 and we were like, crap we need to slow down and SAVOR THE MOMENT. The degenerates passed us. We were taking 15 minute shifts with Rainier Baby. So many freaking Day HIKERS. UGH. Dada took the baby for the last .6 But it was slow going, after that one lovely gradual mile it was steep rock climbing stuff. .3, .2 and finally .1 till tree line! got to a table top rock place with a view and the degenerates were there, Hudson

We all felt a huge spectrum of emotions when we finished the trail, and there was no "one" perspective. Everyone, like Dove (17) here, processed it in their own way.

he was concerned, we still had two miles to go back down the hill followed by a thirty-minute car ride before we got dinner or ice cream, which was the only victory he would feel.

Our journey had ended just like it began that cold, gray first day: nothing like we expected, rather underwhelming, and rainy.

But it was also the first time I'd relaxed in five months. We'd achieved our goal, and I felt good.

I thought back to Silver's adage: "The trail provides."

The trail will only provide if you accept its offer. All of it. You must leave home. You must be broken. It will cost you your entire life as you know it. And then, and only then, can you receive. What you receive will be far greater than anything you had or anything you lost. It will change you. It might even heal you.

Touching the sign wasn't the end of our journey. Winning the fight for together—that was truly our destination all along.

CHAPTER TWENTY-EIGHT

Life After
the Adventure

"And once you live a good story, you get a taste for a kind of meaning in life, and you can't go back to being normal; you can't go back to meaningless scenes stitched together by the forgettable thread of wasted time."
—Donald Miller, *A Million Miles in a Thousand Years*

The night we finished the trail, The Degenerates invited us to a celebration dinner at a country club resort. Some of their parents and family had come from out of town to celebrate their accomplishment. It all started with a champagne toast from Not Dead.

"Here's to a long-ass walk, meeting some cool-ass people, and celebrating something we never thought we could do...but we did it!" she said. We shared stories around the table, and Fun Facts' parents, both PhDs, paid for our entire family's lobster dinner. Her mother thanked us for the role we played in her daughter's hike.

"As a psychologist," she said, "I so appreciate you exposing your process as a family: anticipating some unknown ahead and laying it out to your kids, inquiring about their expectations and feelings, checking in with each other frequently and consistently, encouraging and supporting each other through steps and phases, making adjustments as necessary for the well-being of your family, and anchoring yourselves in your clear values. Your curiosity, respect, and love is abundantly evident. As much as hiking two thousand, two hundred miles, that building of self and family is a tremendous accomplishment in being fully human. It brings its own compelling and irrevocable reward. 'Well done' seems so inadequate."

The next day, we paid for a shuttle driver to take us to Portland, Maine, so we could catch our flight. We had some spare time before the flight, so we went down to Portland's waterfront, where we met Kate from DC. She and her husband just happened to be there on vacation. We shared lobster rolls with them on the pier.

A stranger walked up to us and said, "Don't listen to the Baxter officials. I'll help you pay the fine." Since our videos were being released on delay, he didn't know we'd already made our decision and finished. Three hours later, the same scene played out in the airport. It felt strange that people knew who we were and were so opinionated. We hated to let them down, but it wasn't their story. It was ours.

Online, a political debate had erupted around our family not being allowed to summit. People were petitioning the governor of Maine and bombarding the park offices with requests, hate mail, and threats. Some people argued it was unfair and nonsensical to rob us of the summiting experience. Others applauded Baxter State Park for sticking to their guns and said we were spoiled and entitled for even requesting an exception.

Jennifer Pharr Davis, author of *Becoming Odyssa: Adventures on the Appalachian Trail*, National Geographic's Adventurer of the Year, and one-time world record holder for the fastest unsupported Appalachian Trail hike, commented in an online article. She referenced two previous exceptions that had been made for underage hikers to summit, saying, "If a child is able to traverse the entire Appalachian Trail—unassisted or in a carrier—they should be allowed to summit Katahdin."

The legend Warren Doyle, Hudson's hero and record holder for eighteen completions of the A.T. and Appalachian Trail Hall of Fame member, even chimed in:

Dear Baxter State Park,

Your legal authority takes priority over the more important moral authority. You make a mockery of the "wilderness experience."

He later said:

The mistake that the Crawfords made was to call Baxter State Park to ask permission.

We could see both sides of the online debate, and in the end, we didn't care about either. These commentators didn't know us. They were using our story for their own beliefs, causes, and fights. That was their hike. The success of our hike had consistently been determined not by fighting and defending our status within systems of finances, legality, and accomplishment, but by stepping away from these systems.

This didn't stop us from posting a picture of Rainier on Hudson's sign with the caption: "Thanks, Baxter, for a good time. Sorry our sign is better than yours. If you ever want to borrow it, you can, but only if you're under the age of six."

Jennifer Pharr Davis ended her article by saying, "Katahdin is an incredible place. Its name is translated as 'the greatest mountain,' but its summit—or lack thereof—does not define an Appalachian Trail thru-hike. Especially when you travel 2,189 miles to reach her crest and are told that you don't belong there."

Ironically, not being able to summit gave us a summit experience that we never could have planned. It was beyond our wildest dreams and depicted our highest value: togetherness. If our story had only been about a hike, then sure, Baxter's decision would have ruined that story. But because we opted for a different story about togetherness, Baxter's decision just made it that much better. In the months and years that would follow, we fielded no end of comments and messages from people expressing their certainty that one day, when Rainier was old enough, we'd all go back and summit together to complete our mission. "You'll get to the top of Katahdin someday!" "You'll be back!" We shrugged these comments off. Our summit experience was already better and more satisfying than we ever could have imagined, and it was unique to our family. We didn't dream of going back to the mountain to edit or complete it. It was already perfect.

OUR FINAL DESTINATION

We finally made it to Lakeside Bible Camp in Washington. We had a great time, but it was hard to shift into life off the trail. The first week there, we barely saw our kids. They were off having fun with

Friday August 10th 2018

ON an airplane to Colorado. This morning it was so wierd waking up with not a worry or mile in the mind. I woke up at 5:30 and spot slept till around 7:15 and then got up and went downstairs to start packing. 7:15 felt so late. Went out to breakfast at the AT Cafe. Last night was so much fun. the 4 hour ~~car~~ shuttle ride to Portland ME wasn't bad at all. Had lunch with Kate and her fam. That was a trip. And super fun. This plane ride rather sucks. In the middle between Eden and a ~~childish~~ guy for 4 hours. Frontier ~~p~~ planes are ~~very~~ v crappy. I CAN'T BELIEVE TONIGHT WE'LL BE IN SEATTLE!!

Like the rest of us, Dove (17) experienced the surrealness of not having to think about walking for the first time in more than five months.

their cousins. After spending every day together for the past five months, we felt the stark contrast harshly; we missed them.

At one point at the camp, a friend saw Rainier running with a stick and instinctively told him to stop. For the past five months, Rainier had been playing in waterfalls, fording rivers, and navigating boulder fields. Much of the time, we had little access to medical care or cell service. Now, here on a soft, grassy hill, Rainier had a dull stick in his hand. By one definition, he was the safest he had been in half a year. When our friend saw that Kami and I were totally unalarmed, he rolled his eyes and said, "Or you can just let him run with a stick."

With our hiking friends, we were heroes. Here, we were irresponsible parents, and maybe crazy. We realized it would be hard to explain our 2,200-mile journey to those who hadn't been there.

While many of our friends at camp begged to hear the details of our story, those on Whiteblaze found new ways to dismiss our accomplishments.

*"Too bad they didn't just walk for the sake of walkin'. the media circus was by design. Not impressed." —*Lone Wolf

*"Good for them. The parents are still weirdos." —*FrogLevel

*"I'm just wondering what holy mission the do-gooders have moved onto now that we know the toddler survived with all of his fingers and toes (and cheeks) and hasn't suffered any permanent damage from his period of inactivity..." —*Lonehiker

*"Designed to get handouts—the guy makes six kids, has money to get all tatted up—yet wants others to subsidize the six month vaca—in other words, about typical" —*George

We had come to accept that our journey was not for everyone, and that for some people, there would never be any amount of effort that would be enough to prove a point or change their mind.

After camp, we drove back across the country. Six months after leaving home, we walked into our house, which was in pristine condition after having been used as a vacation rental, and set our backpacks on the floor. They still had dirt from Maine on them.

At the end of hiking such a long way, it's easy to think, *What am I going to do now?* Walking gives you purpose. What it lacks in comfort, it makes up in simplicity. Every day, you wake up and know exactly what you need to do. It's all laid out for you. Off the trail, we had all kinds of things on our calendar to manage. Without a clear goal each day, it was easy to feel depressed about life. Ambiguity returned to life. It was hard to know what to do with all our stuff. For so long, we'd just had our backpacks. That was all we were responsible for. Now, we were again responsible for all these additional items—books, clothes, computers, our car. It felt overwhelming, and it changed how we looked at our possessions. We threw out some of our clothes, and we took stock of how much it cost to manage so much stuff.

RECOVERY

There were some clear physical consequences to our trip. We had all kinds of soreness. Even months later, some of us still felt sore in our legs and knees.

On the plus side, we immediately started putting on weight. The kids were all back to their original weights within two months. We have a picture of us before Lakeside and after, and we look completely different. In the before picture, I have a beard, you can see all our shoulder bones and ribs, our abs are chiseled, and there is no fat on our bodies—except for Rainier, who was, of course, fatter.

A cousin who had just received her degree in substance abuse counseling said if it wasn't for our nails and skin, she would have thought we were all on meth.

There were a few lasting physical changes too. Filia had her teeth checked, and sure enough, she had a cavity that required a filling. The dentist said it was nothing serious. Memory tested positive for Lyme disease and was put on antibiotics.

Overall, though, we came out of the trip relatively unscathed. Our family started running again three times a week. It felt more natural for our bodies to move than to sit staring at a computer screen. Altra sent us road shoes to run in.

For six months, Kami and I slept in every day. We woke up and enjoyed coffee together. We didn't take it for granted. On the A.T., we thought constantly about optimizing nutrition, rest, and miles, and now we enjoyed just sipping coffee, reading a book, and using my fountain pen to copy text in the morning. It made me feel human again.

Over the next year, Rainier turned three, and Dove turned eighteen and got her driver's license. When it came time for Dove to get her first car, it didn't come from any of our old friends. It didn't come from family members or anyone at a church. It came from Fresh Ground. A man who feeds hikers. He had since upgraded to a van, and almost two years after we started our hike, Fresh Ground drove ten hours from North Carolina to deliver Stinkbug—his smelly, beat-up Camry, covered in bumper stickers—as a gift to Dove. As usual, he wouldn't accept any payment.

WAS IT WORTH IT?

People often told us, "Someday, your kids will look back and appreciate the trail."

Right now, two years later, our kids have mixed feelings about the A.T. When Eden is in a cranky mood, she'll say, "It's your fault. You killed my soul on the A.T." We've all joked about never hiking again.

Eventually, Seven went through all of the footage we filmed from the trail. There were 125 videos that, at first, seemed too painful to watch. We put them together into a one-hour-long-documentary and had the kids record a voiceover. It shows the snow, the meals, and the faces of the people we met. Every week we walk past some-one in our house watching it, and we can tell they miss the trail.

As time went on, our feelings became more nuanced. We didn't want to hike again, but we could not deny the power of the experiences and feelings we had on the trail. The hike started to feel like a faraway fairy tale that we had been a part of, something epic and precious that maybe we would someday recapture. It was a weird, conflicting set of feelings—we didn't want to go back to the A.T., but we craved what thru-hiking had given us, to the extent that we wondered if we'd be able to stay away.

While on the trail, Odie had shared with us a poem he wrote about thru-hikers. It captured the glory of what thru-hiking has done for so many people, and captured the transformation our family experienced together.

> We ate like fat kids, partied like rock stars and looked like
>   athletes.
> We climbed mountains for breakfast, then beat the sun to the
>   horizon.
> We trusted our lives to strangers and called them family.
> We changed our socks weekly and our minds courageously.
> We believed in magic and would often laugh at the moon...

To this day, we've been unable to find another activity that can change you, transform how you see the world, build your confidence, and bring a group of people closer together than thru-hiking.

Looking back now, we ask ourselves if hiking 2,200 miles was worth it. We would love to say it was the best experience of our lives, that we have no regrets, and that the trip stands as a shining beacon of positivity in all of our memory banks. But that's not entirely true.

Even in writing this book I encountered doubt about decisions and actions that at one time, felt normal. We simply did our best with what we had, unsure how it would turn out.

We're still unsure. Once home, we reread the comments on Reddit about pushing our kids too hard and ensuring they would eventually hate us. Even though the commenters quickly moved on to critiquing someone else, their comments still made me wonder if we did push too hard.

Our hike on the A.T. is just one picture of what's possible for the average family. We say "average" because hiking is a fairly average activity; it wasn't like we were going to the moon. We were simply walking. And after we calculated the entire cost of our trip, including the meals that had been delivered, all of the hotels, and the shoes, and the shuttles, the total came to ten dollars a person a day. Financially, walking through fourteen states isn't that far out of reach for the average family.

The trail gave us an opportunity to let our kids truly shine. And they shined in the most simple and normal activities that anyone can do: sharing, cooking, laughing, and walking. If we were only able to focus on our fears, prioritizing safety, we may have never been able to see all they were capable of doing, and we would have sold both parenthood and childhood short. And most importantly, we would have missed out on the relationships that bind them together.

The rough and intense moments on the A.T., when we were pushed to our limits, were a rare glimpse into what our relationships were truly made of and what they could be. Could we respect and honor our kids and their preferences for who they really were, even if it cost us our dream of sixteen years that we had been working five months for? Could they respect and care about us when they saw us at our worst? Could you smash eight people this close together for this long and have it actually work out, or were the walls and doors and devices back home there for a reason?

How do you decide if something is worth it? For Filia, she has spent five percent of her life on the Appalachian Trail. That's one out of every twenty days of her life spent enduring extreme exercise under extreme conditions. Rainier has spent closer to ten percent, one out of ten days, of his life on the trail. These were days our family spent suffering, crying, sweating, shivering, and even literally starving. This time on the Appalachian Trail was a time when we gave up comfort, school, and income; all normal life as we knew it. The cost of hiking was high. In a way, it literally cost us everything.

But every lifestyle choice requires a sacrifice. Back at home, the cost of stability and comfort was missing out on adventure and challenge. Even though the price we paid on the trail *seemed* higher because it was further from the status quo, now that some time had passed, we were able to feel the cost less and see some of what we'd received in return.

Our time spent hiking was an investment toward turning us into the type of people we wanted to become. People who are free; people who care about moments, experiences, and relationships; people who are fearless, yet sensitive enough to truly appreciate the small things. We had each become stronger, but also humbler. Our lives and the relationships we had with each other felt more real.

So, when asking yourself if something is worth it, I've learned that you cannot just look at the cost. You have to look at the full equation of what you get in return. Only then can you answer that very complicated question.

They say that five years after a fight with your spouse, you won't remember what you fought about, but you'll remember that you fought.

No matter how important the title of "thru-hiker" seemed or how good it could feel to touch the sign on Katahdin and hold the record for largest family to complete the A.T., we had a collective feeling we wouldn't care about any of these things in twenty years. What we would care about is how we had seen and treated our children and the relationships we had built.

For that, there was no better learning tool than walking 2,200 miles with two tents through three seasons. Not that we had found, anyway. And our fight wasn't over; once we were home, we'd need to find new adventures to bring our family closer for the rest of our lives.

Here's the truth.

There was not one moment we seriously considered quitting.

Sure, we thought about it. And we knew it was an option. But we knew we wouldn't.

We'll never regret taking the risk of thru-hiking the trail with our kids. We'll never regret risking our relationship with them in pursuit of togetherness. We might wake up one day in ten years and realize the cost was too high—because, honestly, it was way higher than we could have imagined. If that happens, we're prepared to admit our weaknesses, apologize to our kids, and course correct for the future. Whether it's a hike or an apology, any step toward togetherness is a worthwhile one.

After all, parenting is a gamble either way. At home, you play it safe and risk losing togetherness, care, and adventure. In the woods, you gamble with bears, blizzards, and reaching the end of your rope.

We know which side we'll bet on.

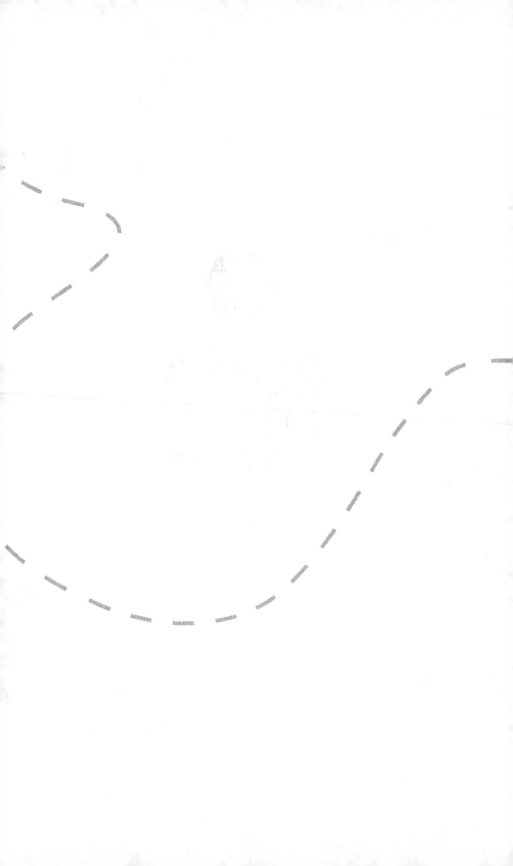

2000
MILES
TOGETHER

MARCH

START **1**   2   3   4

5 ZERO MI   6   7   **8** HIGH 40 F   9   **10** ZERO MI FREEZING RAIN   11

NEW HIGH **15.8** MI
12   **13** N☆C   **14** SNOW   15   16   17   18

ENTER **SMOKIES**
19   **20**   **21** BLIZZARD   **22**   **23** ZERO MI / GATLINBURG WITH PARENTS   24   25

OUT OF **SMOKIES**
26   **27** NEW HIGH **17.3** MI   28   29   30   31

AVERAGE
10.3 MILES PER DAY
4 ZEROES

APRIL

EASTER ZERO MI
1   2   3   4

ENTER **TENNESSEE** NEW HIGH **17.6** MI
5   **6**   7   8   9   10   **11** NEW HIGH **19.1** MI

KAMI'S BIRTHDAY ENTER **VIRGINIA**
12   13   14   **15** NEW HIGH **20.5** MI   16   **17** NEW HIGH **21.5** MI   18

HIGH 40 F SNOW
19   20   21   22   **23** ZERO MI   **24** ZERO MI SICK   25

26   27   **28** FOREST FIRE   **29**   **30** BYE, HOPS!

AVERAGE
13 MILES PER DAY
3 ZEROES

JULY

86 F
1   2   3

RECORD BREAKING HEAT
4 91 F **5**

SLACKPACKED BY PARENTS
6   **7**   **8**   9

BEN'S BIRTHDAY
10 **11**

ENTERED THE WHITES

12   13   14   15   16

JOE DODGE LODGE
ZERO
MI **17**   18

DIRIGO
ENTERED MAINE
19   **20**   21   22   23   24   25

FINISH TECHNICAL 200

AVERAGE
14.2 MILES PER DAY
1 ZERO

26   27   **28**   29   30   31

AUGUST

1   **2**   **3**   **4**

100 MILE WILDERNESS

DAY 161
OUR SUMMIT DAY

FLY TO SEATTLE

5   **6**   **7**   8   **9**   **10**

AVERAGE
13.5 MILES PER DAY
13 TOTAL TRIP ZEROES

EPILOGUE

Hops overcame the broken bone in his foot and summited Mount Katahdin one week after we did, fulfilling a dream he had since he was eleven years old. He was sixty-eight.

Silver went on to hike across New Zealand and also thru-hiked the Pacific Crest Trail.

Harvey Lewis finished the A.T. in forty-nine days, placing eighth as the fastest completion of all time.[2] He would later invite us to do our first ultramarathon and run next to Filia as she ran forty miles in twenty-four hours. She was eight. Harvey placed first, running 120 miles in total.

Pappy, the oldest hiker, did not finish. He said he would be back next year.

Five months after finishing the trail, we released a full hour-long documentary on YouTube called *To the Tree Line*. We used the best video footage from our entire hike combined with the kids' narration.

---

2   Warren Doyle, who also unofficially keeps track of trail records, reports Harvey's place as ninth.

It took Seven and I weeks of editing, and to date, it has been watched more than nine hundred thousand times.

On our one-year anniversary, we returned to Winding Stair Gap, the location where Kami changed Rainier's diaper in the freezing cold three miles before we got picked up by Arnie-1-Mile. We met Fresh Ground there and set up a kitchen and fed hikers blueberry pancakes, homemade corndogs, fettucine Alfredo, and Kool-Aid (the menu was based on what the kids would have wanted to stumble across most when they were on the trail).

And not just because of some of the hate comments we still get on our videos, years later. This one's as of May 2020:

> "Geez...greedy much?! Perhaps you can be the one donating Altras and food and helping others that are less fortunate than you... considering you are wealthy and retired before the age of forty. So gross! I was actually rooting for your family while watching you do the A.T. trail...however...upon realizing you are just a greedy, selfish, pig family, it just made me sick to know you gobbled up food from people who were providing trail magic and have less money than you do, are still working for a living, still owe mortgages on their homes, have poorer health than you all...yikes...Pigs! Opportunists! Honestly, did you give anything back to the wonderful A.T. trail people, or were you just takers?" —da doe

Well. If we've learned anything documenting our adventures, it's that haters are most definitely gonna hate and our story is not for everyone. We're learning to be okay with that.

On September 29, 2018, less than two months after we had stayed with him, Earl "Bear" Towne died peacefully at his home and hostel–The Cabin. At a memorial service, Odie from *The Hiker Yearbook* served moose tracks ice cream to hikers. Gifford's (Bear's favorite brand from Maine that he served to us) donated twice the amount that was requested.

When I took Dove on a surprise trip to NYC for her eighteenth birthday, we stayed with Eddie and Kat. Kat took us to an underground improv jazz club, where we watched Eddie jam with other world-class musicians—on his saxophone, instead of on a tin whistle.

The year after we hiked, as always, our family was signed up to cook at Lakeside. A couple of months before we were set to go, we got a call from the camp organizers. They'd seen a vlog we'd posted on our Fight For Together channel where we spoke openly about our changed beliefs about sexuality—that we no longer believed it was a sin to be gay. Because of these beliefs, Lakeside had decided to rescind our invitations. We were no longer welcome to cook at the camp where all our kids, and where Kami and I, had grown up. Fresh Ground, who was visiting at the time, comforted the kids through their tears and helped us process the loss.

Tim "Fresh Ground" Davis has continued to feed hikers on the A.T. each year, starting during the coldest month of February and heading north until he runs out of money. If you would like to support him, you can find him on Facebook at FreshGroundLeapfrogCafe, or donate at:

Venmo: @freshgroundleapfrogcafe
PayPal: Friends and Family, davistimdavis3@hotmail.com

In 2020, Dr. Warren Doyle was admitted into the Appalachian Trail Hall of Fame.

The custom summit sign that Hudson handcrafted for us is on display at The Bearded Woods Hostel, and to this day, people ask to get their picture taken with it.

To date, we have not applied for our 2,000-Miler certificates and patches from the ATC. We didn't need the validation of an organization to feel accomplished, and the kids didn't seem to care about it.

About eighteen months after we stood on Katahdin, Kami and I asked the kids each to write a reflection on their hike.

> Dove 18
>
> I really miss the AT. I miss the people, I miss the feeling of getting closer and closer to something we'd been working towards for so long. I miss the way food tastes and how much I could eat of it.
>
> The AT comes up a lot in our everyday life. We referance it all the time.
>
> Sometimes we'll mention It, It in that something can't be worse than when we were hiking 12 miles through a blizzard on the AT and sometimes we'll talk about how it felt relaxing at a trail magic stop with out friends.
>
> The AT made me stronger. More patient, more tough, more open-minded and free. Theres a lot of things that are less hard than the AT, and because ive done that, I feel like a lot of other things are possible to do too.
>
> We head to the trail in a week to make food for some hikers. I know I'm really going to want to start walking with them.

Eden (17)

It's hard to believe that two years ago I was going through one of the hardest parts of my life so far. I remember the first day. How it kind of felt like the end of the world I knew that the Appalachian Trail would change my life but I thought that the change would be mostly negative And there were, MOST DEFINITELY negative, crappy, very, very crappy moments. Too many to count. But there were also, the moments I miss, going to red robin after 23 miles hiking squishing in an uber, counting orange newts, peeling off shoes and socks to cross rivers, packing out subway sandwiches, washing dirt ~~out~~ out of my hair.

Seven (15)

The Appalachian trail

Im really glad I did it because I got to see my family in a ~~us~~ entirely different way working together

I mostly miss the people on the trail because I feal like I have gone through so much with them

I dont really want to hike anything any more though (only short hikes)

Its weird watching old videos from the AT because I miss it and I dont at the same time and I remember the best moments and some of the hardest moments

My perspective has changed a lot about the AT before hiking it I really didnt wanna do it but taards the end I really enjoyed it and now I appriciate it all

the first 3 or 2 months were the hardest but the last 2 months made it all worth it

Memory   (13)

Looking back is strange. because is feals like it was hasent been that long. and its hard to remember the hard stuff. but I remember most of the good things like hanging out with fresh grounds, culigan, not dead, nubs, fun facts, and Zultan, Babyface in main. I remember fresh grounds doing trail magic for us in the 100 mile Wilderness and that was probably one of my favorite parts. And I think I'm starting to miss it a little. but only the good parts.

Filia's Response: (9)

Looking back is weird. I really liked that people hosted us in their house.

I loved looking forward to a nice warm shower and a hotel.

I don't miss anything. Except the days we saw Fresh Ground and it was sunny.

I don't miss the rainy or stormy or sick days. Waking up and you felt hot and wet. And you had to wake up and your tent was wet and it was so miserable.

If it was a rainy day it could be fun b/c of a river ~~Memory and I w~~ down the trail + Memory + I would move stuff on the trail so the river would be bigger.

Me, Memory, + Seven would pop the sap bubbles on the tree.

~~I did~~ My least favorite part was the top parts where there was no trees + it was misty + rainy.

If it was a really hot day I loved how we went in the river or stream.

I love when Fresh Ground meets us + made lunch for us or bfast or dinner.

> Rainier (4)
>
> I remember that we go to Fresh Ground and eat some food. That's really fun. I like that. I like that time.
>
> I remember having a new house. That was really fun too. (We think he's talking about the hostels.) I asked him which new house? He said it has one, two, three, four, five, six, seven beds.
>
> And I remember when Fresh Ground gave us new candy in the house or something. (This was the following year when we went back to do trail magic.) We found red rocks on the Appalachian Trail and I think that's all. Put them in the river.

SPECIAL THANKS

Our entire family would like to thank this incomplete list of people who helped us on our journey. I wish we could have written about each one of them in this book—you all deserve recognition. Here are a few stats that show just how much support we received.

We stayed in thirty-four houses or hostels that were paid for by other people.

We had eighty-six meals provided for us for free—delivered on the trail or at people's houses.

Others slackpacked us a total of twenty-three days.

The support, of course, went beyond statistics. We have so many memories to be grateful for.

First, thank you to Halmonee and Papa for your endless hours of driving and support. You were the key to our happiest moments on the trail.

Thanks to Hanna for managing our property.

And a massive, heartfelt thank you to everyone who offered us housing, food, and cigars, hiked with us, or slackpacked us:

Nicole & John Mahshie

Tonya Braswell

Eric & Julia Lutkenhoff

Mike & Claudia Grenier

Gordon & Nancy Priddy (Arnie-1-Mile & G)

Arnold "Bloodhound" Guzman for the writing

Jordan & Kristen Chang

Kenny and Manon

Melissa Coleman (and family)

Gavin & Kim Inson

Jeff & Lanhee Harrington

Lyndsey & Adam

Kate & Steve Bowen

Sue & Mark Brenneman

Stan "The Man" Sutter

Shauna Dickson

Heidi & Jeffrey Varner

Bill & Denise Hirn

Becky & Tyler Luzier

Erin & Matthew Blank

Bernadette Leibensperger

Tylor, Chris, & Sandy Hess

Misty Mott

Megan & Dan Washer

Heather McHale

Ralphferrusi Ferrusi

Susan & Billie-Jo Bradley
Jennifer Gonzalez
Bobby & Wendi Love
Julie Lombardi
Hudson and Lu Young
Lisa & Nancy
Kendi Ethier
The Bissaillons and everyone at CrossFit Great Barrington
The Folks at Bola Granola of Great Barrington: *https://bolagrano-la.com/*
Paul Yeomans
Jennifer Robbins
Martin & Russ Cote
Sarah & Matt Stanishewski
The Prettymans
Brock & Sara Quesnel
Pat & Paul Killigrew
Jay "Ziploc" and Betsy Brooks
Carl "Omelet Guy" Spring
Sage McReynolds
Caitlyn & Jodeob
Serena & Justin at the Notch Hostel
Harm Scherpbier
Sandy & Mark Wagner
Whitney Silberblatt
Deb & "Granite State" Gaskin
Sharon & "YOLO" Akers
Matt "Odie" Norman
Tim "Fresh Ground" Davis—you're famous!
Benjamin & Melissa Bayley

Bob & Barbara Dunne
Karen Reilly
Brad & Beth Herder
Beth Reuman & Rick Hemond—thank you for the lobster!

All of the hostel owners and shuttle drivers that made special accommodations for large families and small kids. You are the life-blood of the trail.

And everyone else who fed, housed, and slackpacked us. Many people left drinks or water on the trail; some people's names we never knew, and others were written on little scraps of paper, never to be found or mentioned. You changed our day, and you made our hike.

To the following companies who came out of the woodwork and supported our family:

The folks at Altra who provided us with shoes.
The Trek and Arnold for publishing the wonderful article that
caused so many people to reach out.
Zpacks for the amazing and light tent.
Biddle & Bop who supplied us with a new rain suit for Rainier.

To everyone who left a comment or like on our hiking videos—you contributed to the conversations, and your online presence reminds us that we are not alone.

NOBO class of 2018—you guys are especially my heroes!

Hops—Thanks for being our trail grandpa. You made our hike richer. Oh, and thanks for the Chinese food!

The Degenerates: Culligan, Not Dead, Fun Facts, Nubs, and Mama Kish: "Enghh, enghh, enghh, enghh, enghh...enghh, enghhhhhh-hhh!" (That's a broken-ass conch call.)

David Axel "Silver" Kurtz—you still owe me a cigar.

Eddie and Kat!

The Trailer Park Boys: Zoltan and Baby Face, who cheered us at the finish!

And finally, thank you to everyone who supported us and continues to support us on Patreon.

EDITOR'S NOTE

When I was first offered the opportunity to work with Ben on writing and editing 2,000 *Miles Together*, I wasn't exactly excited. The book was behind schedule, and the draft I was handed bore little resemblance to the story you've just read (in fact, it read kind of like a Wikipedia article, an exhaustive factual account of locations and dates). But at the same time, I could tell that there was something unique about this project—an opportunity to make a unique story come alive. The book's potential went beyond a traditional adventure memoir. It was more like a sprawling quest epic with a cast of a dozen main characters across a two-thousand-mile setting. It pitted man against nature, instinct against criticism; it was about all the emotions and tensions between parents and kids. The first time I read through Ben's account of events, I thought, *Seriously, is he crazy?* I knew it would take all of my experience and skills as a writer to identify and flesh out the right narrative.

I started by interviewing Ben, but I soon found that his perspective wasn't enough. I needed to hear from Kami and each of the kids.

I needed to actually see the trail. Luckily, this was made easy for me, in the form of the Crawford family's YouTube channel. I went head-first down the rabbit hole, watching every single trail video from the A.T. in chronological order. I winced as I watched them struggling through freezing rain on Springer Mountain, and then dozens of hours later, I cried when they finally reached Katahdin. Throughout, I took several side adventures through their other videos, too, painting myself a picture of their lives before and after the hike. It wasn't really work—it was entertainment. We're talking pajamas and popcorn, yelling at the screen, the whole nine yards. It was kind of like discovering a new show on Netflix that already had five entire seasons up; I binge-watched the hell out of the Crawfords. What struck me most about the family was the way they presented their unconventional life totally without explanation, justification, or a hint of defensiveness. Just, *This is who we are. This is the way we choose to live.*

As I watched the trail videos, I began to get an idea of how to present the complicated events and themes in a way that invited the reader into the story. The arc of the narrative was all right there in the meticulously edited footage (thank you, Seven), but translating it to the page was its own epic journey. It was an incredibly daunting task, and I was frustrated for a *very* long time, just because there was so much content, feeling, and color to try to wrangle. It was the world's biggest jigsaw puzzle, and I was keeping all the pieces essentially inside my head as I sorted through the story and laid it out in a way that made me feel as compelled and excited as I had watching the videos.

Once we had the structure of a real story broken out, with a central theme and arc, Ben and I truly worked in tandem to bring the story to life: his story, his words told over many hours of interviews, and my wordsmithing, advice, and occasional vehement rejections.

"This is passive voice." "But I like it!" "No. Tough." Through thirteen drafts, we painstakingly considered every sentence, event, and anecdote. Ben had written long multi-page sermons on parenting, and I cut them mercilessly, to which he'd reply, "Oh good, I hated that, fuck that section!"

As we worked, Ben committed himself to the craft of writing, learning as much as he could. Every time we got on the phone, he'd have read another book on storytelling; Stephen King, Joseph Campbell. Because of his commitment, the most important contributions to the narrative arc were undoubtedly his. And for me, as a professional writer, it was incredibly energizing for a client to morph into a true collaborative partner. Writing is very much a "lone wolf" experience most of the time. It's hard to explain what I do, and few people who aren't writers get it. It's not often a shared experience. So for this project to *become* that was part of why it became so special to me, and why I looked forward to the work so much—work that increasingly felt like creative play as the months went on.

I think I turned in four of what were supposed to be "touchdown edits" to Ben. But when we'd get on the phone to discuss, he'd say, "Okay, but...I just had this idea for another theme we should build in..." Typically, if I hear that from a client, I'm dreading what comes next. But that didn't happen with this book because he was always right, and I had a personal stake in making the story not just great, but as phenomenal as it possibly could be.

In the time I spent working on *2,000 Miles Together*, I went beyond the words. I dove deep into the world of the Crawfords, learning their individual quirks, their likes and dislikes, their speech patterns, their favorite foods, and the deep and often-shifting intricacies of how they felt about their epic adventure. I started to understand this book not as a series of anecdotes, but as a narrative as rich and exciting as any writer could ever hope to stumble across, and a story few writers ever get the pure writerly joy of helping to craft.

Working on this book changed my life. For one thing, it showed me what's possible in the world of outdoor adventure, and my side hobby of short day hikes morphed into a full-blown backpacking addiction. But more importantly, it showed me what's possible for family. It showed me what it looks like when parents listen to and respect their children. It showed me the priceless connection that choosing *together* can create.

My hope for readers is the same—that this book expands your idea of what's possible.

—Meghan McCracken

ACKNOWLEDGMENTS

I would not have been able to write this book without the support of the kids, who filmed their honest reactions through tears, laughter, and disappointment, edited and published videos, and allowed me to use their journals to understand and share the trail from their perspective. I appreciate your honesty, trust, and willingness to share all aspects of your journey with me.

Thanks to Kami for working with me through the pain of the experience to tell and retell the stories that have shaped our family.

Thanks to Matthew "Odie" Norman for permission to use his poem. Hikers Hike!

Thanks to Whiteblaze.net for permission to use material posted on their website.

Thanks to Em Sites Karnes: for help with cover concepts and keepin' it real!

Carrie, Amy, Dirk, Caleb, Tim, and Bryan for reading early versions of the book and providing feedback, and especially Robin, who encouraged me to share my feelings, not just my thoughts.

Thanks to Warren Doyle for being an inspiration to the hiking community and being willing to lend your voice and thoughts to this project.

Thanks to everyone who left a comment on Reddit, YouTube, Instagram, Facebook, Whiteblaze, and other sites that were used in the book. Whether you agreed with us or not, your opinions added to the conversation and helped make this book what it is.

Thanks to the team at Scribe: John Mannion, Natalie Aboudaoud, and Josh Raymer. Thank you to Anton Khodakovsky for the beautiful map and calendar illustrations. And especially Erin Tyler: thank you for your work on the cover and for giving me twenty revisions without giving up. Making something look scrappy *and* professional wasn't easy, but you did it.

Meghan. I wanted to tell the story chronologically and leave nothing out. You helped me to craft a narrative held together by thematic elements and helped delete the stuff that would have driven people (including myself) crazy. The care and effort that you brought to the project with the late nights and hours of re-writing was much appreciated. Your desire to dive deep into our lives, stories, and videos helped me to trust that you were the best person for this project. Thank you for being willing to blow apart any deadline, contractual constraint, and professional boundary in service of the best story.

WHERE TO FIND THE CRAWFORDS

We would love to hear your feedback and *your* story of how reading this book has impacted you! The most helpful way is if you write a review on Amazon sharing your experience.

You can also interact with us more at the following places:

1. Our family's YouTube channel, Fight For Together: *www.youtube.com/c/FightforTogether*

2. On our channel, you can find the documentary we made about our hike, *To the Treeline*: *youtu.be/JtickT2tCwo*

3. You can also find the full playlist of our daily hiking videos: *www.youtube.com/playlist?list=PL8jVL_i9OvEF_GWO4E1AneMON_IFLqci*

4. Find us on Instagram! Our family's channel: *@fightfortogether*, Ben Crawford's channel: *@3enCrawford*

5. Go to *fightfortogether.com* to find all the links in this book, additional resources, and our Fight For Together merch

6. And finally, we're on Facebook at *www.facebook.com/fightfortogether*

ADDITIONAL NOTES AND RESOURCES

For direct links to all the below resources,
go to *www.fightfortogether.com.*

INTRODUCTION

STRINGBEAN—Appalachian Trail FKT Documentary [video]. Video of Stringbean's unsupported record on the A.T. The quote we use in the intro is from this video. https://youtu.be/fCy7ASKYLto

The Appalachian Trail Conservancy describes the Appalachian Trail as the longest hiking-only trail in the world. https://en.wikipedia.org/wiki/Appalachian_Trail.

Into Thin Air: A Personal Account of the Mt. Everest Disaster by Jon Krakauer was an influential book I read in my twenties that describes the life-threatening phenomenon called "summit fever" in great detail.

CHAPTER 1

Through Painted Deserts: Light, God, and Beauty on the Open Road by Donald Miller: where we got the title quote.

Week 1: WE ALREADY WANT TO QUIT [video]. Our first day in the rain. At this point, we were planning on publishing one video a week. https://youtu.be/QDEy3tVwl8w

CHAPTER 2

Week 1: WE ALREADY WANT TO QUIT [video]. At around the 10 minute mark, you meet MacGyver and hear him talk about Fresh Ground. It wouldn't be for months later that we knew who he was talking about, and it wasn't until one of our viewers commented that he was mentioned on Day 3 that we knew this reference existed. https://youtu.be/QDEy3tVwl8w

Day 5: Something Terrible Happened [video]. Our lowest moment with kids sick in the cabin and we decide not to quit. This is the video where I realize we do not have what it takes to finish, just to keep going. https://youtu.be/RSmAh5xp2uU

CHAPTER 3

Dissolution speech given by J. Krishnamurti: source of chapter title quote. https://jkrishnamurti.org/about-dissolution-speech

Day 9: WE MADE THE DEADLINE [video]. We arrive in Hiawassee, our first town. https://youtu.be/qTNynA2Cz9E

Day 14: THEY RESCUED US [video]. Meeting Arnie-1-Mile. https://youtu.be/aEpbCf7tr_c

Arnie-1-Mile's video of meeting us (happens around the 18 minute mark). https://youtu.be/xJ3q-ztM8S4

CHAPTER 4

Mere Christianity by C. S. Lewis: source for chapter title quote.

Day 8: PARENTING MISTAKE [video]. An apology to Rainier. https://youtu.be/s7ymIT29i7g

CHAPTER 5

Training for the New Alpinism: A Manual for the Climber as Athlete by Steve House: source of chapter title quote. Steve House has been influential to me because of his ethos around adventure, speed, gear, and minimalism.

Day 20: HARDEST PART OF THE TRAIL [video]. We get accepted into an over-capacity shelter in the Smokies. https://youtu.be/VYIhx26MQVw

Day 21: CRAZY SNOW [video]. We wake up to frozen gear, share what it was like to be taken care of in the shelter, walk through a blizzard, and end up in a bathroom. https://youtu.be/77twOzg-F1M

CHAPTER 6

Building a Bridge to the 18th Century: How the Past Can Improve Our Future by Neil Postman: source for chapter title quote.

Day 22: BEST DAY EVER [video]. We wake up in the bathroom, get rescued by my parents, and discuss CPS. https://youtu.be/UPt_ooqhcQg

CHAPTER 7

The War of Art by Steven Pressfield: source of chapter title quote. Steven Pressfield has been one of the most influential authors in my life, and his nonfiction books beginning with this one were key in me moving toward writing and even the completion of this book.

Crawford Family on the Wonderland 2009 [YouTube playlist]. This is a series of videos we made from our first hike when the four kids were two, four, six, and eight. The video quality and editing is pretty bad, but we had never made videos like this and were very proud of it at the time. https://www.youtube.com/playlist?list=PL96CC809A919BDF85

Wonderland Trail 2015 [vlogs; YouTube playlist]. This is a video series of our fifth and most recent time hiking the ninety-five-mile Wonderland Trail around Mount Rainier when our kids were four, eight, ten, twelve, and fourteen. Kami was four months pregnant. https://www.youtube.com/playlist?list=PL8jVL_i9OvEF9t4AY3eWpGXbiiJWUkJtJ

Dixie's Channel, Homemade Wanderlust, that motivated Kami to hike the Appalachian Trail with six kids. *www.youtube.com/channel/ UCQhqmV26773qZhzqJz4VFcw*
Reddit comments taken from these threads:

"Fight For Together/Crawford Family's Appalachian TrailWreck 3/26-4/1: Will the baby lose toes to frostbite? Will Mom Crawford get pregnant on the trail? Will these dumbasses have their kids taken away? Discuss!" The first discussion thread we found that was really difficult for us to deal with. https://www.reddit.com/r/blogsnark/comments/878szp/fight_for_ togethercrawford_familys_appalachian/

"Fight For Together/Crawford Family's Appalachian TrailWreck 4/2-4/8: Another week on the trail. Who will get sick? Will anyone go missing?" https://www.reddit.com/r/blogsnark/comments/892w3e/fight_for_ togethercrawford_familyappalachian/

CHAPTER 8

The Art of Asking; or, How I Learned to Stop Worrying and Let People Help by Amanda Palmer: source of chapter title quote. I love Amanda Palmer's work and her storytelling around success looking like increased dependence and connection to your fans. If interested, check out her TED talk by the same title ("The Art of Asking").

Day 28: WE FINALLY WEIGH OUR PACKS [video]. After reading the comments on Reddit, we walk into Hot Springs. https://youtu.be/ wnzso9z5YLA

ONE MONTH REVIEW [video]. Staying at John and Nicole's house and farm. https://youtu.be/hHvhoZrFvOQ

New BABY! Home Birth with Family [YouTube video]. Video of Rainier's birth that Nicole saw and led to her reaching out to us. https://youtu. be/fPGPkbsA-8I

Child Protective Services MESSAGE FROM THE KIDS [video]. Our kids record a message at the farm to the people who reported us to CPS. https://youtu.be/tyKp1Gjia_M

It Is The People | A Pacific Crest Trail Film [video]. Elina's masterpiece where she referred to thru-hiking as "privileged homelessness, with intention." This is a must watch if you want to get a feel for what thru-hiking is like. https://youtu.be/hiVbB7Pf2lY

CHAPTER 9

Day 43: BIRTHDAY IN DAMASCUS [video]. Tonya delivers us trail magic and surprise birthday cake for Kami, and we tell the story of Damascus. https://youtu.be/jAOlH9eKI8s

How I Went From Waiting Tables to Being a Professional Blackjack Player (on Accident) [Kindle E-book]. The story of our bike trip in our first year of marriage and how it changed our life. https://www.amazon.com/dp/B07KTG94KM/ref=cm_sw_r_tw_dp_x_Z6idFbKPEoFNT

Day 42: BLOWN AWAY BY ENCOURAGEMENT [video]. Interview with Grace and the Old Guys Hiking Club, who encouraged us. https://youtu.be/ykn2k4Zf1Eo

Day 50: SO SICK OF THE COLD [video]. Gnome encourages us. https://youtu.be/Drnrao1I39g

Day 44: GEAR UPGRADES, ULTIMATE RESUPPLY AND INTERVIEW WITH TRAIL ANGELS [video]. My first day with Altra shoes. https://youtu.be/lLZzK6TD_lo

Dear Altra, We love you! [YouTube video]. The video we sent to Altra that led to them sending us free shoes. https://youtu.be/9SkTNxf4t1w

CHAPTER 10

Day 48: MOTIVATING KIDS—LONGEST DAY YET [video]. Around the 13 minute mark, the video shows us finishing our longest day yet and giving a tour of Quarter Way Inn. https://youtu.be/8WF6wNhlRg4

Day 49: WE NEED A BREAK [video]. Gourmet breakfast at the Quarter Way Inn. https://youtu.be/FzfVURgOgYI

Day 51: AWESOME PEOPLE WE'VE MET ON THE TRAIL [video]. Brushy Mountain Grill and interviews with The Degenerates: Culligan, Not Dead, Mama Kish, Fun Facts, Nubs, and Hops and Silver. https://youtu.be/YpscGg-m47I

CHAPTER 11

Thru-Hiker definition [Wikipedia]. Thru-hiking, or through-hiking, is to hike an established end-to-end hiking trail or long-distance trail with continuous footsteps in one direction. https://en.wikipedia.org/wiki/Thru-hiking

Day 61: CAUGHT IN FOREST FIRE [video]. Spending an extra night at Jordan and Kristen's house because of the forest fire. And then getting dropped off in Daleville after skipping nineteen miles of trail. https://youtu.be/Scb_Q1p7A1w

Day 56: EVERYONE GOT SICK [video] Hops shares his story of when he decided to hike the A.T. https://youtu.be/wiUARKyUehI

We need your HELP: QUESTION FOR THRU Hikers [video]. Us asking for help from thru-hikers to decide if we should go back and hike the nineteen miles of trail that we missed. https://youtu.be/ELm54hT1jV4

Day 69: WHY WE'RE SKIPPING PART OF THE TRAIL [video]. We announce our final decision to skip the section of trail on fire. https://youtu.be/ivABRY4UQxY

CHAPTER 12

Reinhold Messner (source of chapter intro quote) is an Italian mountaineer who has been instrumental to me in his perspectives of adventure, risk, and the essence of adventure and finding the limits of human potential. He is credited with the first solo ascent of Mount Everest without supplemental oxygen, among many other physical accomplishments.

Day 65: GOING HOME [video]. We get our first shipment of free shoes from Altra and announce our plan to run a marathon. https://youtu.be/f3lXfHvA7iM

RUNNING A MARATHON DURING AN APPALACHIAN TRAIL THRUHIKE [video]. Our family runs the Flying Pig Marathon and then discusses if it was worth it. https://youtu.be/PpG6MRNccPE

UNBELIEVABLE Six Year Old runs FULL MARATHON! [video]. Filia's first marathon the year before. https://youtu.be/44v1JV-OSJY

A Million Miles in a Thousand Years: How I Learned to Live a Better Story by Donald Miller: the book that inspired us to ask different questions when we plan an adventure.

CHAPTER 13

Day 75: THIS CHANGES EVERYTHING [video]. Dove starts carrying Rainier. https://youtu.be/YGAQdX_zcWQ

Day 74: She Turns 17 [video]. Dove's seventeenth birthday celebration surprise breakfast of eggs Benedict. https://youtu.be/w9RThXJgHyc

Day 76: STAYING IN A MANSION [video]. We stay at Claire and Griffin's vacation house with Silver. https://youtu.be/EfJRljHX7DI

CHAPTER 14

Day 82: ENTER THE ROLLERCOASTER [video]. One of the funniest sections of video editing is at 8:40 and how we dealt with one of the most difficult sections of trail. Also, this shows us arriving at Bear's Den hostel with Silver. https://youtu.be/-dVrUu3NsJA

Day 83: BLOWN AWAY BY ENCOURAGEMENT [video]. We say goodbye to Silver, not knowing it's the last time we would see him. We arrive at Kate's house. https://youtu.be/weuUtQIBuis

Day 71: WE'RE ACTUALLY NORMAL [video]. We start the morning off at Devil's Backbone Brewery, getting a ride from the founder and CEO. https://youtu.be/KKjSs46cdCw

Day 89: HALFWAY THRU!!! [video]. Roberta the Mennonite. https://youtu.be/2nT1kWEviNI

Day 84: A DAY IN WASHINGTON DC [video]. Our day as tourists in the nation's capital and the last zero day we would take in fifty-four days. https://youtu.be/AxAaPkR_ZZM

Day 85: WE MADE IT TO HARPERS FERRY [video]. Our time at the ATC headquarters. https://youtu.be/Yz3SlYgJTIM

CHAPTER 15

The term "cult" has been controversial and highly debated when applied to the particular organization we stayed with. When we did our own research, we found that they have multiple locations that are owned and, to a certain degree, controlled by a parent organization. There are many levels of secrecy and information that are not made public, and many people are participating on many different levels of commitment and involvement. I have found "cult" as a definitive label to be not helpful—because the term is not well defined—and mostly use it in this book as a literary device to describe our experience to the reader.

I have found the following eight criteria to be helpful in determining where on the "cult" spectrum an organization lies. These criteria are based upon research by psychiatrist Robert Jay Lifton as published in his 1961 book, Thought Reform and the Psychology of Totalism.

- Milieu control
- Mystical manipulation
- Demand for purity
- Confession
- Sacred science
- Loading the language
- Doctrine over person
- Dispensing of existence

Based on these criteria, I would score the organization we stayed with an 8 out of 10. This is a subjective and personal rating based upon our history and limited experience. A summary of the 8 points can be found here: https://en.wikipedia.org/wiki/Thought_Reform_and_the_Psychology_of_Totalism

Day 85: WE MADE IT TO HARPERS FERRY [video]. The end of this episode is filmed at the cult. I didn't want to show it much because I didn't want to make it look bad and we were very grateful for their hospitality. https://youtu.be/Yz3SlYgJTIM

Cults podcast on Spotify: "Twelve Tribes—Elbert Spriggs Part 1." Twelve Tribes is the organization that owns the farm we stayed at. Although the parent organization is not a complete overlap with what we experienced, the influence is tangible. https://open.spotify.com/episode/46u5tPu3dCSqio8pOP8otP

Cults podcast on Spotify: "Twelve Tribes—Elbert Spriggs Part 2." Twelve Tribes is the organization that owns the farm we stayed at. Although the parent organization is not a complete overlap with what we experienced, the influence is tangible. https://open.spotify.com/episode/2Cjx1dx7D5k87HAy5oMEcE

"Being in a Cult: Our Story" [Podcast on our Everyone Belongs Channel] We tell our story of our experience with cult-like behavior and use Robert Lifton's 8 Criteria for Thought Reform to evaluate our own experiences. https://youtu.be/KidRDO_nkw4

CHAPTER 16

Sabbath as Resistance by Walter Brueggemann: source of chapter intro quote. A book that helped us reframe rest as a proactive rebellion against a culture of productivity and monetization. Content is presented from a biblically defensive position. https://www.amazon.com/dp/0664263291/?ref=exp_fightfortogether_dp_vv_d

Day 96: CONQUERING PENNSYLVANIA ROCKS [video]. Our longest day of 23.7 miles, where we end up at Red Robin. https://youtu.be/vHQcPpT8Pzs

CHAPTER 17

The Shack: Where Tragedy Confronts Eternity by William P. Young: source of chapter intro quote. I have never read this book, but we were highly cautioned for how dangerous it was while in certain religious circles that were especially leery of using feminine gender pronouns while referencing deity.

Dumb Ways to Die [video]. Original song by Metro Trains Melbourne. https://youtu.be/IJNR2EpSojw

Day 99: SO MANY DUMB WAYS TO DIE [video]. Eden carries Rainier up Lehigh Gap and we sing "Dumb Ways to Die" starting around 6 minutes. https://youtu.be/5oDdhUZVG3g

Day 103: WE DO THIS EVERY NIGHT [video]. An example of what tent time looked like every night. https://youtu.be/BpuLpmVYLwg

Day 102: OUR FAVORITE SHOES [video]. In the very beginning of this video, we say goodbye to the Hesses. https://youtu.be/qUzOoaAGc50

CHAPTER 18

Backpacker magazine: "Madman Walking?" Source of chapter intro quote. Article about Warren Doyle. Much more info provided in chapter 19 notes. https://www.backpacker.com/stories/madman-walking

FINAL GOODBYE: Going hiking for 6 months [video]. Our final video before leaving for the trail. At around 28 minutes, you can hear the offer from Stan the Man to buy us ice cream. https://youtu.be/wopUQtXOsz0

Day 106: NEVER THOUGHT THIS DAY WOULD COME [video]. Our day being slackpacked by Stan the Man, eating ice cream, and surprising the kids with Incredibles 2. https://youtu.be/eA7JMXidh8A

Day 109: EPIC REUNION [video]. Heather brings us pizza from NYC, we reunite with Hops and celebrate with Chinese food. https://youtu.be/4or_bqOgWo8

CHAPTER 19

The Fellowship of the Ring by J. R. R. Tolkien: source quote for chapter intro quote.

Day 113: THREE KIDS SICK [video]. We start off at Hudson and Lu's Bearded Wood's Hostel with breakfast and a tour. At 5:45, Hudson vows to meet us at Katahdin. And contains our decision to hike with sick kids. https://youtu.be/DntFSLqoVXM

Warren Doyle Wikipedia page. https://en.wikipedia.org/wiki/Warren_Doyle

Outside magazine article about mental preparedness. https://www.outsideonline.com/2412271/warren-doyle-appalachian-trail-thru-hikes-lessons

Speed record holder Jennifer Pharr Davis reflects on Doyle's influence
and inspiration. https://www.blueridgeoutdoors.com/hiking/outdoor-
person-of-the-year/

Backpacker magazine: "Madman Walking?" This was the article I read that
really showed the depth and complexity of Warren Doyle and showed
me that he has dealt with many similar dynamics during his life that
we have: facing government regulations, thinking outside the box,
finding new frontiers of group dynamics, and being called crazy. It
was after reading this article that I knew I wanted him to write the
foreword to this book and was overjoyed when he said yes. https://
www.backpacker.com/stories/madman-walking

"The Appalachian: 30,000 Miles and Counting." https://
theappalachianonline.com/30000-miles-and-counting-longtime-hiker-
leads-the-way-on-appalachian-trail/

"2020 Appalachian Trail Hall of Fame Inductees Announced." https://
www.atmuseum.org/news/2020-appalachian-trail-hall-of-fame-
inductees-announced

"Walking the Entire Appalachian Trail: Fulfilling a Dream by
Accomplishing the Task" by Warren Doyle, 36,000-miler (33rd edition
2016). Warren's one-page book on hiking the A.T. https://static1.
squarespace.com/static/56a590ee1a5203313c3859be/t/56a7e11a89a60a7
21010fc53/1453842714741/Warrens+Book.pdf

Day 116: SLEEPING IN A GYM [video]. Tour of the CrossFit gym we spent
the night at. https://youtu.be/hAsET6JHPoI

Day 120: WHEN DO YOU GO TO THE HOSPITAL? [video]. At the end of this
video, we finally catch up with The Degenerates. The video is not that
great, and we don't actually film meeting up with them. https://youtu.
be/17C-KrXFvHM

Day 141: WE MADE IT TO MAINE [video]. At 7:30, we get a private concert
from Eddie the professional saxophone player from Brooklyn on his
penny whistle. Often, he would play while we walked and take requests
from Rainier. https://youtu.be/XAnxJiI4xOI

Day 126: MEETING HARVEY LEWIS [video]. Our meetup with Harvey
Lewis and his father on his FKT (fastest known time) attempt of the
A.T. Harvey is from our hometown of Cincinnati and wore a Flying

Pig Marathon jersey in preparation for meeting us. https://youtu.
be/9zULYYe1B6E

Like Harvey, Like Son [documentary]. Movie about Harvey's attempt and
relationship with his father. https://www.likeharveylikeson.com/

Day 127: MEETING PAPPY [video]. At around 6:20, we meet eighty-eight-
year-old "Pappy" on his attempt to be the oldest person to hike the A.T.
https://youtu.be/TgOZhwVUsSg

CHAPTER 20

Day 123: WE'VE BEEN OUT HERE FOR 4 MONTHS [video]. Around 6:50,
we meet The Degenerates and Hops at the lake. https://youtu.be/-
BT2B6mwxEk

Day 127: MEETING PAPPY [video]. Around 8:50, we meet up with my
parents for the fourth and final time of our trip. At 18 minutes, we
receive our second and final pair of Altra shoes. https://youtu.be/
TgOZhwVUsSg

Day 130: 18th WEDDING ANNIVERSARY [video]. Episode starts off
saying goodbye to my parents for the final time. https://youtu.be/
HR110qK5VTg

CHAPTER 21

Day 131: CAN'T GIVE UP NOW [video]. At around 13 minutes, we meet
the Omelet Guy, Carl. At around 3:50, we are awarded a conch shell
and named honorary Degenerates. (I must say that in the book,
we share this story as happening the next day on the top of Mount
Moosilauke, which is where the ladies, Fun Facts, Not Dead, and
Mama Kish, received their necklaces, so this part of the narrative is
NOT chronologically true, but Meghan, my cowriter, insisted that it
made for better reading and was factually negligible, so she won out.)
At 4:45, there's an episode of *Meet That Degenerate* interviewing Fun
Facts. https://youtu.be/uPnzx2yT4qc

The Omelet Guy [video]. A profile of Carl the Omelet Guy made by Osprey
Packs that uses video footage from our family. Also, the couple

with the dog in the film are Caitlin and Jodeob. https://youtu.be/
xq5DATG44R8

Day 132: HAPPY BIRTHDAY BEN [video]. In this episode, we climb Mount
Moosilauke—our first mountain in the Whites and Technical 200—
and climb down to my birthday in the parking lot, where I shotgun my
first beer. https://youtu.be/UoZrpz1NUZk

Day 133: THE WHITES ARE KICKING OUR BUTTS [video]. We wake up at
the Notch Hostel, which Serena and Justin let us sleep in for free.
We hike with Caitlin, and Jodeob slackpacks us. https://youtu.
be/4Lr27E9bEhI

CHAPTER 22

Ed Viesturs: chapter intro quote attributed to him. One of my favorite
mountaineers and the only American to have climbed all fourteen
of the world's eight-thousand-meter mountain peaks without using
supplemental oxygen. I especially liked him because he was a local
Mount Rainier (my favorite peak that we named our two-year-old
after and I have summited five times) guide and had crazy stories of
his time there.

List of people who died on the Presidential Range Wikipedia page.
https://en.wikipedia.org/wiki/List_of_people_who_died_on_the_
Presidential_Range

Day 137: SUMMITING MT WASHINGTON [video]. In this episode, we
summit Mount Washington and make the hustle to Joe Dodge Lodge,
tapping into "orcs in daylight mode" and ransacking the buffet.
https://youtu.be/QbO32almFSM

Day 138: WE BOUGHT PLANE TICKETS [video]. Our first zero in fifty-four
days, we buy plane tickets in the rain; around 13:50, the kids play the
piano. https://youtu.be/KZvMGQ2yWlc

Day 140: BEST FOOD ON THE TRAIL [video]. Around 6:30, we meet Fresh
Ground for lunch as we complete the Whites, and we see Hops for the
last time. https://youtu.be/uBLo3xOGDGM

CHAPTER 23

Percival Baxter was the governor of Maine from 1921–1925. A very interesting character who bought up all the land that makes up Baxter State Park—home of the terminus, Mount Katahdin. Baxter died at the age of eighty-seven after donating the park to the people of Maine along with $7 million to maintain it as long as they followed a *very* specific list of requirements. According to Park Superintendent Eben Sypitkowski, it functions "like a cult" because the park and money are dedicated to carrying out the vision of one man. The goal of Baxter and the park was to keep it "forever wild," which means that instead of the main goal being access, the primary directive ends up being more prohibitive. Other strange rules include all employees must be from Maine, no paved roads, and, of course, no one under the age of six is allowed above the tree line.

Baxter State Park Wikipedia Page: Contains the history of Baxter State Park. https://en.wikipedia.org/wiki/Baxter_State_Park

Baxter State Park Homepage: Contains the history and mission of BSP. https://baxterstatepark.org/shortcodes/history/

Additional Resources on Scott Jurek's Summit

"Scott Jurek to Pay $500 Fine for Public Drinking in Baxter State Park" [Runner's World Article] Describes Jurek's citation, including the two that were dropped. https://www.runnersworld.com/news/a20852777/scott-jurek-to-pay-500-fine-for-public-drinking-in-baxter-state-park/

"Scott Jurek Responds to 'Personal Attacks, Misinformation' Surrounding State Park Citations" [Runner's World Article] Jurek's response to BSP's citations and accusations. https://www.runnersworld.com/news/a20847021/scott-jurek-responds-to-personal-attacks-misinformation-surrounding-state-park-citations/

"Fussing: Appalachian Trail Conservancy & Baxter State Park" [blog post] A well-thought-out and well-presented article about the conflicting interests of the ATC and BSP and the future of the A.T. This writing shows why the tensions were high around our decision, as many feel that the future of the hiking community lies with a few individuals that

BSP can make an example of. https://appalachiantrail.com/20150724/
fussing-appalachian-trail-conservancy-baxter-state-park/
"Baxter State Park vs. Scott Jurek: The Clash of Commercial Sports and
Wilderness Preservation" [blog post] Article highlighting BSP and
the problem they have with Jurek's sponsorship and the increased
popularity of the usage of its park as the terminus of the ATC.
https://thetrek.co/baxter-state-park-vs-scott-jurek-the-clash-of-
commercial-sports-and-wilderness-preservation/
"Ultramarathoning in Baxter Park – another perspective." [Facebook post]
Baxter State Park's Vitriolic response regarding Scott Jurek's finish.
https://www.facebook.com/baxterstatepark/posts/1682502611969384
"As Hikers Celebrate on Appalachian Trail, Some Ask: Where Will It End?"
[NYT Article] Articles like this provide the backdrop for a lot of fear and
judgment around anyone that threatens to break a rule in BSP and "ruin
things for everyone." https://www.nytimes.com/2015/08/30/us/as-
hikers-celebrate-on-appalachian-trail-some-ask-where-will-it-end.html
"A Dispute Over the End of the Appalachian Trail" [open letter from
director of BSP to the ATC] Information from BSP's perspective of
the dangers of the A.T. ending at Katahdin. Sources we have talked to
say there is no real risk for BSP to deny A.T. hikers in the immediate
future, but the letter served as a signal to increase tensions from the
hiking community, warning them of the looming threat.
https://www.nytimes.com/interactive/2015/08/28/us/document-at-
ron-tipton-wendy-janssen-letter-11-19-2014.html

Day 141: WE MADE IT TO MAINE [video]. At 7:30, we celebrate as we walk
into Maine with Eddie and Kat. https://youtu.be/XAnxJiI4xOI
Day 142: MOST DIFFICULT MILE OF THE AT [video]. PeeWee vlogs
our family hiking through the most difficult mile of the A.T.—the
Mahoosuc Notch. https://youtu.be/oXFoh57wRSg
Day 163: To Crawford Notch with the Crawfords [video]. Amanda "PeeWee"
Bess's trail vlog from the day she hikes with us. https://youtu.be/
JMpoKPeQies
Day 145: TERRIBLE NEWS [video]. Interview with Odie as he slackpacks us.
We return to The Cabin and have dinner and interview Honey. Then we

call Baxter State Park and are told that we are not allowed to finish the trail. https://youtu.be/okX7hGVFm1g

APPALACHIAN TRAIL SPEECH: "YOU ARE ROYALTY" [video]. The speech Odie usually delivers at the Trail Days Festival in Damascus. https://youtu.be/bMxRIzjrNDk

CHAPTER 24

Day 164 [video]. This is a video from PeeWee's (Amanda Bess) channel that shows her difficulty toward the end and the homesickness she dealt with, especially from 1–3 minutes. https://youtu.be/XYf7541DreQ

Day 147: DANGEROUS RIVER FORDING [video]. We head out, hiking into a storm, and say goodbye to PeeWee for the last time. 2:45 and 6 are good examples of the wet terrain we dealt with, and 11 shows one of our harder stream crossings. https://youtu.be/631vNmPzT_M

Day 148: MALNOURISHED KIDS [video]. Interview with Beth, who shared about her dad, and was one of the most encouraging points of our trip. https://youtu.be/mh9csZ45Pwg

A Walk in the Woods: Rediscovering America on the Appalachian Trail by Bill Bryson. The book that was turned into a movie where the author says that Shaw's is the most famous guesthouse on the A.T., partly because it's the last comfort stop for anyone going into the Hundred-Mile Wilderness and the first for anyone coming out, but also because it's very friendly and a good deal.

Day 151: HE PAID FOR EVERYTHING [video]. Around 15 minutes, I talk about getting sick, and then Kami shares about her worries. https://youtu.be/42SkTPmD46Q

Day 152: HUGE SURPRISE [video]. At 8:15, we get a text message from Fresh Ground. We find out that we're going to be supported by Fresh Ground through the entire Hundred-Mile Wilderness. https://youtu.be/AP2REgbOYcI

CHAPTER 25

Story: Substance, Structure, Style, and the Principles of Screenwriting by Robert McKee: source of chapter intro quote.

Day 153: HARDEST DECISION WE'VE HAD TO MAKE [video]. Starts off with Shaw's Hostel Famous Breakfast and the kids making a decision to not hike to the top of Katahdin. https://youtu.be/AmhHMwAfmUs

CHAPTER 26

Day 154: AN INCREDIBLE ARRANGEMENT [video]. At 2 minutes, I share the story of trying to pay for Fresh Ground's meal, but Poet won't let me; at 4:50, Poet recites his poem about seeing Katahdin; at 5:30, we reunite with Culligan right before going into the Hundred-Mile Wilderness; at 6:30, you can see the one-hundred-mile sign; at 13:40, you can see the kids' reactions to Fresh Ground supporting us in the Hundred-Mile Wilderness. https://youtu.be/QZq7EYB_U_g

How I Went from Waiting Tables to Being a Professional Blackjack Player (on Accident) [Kindle edition] by Benjamin Crawford. The inspirational story of how I went from a bike accident to playing blackjack professionally. https://www.amazon.com/gp/product/B07KTG94KM/ref=dbs_a_def_rwt_bibl_vppi_i1

The 29-Minute Card Counting Book [Kindle edition] by Benjamin Crawford. A guide I wrote for our website that explains most everything you need to know to beat the game of blackjack. https://www.amazon.com/gp/product/B07KT5VRDH/ref=dbs_a_def_rwt_bibl_vppi_i2

Day 155: LESS THAN 100 MILES TO GO [video]. At 2:20, we meet Fresh Ground for the first time and he takes our packs so we can slackpack. https://youtu.be/3E2iXtTAJ3A

Day 158: PARENTS GET LOST [video]. At 15:15, we have an episode of Meet That Degenerate with Not Dead enjoying Fresh Ground's trail magic. https://youtu.be/W_bO4vCTq94

CHAPTER 27

Day 159: WE CAN'T BELIEVE IT [video]. At 12:45, Hudson drives eight hours to meet us. https://youtu.be/5_XLrdajyVo

Trail Day 160: TWO MILES FROM THE FINISH [video]. At 14:30, we open up our vinyl sign for our picture at the top. https://youtu.be/WAczvu6izfQ

FINAL DAY: WE MADE IT [video]. At 13, we make it to the tree line and finish our journey and get our picture at Hudson's sign. https://youtu.be/DdYrGUHRFk8

OUR FAMILY HIKES the APPALACHIAN TRAIL [video]. 1:04:15 has my favorite version of the ending with better editing, music, and narration because we had much more time to make this video. https://youtu.be/JtickT2tCwo

CHAPTER 28

THE DAY AFTER [video]. At 3:30, we take a shuttle to Portland, Maine, and have lunch with Kate, Steve, and kids on the pier and conclude that butter lobster rolls are better than mayonnaise. At 10 minutes, we catch our flight to Seattle. https://youtu.be/97kbUl9e_Vs

1 WEEK AFTER FINISHING [video]. We finally make it to our goal, Lakeside Bible Camp on Whidbey Island in Washington. https://youtu.be/vwlE4KQattk

HE GAVE HER A CAR [YouTube video]. Fresh Ground gives his car, Stinkbug, to Dove. https://youtu.be/XN5I-lWBolg

HOW MUCH WE SPENT ON THE APPALACHIAN TRAIL [video]. In this video, we detail every expense and how much it cost our family to hike the entire A.T. https://youtu.be/9kwJSFMA3_4

EPILOGUE

Flying to *NEW YORK* to get a slice of pizza [video]. We go to NYC on a surprise trip for Dove and stay with Eddie and Kat, and see Eddie play saxophone in an underground jazz club. https://youtu.be/Oez3eFBWkJE

BANNED FROM BIBLE CAMP FOR AFFIRMING [video]. Our story of getting denied the opportunity to cook at camp. https://youtu.be/M7KHR8hJY9A

Our Beef with Religious Exclusion [video]. The longer version on our other channel about the problem we have with religious exclusion. https://youtu.be/_tVoP35au1E

WE'RE GOING BACK to the APPALACHIAN TRAIL [video]. Trail Magic: one year later, we go back to the trail to feed hikers. Fresh Ground surprises Kami and the kids by showing up. https://youtu.be/3igkiZOq_Kk

FINALLY Back on the Appalachian Trail [video]. Our first day feeding hikers and an interview with the kids. https://youtu.be/meWKlRZxeyM

Sleeping in a van for 6 months on the Appalachian Trail [video]. Feeding hikers and an interview with Fresh Ground. https://youtu.be/-PNqNDJcGNM

Best Meal on the Appalachian Trail [video]. Interviewing hikers. https://youtu.be/-cuB-1hLhwU

What makes hikers unique [video]. Extended interview with Fresh Ground and his reaction to reading an early manuscript of this book. https://youtu.be/TDw97hlnYJY

How to Run 24 Hours WITH KIDS [video]. Running an ultramarathon with Harvey Lewis. https://youtu.be/v_gF5O4VJa4

GENERAL

Appalachian Trail Thru Hike [YouTube playlist]. A playlist of every one of our Appalachian Trail videos. https://www.youtube.com/playlist?list=PL8jVL_i9OvEF_GWO4E1AneMON_IFLqciu

WhiteBlaze.net:

"Thru Hiking Family of 8 - Your Thoughts?" The main thread that discussed our hike and vlogs from the beginning. https://www.whiteblaze.net/forum/showthread.php/128847-Thru-Hiking-Family-of-8-Your-Thoughts

"Did the Crawford Family (7 of 8) really summit?" Thread discussing the completion of our hike. https://www.whiteblaze.net/forum/showthread.php/130386-Did-the-Crawford-Family-(7-of-8)-really-summit

ADDITIONAL READING

1. *Unconditional Parenting: Moving from Rewards and Punishments to Love and Reason* by Alfie Kohn. Alfie Kohn is one of the few people I have found who writes about the dangers of short-term rewards and consequences. He also has a DVD lecture with the same title that is very good.

2. *Hold On to Your Kids: Why Parents Need to Matter More Than Peers* by Gabor Maté. Dr. Maté explains how crucial it is and why it is so difficult that parents fight to remain the primary influencers in their children's lives.

3. *The Conscious Parent: Transforming Ourselves, Empowering Our Children* by Dr. Shefali Tsabary

4. "Do Schools Kill Creativity?" by Sir Ken Robinson. My favorite TED talk of all time that gives another take on education, trusting kids, allowing them to make mistakes, and releasing creativity.

5. *Family Business: A Book about Patagonia's Innovative On-Site Childcare* by Malinda Chouinard and Jennifer Ridgeway. This book is one of my favorite parenting books with great examples of how to craft contexts for growth, especially for young ages.

6. *A Million Miles in a Thousand Years: How I Learned to Live a Better Story* by Donald Miller. This book really helped me ask questions about whether or not our family was living the type of story that was worth writing about. It gave me a framework for finding purpose and finding adventures.

7. *How to Talk So Kids Will Listen & Listen So Kids Will Talk* by Adele Faber and Elaine Mazlish. A classic about communication with smaller people.

8. *Selfish Reasons to Have More Kids: Why Being a Great Parent is Less Work and More Fun Than You Think* by Bryan Caplan. I love this book because of its chapters on twin studies. It shows that much of the work we put into parenting doesn't change the outcome of the kids.

9. *Unleash Your Family: Chaos to Creativity in One Week*. I wrote this book when our family entered lockdown during the COVID-19 pandemic. It documents how we avoided panic and turned what could have been a time of boredom and interrupted plans into a new framework for productivity and creativity in a practical step-by-step format that fits within one week.

ABOUT THE AUTHOR

Ben Crawford is an entrepreneur, author, and influencer who, along with his wife, Kami, and their six children, set the record in 2018 for the largest family and youngest female (7-year-old Filia Crawford) to thru-hike the Appalachian Trail. His greatest goal is to discover the full potential of the human family, and to empower people to find freedom by questioning the status quo. Ben's previous book, *Unleash Your Family*, details the Crawfords' approach to turning the chaos of quarantine life into structured creativity. On his YouTube channel, *Fight For Together*, Ben aims to challenge existing perspectives on marriage, family, parenting, and self-awareness—through every-thing from running ultramarathons with young children, to experi-menting with authority by living a year with no rules. The Crawfords live just outside Cincinnati, where they are currently planning their next adventure.

CPSIA information can be obtained
at www.ICGtesting.com
Printed in the USA
LVHW040232251120
672446LV00025B/601/J